SHARED RECIPES

Among Friends

P. 90 Stroganoff
P. 100 Pork chops
P. 101 Chicken
P. 83 Fruit Salad Dressing

P. 187 Soda Cracker Pie

P. 61 Swiss onion soup

Additional copies of ***Among Friends*** may be obtained at the cost of $14.95, plus $2.50 postage and handling, each book.

Send To:

JUNIOR AUXILIARY OF RUSSELLVILLE, AR, INC.
P. O. Box 1011
Russellville, Arkansas 72811

ISBN: 0-9634925-1-9

1st Printing	5,000 copies	October, 1993
2nd Printing	5,000 copies	December, 1995

Printed in the USA by

SHARED RECIPES

Among Friends

Junior Auxiliary of Russellville is a community service organization that encourages trained volunteers to help in meeting community needs. Various planned projects are supported in several fields such as welfare, health, recreation, civic, culture, and education. While services are beneficial to the general public, there is a particular emphasis on children. All proceeds from the sale of *Among Friends* will go toward funding our many community projects.

Russellville, Arkansas, is located on Scenic Highway 7 in the foothills of the Ozark Mountains in the Arkansas River Valley. Russellville is a committed, caring community that generously supports the efforts of many charitable organizations.

Sharing recipes among friends has been a time honored tradition through history. In working on *Among Friends*, we have tried to convey the feeling of warmth and friendliness that comes from sharing with friends. We hope you will share these recipes with your friends, whether it's over a cup of coffee and warm muffins, a champagne brunch, a backyard barbecue or a family holiday meal. We invite you to share *Among Friends*.

THE JUNIOR AUXILIARY OF RUSSELLVILLE, ARKANSAS

Cookbook Committee

Barb Allen	Tamara Laws
Kay Armstrong	Ruth Narveson
Tonia Beavers	Connie Neumeier
Debbie Bell	Susie Nicholson
Betty Brown	Pam Rushing
Shannon Duke	Carloyn Srygley
Bonnie Haines	Maysel Teeter
Leslie Hill	Teresa Wilkins
Janice James	

Acknowledgements

Cover design by Richard Stephens.

We thank all the members of the Junior Auxiliary of Russellville who shared recipes with us.

Table of Contents

TEMPT YOUR TASTE BUDS

First Down Cheese Spread

- 2 *8 ounce packages cream cheese, softened*
- 10 *ounces sharp cheddar cheese, shredded*
- 1 *4.5 ounce can deviled ham*
- 2 *teaspoons grated onion*
- *Chopped nuts*
- *Pimiento strips*

Combine cream cheese and cheddar, mixing at medium speed with electric mixer until well blended. Add ham and onion, mix well. Chill. Form into football shape, top with nuts and pimiento to resemble football. Serve with assorted crackers. Yields 3½ cups

Carolyn Srygley

Garlic Cheese Ball

- 2 *8 ounce packages cream cheese, softened*
- 4 *cups (16 ounces) shredded sharp cheddar cheese*
- 1 *large clove garlic, crushed*
- ¼ *teaspoon ground red pepper*
- ⅓ *cup chopped pimiento-stuffed olives*
- 1 *4 ounce jar diced pimiento, undrained*
- 1 *teaspoon Worcestershire sauce*
- ½ *cup chopped pecans*
- *Paprika*

Combine first seven ingredients, stir well. Stir in pecans. Shape mixture into two cheese balls and sprinkle with paprika. Chill eight hours. Serve with assorted crackers. Yields 4¾ cups

Vickie Hale

Marinated Cheese

- ½ *cup olive oil*
- ½ *cup white wine vinegar*
- 1 *2 ounce jar diced pimiento, drained*
- 3 *tablespoons chopped fresh parsley*
- 3 *tablespoons minced green onions*
- 3 *cloves garlic, minced*
- 1 *teaspoon sugar*
- ¾ *teaspoon dried basil*
- ½ *teaspoon salt*
- ½ *teaspoon pepper*
- 1 *8 ounce block sharp cheddar cheese, chilled*
- 1 *8 ounce package cream cheese, chilled firm*

Combine everything except cheese into a jar; cover tightly and shake vigorously until all ingredients are mixed well. Set marinade mixture aside. Cut cheddar cheese in half lengthwise. Cut crosswise into ¼ inch thick slices. Repeat procedure with cream cheese. Arrange cheese sliced alternately in a shallow baking dish, standing slices on edge. Pour marinade over cheese slices. Cover and marinate in refrigerator overnight. Transfer to serving platter, reserving marinade. Spoon marinade over cheese slices. Serve with crackers. Yields 16 servings

Teresa Wilkins

Plains Cheese Ring

1 pound sharp cheddar cheese, grated
1 cup chopped nuts
1 cup mayonnaise
1 small onion, grated
Black/cayenne pepper, to taste
Strawberry preserves

Mix first five ingredients well and place in a lightly greased six cup mold. Refrigerate until firm, at least two hours (preferably overnight). Serve with strawberry preserves poured into the center of the ring.

Sara Goodin

Roquefort Grapes

1 10 ounce package almonds, pecans, or English walnuts
1 8 ounce package cream cheese, softened
⅛ pound Roquefort cheese, crumbled
2 tablespoons heavy cream
1 pound small seedless grapes, red or green, washed and dried

Toast nuts, coarsely chop in food processor or by hand. With an electric mixer, mix cream cheese, Roquefort and cream until smooth. Drop a few of the grapes into the cheese mixture and stir by hand to coat. Roll grapes in toasted nuts and place on a tray lined with waxed paper. Chill. Mound into a cluster on a serving dish. Garnish with fresh grape leaves.

Betsy Harris

Spicy Artichoke Dip

1 14 ounce can artichoke hearts, drained and chopped
1 cup mayonnaise
1 cup Parmesan cheese
1 teaspoon garlic powder
1 teaspoon cumin
1 teaspoon red pepper
1 4 ounce can chopped green chilies, drained

Mix all ingredients. Pour into a ramekin or small casserole dish. Heat in oven at 350 degrees for 20 minutes. Serve with blue corn chips, regular corn chips, or crackers. Serves 8-10

Can be stored in refrigerator up to 12 hours before baking.

Tamara Laws

Avocado Cocktail Ring

3 tablespoons unflavored gelatin
⅔ cup cold water
2½ tablespoons boiling water
Salt
3 tablespoons vinegar
Hot pepper sauce, to taste
1½ cups grated cucumber (remove seeds)
¼ cup grated onion
3 large avocados
Juice of one lemon
½ cup mayonnaise
½ cup sour cream
Dash celery salt
Dash garlic powder
Parsley, tiny cooked shrimp, and watercress, for garnish

Soften gelatin in cold water for 10 minutes. Add boiling water and dissolve. Add salt, vinegar and pepper sauce; stir well. Let cool. Grate onion and cucumber. Mash avocados and add lemon juice. Stir cucumber, onion, mayonnaise, sour cream, celery salt and garlic powder into the avocados. Blend in gelatin mixture and taste for seasonings. Pour into a four cup ring mold, sprayed with oil. Refrigerate to congeal, up to three hours. Garnish with parsley, shrimp and watercress. Serve with crackers. Yields 4 cups

Kay Ewing

Hot Chipped Beef

2 8 ounce packages cream cheese, softened
4 tablespoons milk
1 6 ounce package chipped beef, chopped (corned beef may be substituted)
1 cup sour cream
½ cup chopped green pepper
2 tablespoons onion flakes
½ teaspoon pepper
Garlic powder to taste
1 cup chopped pecans, optional

Mix cream cheese well with all ingredients, except pecans. Pour into a ramekin (sprayed with oil), top with pecans and bake at 350 degrees for 20 minutes, or until it begins to brown. Do ***not*** cook until cake-like — it needs to be spreadable. Spread on crackers.

Susan Lewis *Shirley Leonard*

Crabmeat Dip

½ clove garlic
1 8 ounce package cream cheese, softened
⅓ cup heavy cream
2 teaspoons lemon juice
1½ teaspoons Worcestershire sauce
1 cup boned, flaked crabmeat
Dash pepper

Rub mixing bowl with garlic. Mix in the bowl the cream cheese and cream. Add the lemon juice and remaining ingredients. Stir until well blended. Serve with potato chips or crackers. Yields 2 cups

Mary Dean Lyford

Black-Eyed Pea Dip

1 medium onion, chopped
2-3 tablespoons butter
½ cup mayonnaise
½ cup sour cream
1 package Original Ranch dressing
2 tablespoons Parmesan cheese
1 16 ounce can artichoke hearts, drained and chopped finely
1½ cups cooked black-eyed peas, rinsed and drained
¼ cup chopped pecans
4 ounces Mozzarella cheese, grated

Preheat oven to 325 degrees. Sauté onion in butter. Set aside. Combine mayonnaise, sour cream and dressing mix. Fold in Parmesan cheese, artichoke hearts, peas and pecans. Stir in onions. Pour mixture into a two quart buttered baking dish. Cook 20 minutes. Cover with Mozzarella cheese and return to oven until melted. Serve warm with wheat crackers.

Gaye Croom

Fireside Shrimp Dip

½ pound sharp cheddar cheese
1 4.5 ounce can shrimp
1 small onion
1 cup mayonnaise
1 teaspoon Worcestershire sauce

Grate first three ingredients. Mix with mayonnaise and Worcestershire sauce. Serve as spread on crackers or as a dip.

Cynthia Blanchard

Salmon Mousse

2 tablespoons unflavored gelatin
½ cup cold water
16 ounce can red sockeye salmon
2 tablespoons grated onion
1 cup finely diced cucumber
½ cup diced celery
¾ cup diced green bell pepper
1 tablespoon Worcestershire sauce
Dash hot pepper sauce
Salt to taste
½ teaspoon black pepper
1 tablespoon vinegar
3 tablespoons lemon juice
1 cup mayonnaise
½ pint whipping cream

Sprinkle gelatin over water to soften. Stir over hot water to dissolve. Discard bones and skin from salmon. Mix salmon and its oil with vegetables. Add seasonings and set aside. Whip cream and mix with mayonnaise. Fold gelatin mixture into cream mixture. Pour all over salmon, blending well. Pour into oiled, fish-shaped mold and refrigerate overnight. Unmold onto a lettuce-lined tray and garnish as desired. Baby shrimp for scales, sliced almonds for fins, sliced olives become eyes, and a strip of bright red pimiento for the mouth.

Betsy Harris

Shrimp and Artichoke Dip

2 4.5 ounce cans tiny shrimp, drained
2 cups sour cream
1 package Italian dressing mix
1 can artichoke hearts, drained and chopped

Mix all ingredients together and chill for at least two hours. Serve with chips or crackers.

Bonita Church

Mexican Style Appetizer

1 can condensed bean and bacon soup
1 package taco seasoning mix
¼ teaspoon hot pepper sauce
1 cup sour cream
1 4 ounce can chopped green chilies, drained
½ cup sliced green olives
1 cup shredded cheese (longhorn, cheddar, or Mozzarella)
½ cup chopped fresh tomato
Tortilla chips

In a small bowl, combine soup, taco mix and hot sauce. Stir until blended. On a large serving plate, spread mixture into a 6" round. Spread sides and top of bean mixture with sour cream to cover. Layer chilies, olives, cheese and tomato over sour cream. Cover; refrigerate until serving time, at least four hours. Surround with tortilla chips. Serves 10

Ruth Narveson

Spinach con Queso

8 ounces margarine
1 cup diced onion
2 teaspoons minced garlic
¾ cup flour
2½ cups chicken broth
2½ cups heavy cream
1 teaspoon salt
½ teaspoon sugar
2 tablespoons hot pepper sauce
2 tablespoons lemon juice
2 tablespoons chicken bouillon
1 teaspoon cayenne pepper
2 cups sour cream
2 cups grated Parmesan cheese
2 pounds pasteurized process cheese spread, cubed
1 pound Monterey Jack cheese, cubed
¾ pound fresh spinach, rinsed and chopped

Melt margarine, add onions and garlic, and sauté until soft. Slowly add the flour and mix until smooth. Cook roux for five minutes. Add chicken broth and heavy cream to roux, using a wire whisk; add a small amount at a time to keep smooth, simmer five minutes. Add salt, sugar, pepper sauce, lemon juice, bouillon, cayenne and sour cream. Stir cheeses into mixture and melt (do not boil). Add spinach and mix thoroughly. Serve warm with tortilla chips.

Maysel Teeter

Salsa

2-3 tablespoons ground cumin
1 teaspoon chopped cilantro
1 tablespoon coarse ground black pepper
½ bulb (6-8 cloves) fresh garlic, minced
1 teaspoon salt
2 jalapeño peppers, seeded, minced
4 large tomatoes, diced OR 4 16 ounce cans tomatoes, drained, and diced
1 16 ounce can tomato sauce
3-4 green onions, chopped

Mix all ingredients and refrigerate six hours or longer. Serve with warmed chips.

Maysel Teeter

Tropical Salsa

1 fresh pineapple, cut into medium sized pieces
4 peaches and/or nectarines peeled, and cut into medium sized pieces
1 papaya, peeled, seeded, and cut into medium sized pieces
2 tomatoes, peeled, seeded, and diced
1 bunch scallions, cut into rings
1 tablespoon jalapeño, finely chopped, preferably fresh
2 tablespoons fresh lemon juice
¾ cup olive oil
1 tablespoon honey
6 tablespoons champagne vinegar or cider vinegar

Toss all ingredients together and serve with tortilla chips.

Betsy Harris

Tortilla Chips

3-4 packages fresh corn tortilla
Oil for frying

Cut fresh tortillas into sixths and lightly fry wedges in hot (375 degree) oil. Drain chips well on paper towels. Shake hot tortillas in a bag with table salt and one crushed garlic clove. Serve warm or at room temperature.

Betsy Harris

Vegetable Dip

- *1 can tomato soup*
- *2 8 ounce packages cream cheese*
- *1 3 ounce box lemon gelatin*
- *½ cup water*
- *1 cup mayonnaise*
- *¾ cup chopped bell pepper*
- *½ cup chopped onion*
- *½ cup chopped pecans*

Heat together soup, cream cheese, gelatin and water until cheese completely melts, blending with a whisk. Let cool and add mayonnaise. Stir in bell pepper, onions and pecans. Put in blender or food processor and blend well. Refrigerate overnight. Serve with a variety of raw vegetables.

Marie Biggers

Bacon Roll-ups

- *20 slices trimmed white sandwich bread*
- *1 cup sweetened condensed milk*
- *¼ cup mustard*
- *1 teaspoon Worcestershire sauce*
- *1½ pounds sliced bacon*
- *2 cups shredded sharp cheddar cheese*

Roll bread flat after trimming; set aside. Combine condensed milk, mustard and Worcestershire sauce. Cut bacon in half and lay 3 halves side by side; lay a flattened slice of bread on bacon. Spread one tablespoon milk mixture on bread; sprinkle with one tablespoon cheese. Roll up like a jellyroll and secure with toothpicks. Cut between bacon slices. You will have three pieces out of each slice of bread. Place on broiler pan and bake at 375 degrees for 30 minutes. Yields 60 roll-ups

Susan Dishner

Ham Roll-ups

- *2 pounds white bread*
- *1 8 ounce package cream cheese, softened*
- *2 egg yolks*
- *1 6 ounce can chunky ham*
- *1 bunch green onions, chopped*
- *1 cup butter, melted*
- *1 cup Parmesan cheese*

Cut crusts off bread and roll flat with a rolling pin. Mix cheese, egg yolks, ham and onions. Spread small amount on each slice of bread. Roll up and dip in melted butter, then in cheese. Freeze on cookie sheets then transfer to freezer bag. One-half hour before serving, take out of freezer, cut into thirds and bake in preheated 400 degree oven on cookie sheets for 15 minutes. Serves 15 for appetizers

Susie Nicholson

Smoked Oyster Roll

2 8 ounce packages cream cheese, softened
2-3 tablespoons mayonnaise
2 teaspoons Worcestershire sauce
Hot pepper sauce, to taste
½ small onion, chopped finely
½ teaspoon salt
1-2 cloves garlic, pressed
2 3.66 ounce cans smoked oysters, drained and chopped
Garnish: Paprika, cherry tomatoes, parsley
Crackers

Mix cream cheese and mayonnaise. Add next five ingredients and mix well. Refrigerate until it hardens somewhat. Spread ½″ thick on waxed paper. Spread chopped oysters over mixture. Chill again. Roll up and chill until ready to serve. Sprinkle with paprika and dress up with parsley and cherry tomatoes. Serve sliced on crackers. Serves 10

Jane Barnes

Tortilla Roll-ups

2 8 ounce packages cream cheese, softened
2 4 ounce cans chopped black olives, drained
2 4 ounce cans chopped green chilies, drained
Dash garlic powder
1 tablespoon picante sauce
1 package flour tortillas

Mix all ingredients and spread thinly over 10-12 tortillas. Roll up and wrap in plastic wrap. Chill. Cut into ½″ slices and serve with salsa. Will keep chilled up to one week.

Mary Smith

Bacon Wrapped Peppers with Cheese

3 ounces cream cheese, softened
3 ounces cheddar cheese, shredded
1 tablespoon minced onion
2 tablespoons Worcestershire sauce
12-16 fresh jalapeño peppers
6-8 bacon slices, cut in half

Pour cream cheese, cheddar cheese, onion and Worcestershire sauce in a blender or food processor and mix well. Wash and core the peppers. Stuff each pepper with the cheese mixture and wrap with a bacon half. Place on a cookie sheet and freeze. Do not thaw to cook. Put frozen peppers in a shallow pan and bake in a preheated 475 degree oven until bacon is crisp, turning once, approximately 20 minutes. These can be made ahead and stored in the freezer for several weeks.

Jalia Lingle

Beef Sticks

- 2 *pounds ground beef*
- 1 *cup water*
- 2 *tablespoons Morton's Tender Quick Salt*
- 2 *teaspoons mustard seed*
- ¼ *teaspoon onion salt*
- ½ *teaspoon garlic salt*
- ¼ *teaspoon pepper*
- 2 *tablespoons peppercorns*
- 1 *tablespoon liquid smoke*

Mix all ingredients thoroughly. Let stand in refrigerator at least 24 hours. Mix again. Form into 4-5 long rolls. Place on broiler rack of broiler pan. Bake one hour and 15 minutes at 300 degrees. Cool and wrap in foil.

Sue McCoy

Crab Appetizer

- 7 *ounces crabmeat*
- 1 *8 ounce jar pasteurized sharp cheese spread*
- ¼ *cup mayonnaise*
- ½ *cup soft butter*
- ½ *teaspoon garlic salt*
- 1 *package English muffins*

Mix first five ingredients. This may be done ahead and refrigerated until ready to use. Spread on six split English muffins. Place on cookie sheet and toast under broiler until lightly brown on top. Be careful not to burn. Cut into quarters. Serve hot. Yields 24

Linda Fenech

Crab Croustades

- 1 *loaf unsliced bread (white)*
- ½ *cup butter, melted*
- 1 *5 ounce jar pasteurized sharp cheese spread*
- 1 *egg yolk*
- 1 *6 ounce can crabmeat, drained and flaked*
- 1 *teaspoon Worcestershire sauce*
- ¼ *teaspoon onion powder*
- ⅛ *teaspoon pepper*

Cut bread into 1" slices, remove crust. Cut trimmed slices into 1" cubes. Hollow out each cube, leaving about a ⅛" thick bottom. Brush sides and top with melted butter. Place on cookie sheets. Bake at 400 degrees for 10 minutes or until crisp and brown. Remove to wire rack and cool. Blend cheese and egg yolk, add crabmeat, Worcestershire sauce, onion powder and pepper. Mix well. Fill croustades with crabmeat mixture. These can be placed in foil or plastic container, covered, and frozen. To serve: remove from freezer, place on cookie sheets. Heat in 400 degree oven 10 minutes or until filling just starts to brown. Keep hot to serve.

Sue Streett

Roasted Garlic

- *8 whole heads fresh garlic*
- *1/3 cup extra-virgin olive oil*
- *1½ teaspoons coarsely ground pepper*
- *1½ teaspoons dried thyme*
- *1 teaspoon salt*

Preheat oven to 350 degrees. Trim the point off each garlic head to expose the tops of the cloves. Place the heads next to each other in a shallow baking dish, such as a 9" pie plate. Drizzle the heads with the oil and sprinkle evenly with the pepper, thyme and salt. Roast the garlic for 30 minutes. Reduce the temperature to 250 degrees and cook one hour longer. To serve, pop the cloves out of skins onto slices of buttered French bread and spread. Serve with goat cheese if you like.

Joyce R. Laws

Party Ham Rolls

- *1 cup oleo, melted*
- *3 tablespoons poppy seeds*
- *1 teaspoon Worcestershire sauce*
- *3 tablespoons mustard*
- *1 medium onion, chopped*
- *1 pound of ham, ground*
- *12 ounces Swiss cheese, grated*
- *60 small rolls (in foil tray), about 1" x 2"*

Use grinder or food processor to grind ham, cheese and onion. Add remaining ingredients, except rolls, and mix well. Remove rolls intact from foil tray, slice horizontally with a serrated knife (careful not to separate rolls). Spread mixture on bottom half of rolls and replace top. Return filled rolls to the tray; wrap and seal the whole tray with foil. These may be frozen at this point. Thaw and bake at 350 degrees for 10 minutes. Slice into individual rolls and serve warm. Yields 60 rolls

Kay Stephens

Olive Tarts

- *2 cups finely grated cheddar or longhorn cheese*
- *½ cup margarine, softened*
- *1 cup all-purpose flour*
- *1 teaspoon salt*
- *1 teaspoon paprika*
- *1¼ teaspoons hot pepper sauce*
- *36 small stuffed green olives*

Blend cheese and butter. Stir in flour, salt, paprika and pepper sauce. Wrap one teaspoon of dough around each olive, covering completely. Bake in a preheated 400 degree oven for 15 minutes. These may be made ahead, frozen, and then baked.

Kathy Soto

Bar-B-Cued Meatballs

1 12 ounce can evaporated milk
3 pounds ground beef
2 cups oats
1 cup minced onion
½ teaspoon garlic salt
½ teaspoon pepper
2 eggs

Mix all ingredients and form into meatballs.

Sauce

2 cups catsup
1½ cups brown sugar
2 tablespoons liquid smoke
½ teaspoon garlic powder
½ onion, chopped
2 tablespoons mustard

Mix ingredients and pour over meatballs that have been divided between two 9 x 13 pans. These can be frozen at this point and thawed before baking. Bake at 350 degrees for 30-35 minutes. Makes about 100 cocktail meatballs. These can also be made larger and served as a main dish.

Ruth Narveson

Meatballs in Beer Sauce

2 slices bread, cubed
1 12 ounce can or bottle of beer
1 pound lean ground beef
½ cup shredded Mozzarella cheese
Freshly ground black pepper
1 tablespoon margarine
½ cup chopped onion
2 tablespoons brown sugar
2 tablespoons vinegar
2 tablespoons beef stock
1-2 tablespoons flour, optional

Soak bread cubes in ½ cup beer. Combine beef with cheese, pepper and beer-soaked bread. Mix well and form into 32 cocktail-sized meatballs. Arrange in a single layer on a cookie sheet and bake 15 minutes at 350 degrees. Meanwhile, sauté onions in margarine until tender. Stir in sugar, vinegar, stock and remaining beer. Thicken with flour if desired. Simmer over low heat 10 minutes. When meatballs are done, drain on paper towels, then add to sauce and simmer 20 minutes. Serve with toothpicks. Approximately 55 calories per meatball.

Bonnie Haines

Baked Italian Mushrooms

- 2 *dozen large fresh mushrooms, 1½-2" in diameter*
- 2 *tablespoons butter, melted*
- 2 *tablespoons olive oil*
- 2 *cloves garlic, finely chopped*
- 1 *medium onion, finely chopped*
- 1 *pound bulk sausage*
- 2 *tablespoons fresh bread crumbs*
- 1 *egg, lightly beaten*
- 2 *tablespoons chopped parsley*
- 1 *teaspoon fennel seed*
- ½ *teaspoon red pepper flakes, or to taste*
- 1 *teaspoon oregano*
- 1 *teaspoon basil*
- 2 *tablespoons freshly grated Parmesan cheese*

The day before, cut ends from mushrooms and remove stems, set aside. Return unwashed mushroom caps to refrigerator. Sauté onion and garlic with sausage in a skillet until sausage is done, crumbling sausage with a fork as it cooks. Chop mushroom stems and add to sausage mixture and cook for 2-3 minutes. Drain off fat and let mixture cool for about five minutes. Add bread crumbs, egg, parsley and all seasonings, except cheese. Cool, cover and refrigerate. The next day, lightly wash mushroom caps and drain well. Reheat sausage mixture until heated through. Pour butter and oil into a 9 x 13 dish. Coat all sides of the caps in the mixture and place them cavity side up in the dish. Mound sausage mixture into caps and sprinkle with Parmesan cheese. These can now be refrigerated for 2-3 hours. When ready to serve, bake in 375 degree oven for 20 minutes, or until sizzling and golden brown.

Maysel Teeter

Stuffed Mushrooms

- 1-1½ *pounds mushrooms*
- 2 *tablespoons butter*
- 1 *onion, chopped*
- 2 *tablespoons green pepper*
- 2 *ounces pepperoni*
- ¼ *cup chicken broth*
- ½ *cup bread crumbs, soft*
- 3 *tablespoons Parmesan cheese*
- *Dash salt, pepper, and oregano*
- *Sliced Mozzarella cheese*

Sauté onion and green pepper in butter. Chop stems of mushrooms and pepperoni. Pour into the butter/onion mixture. Add the chicken broth, crumbs, cheese and seasonings. Cook until liquid is absorbed. Stuff mushrooms and top each with a slice of Mozzarella cheese. Bake at 350 degrees for 20 minutes.

Marcia Godown

Ranch Ribs

2-3 tablespoons dark corn syrup
2 tablespoons cornstarch
⅓ cup soy sauce
2 tablespoons Worcestershire sauce
1 teaspoon ginger
¼ cup vinegar
1 clove garlic, crushed
¼ teaspoon salt
½ cup brown sugar
Dash hot pepper sauce
4 pounds spare ribs, have butcher crack into 2" pieces
1 medium onion

Cook the first 10 ingredients for five minutes in a saucepan. Separate ribs and place in a pot of water with onion and simmer, covered, cooking until tender. Drain ribs and chill. When ready to bake, place ribs on a rack in a large baking pan and pour sauce over the ribs. Place in 325 degree oven and bake for 1½ hours, basting often. Cook until tender and glazed. Yields 4 pounds of ribs

Cathy Andrasik

Party Ryes

1 cup finely grated Swiss cheese
¼ cup cooked and crumbled bacon
1 4.5 ounce can chopped black olives
¼ cup chopped green onion
1 teaspoon Worcestershire sauce
¼ cup mayonnaise
1 loaf party rye bread

Mix the above ingredients together in a bowl. Spread mixture onto individual party rye bread. Place on a cookie sheet and bake at 375 degrees for 10-15 minutes. This tastes like pizza. It goes over great!

Terri Knight

Seafood Tartlets

1½ pound loaf thin-sliced sandwich bread
⅓ cup margarine, melted
4½ ounce can tiny shrimp, drained
¾ cup mayonnaise
⅓ cup Parmesan cheese
⅓ cup shredded Swiss cheese
¼ teaspoon Worcestershire sauce
⅛ teaspoon hot sauce
Paprika
Parsley sprigs

Roll each bread slice to ¼" thickness; cut with a 2½" daisy-shaped cookie cutter. Lightly brush each side of bread with melted margarine and place in miniature tart shells. Bake at 400 degrees for 8-10 minutes or until lightly browned. Rinse shrimp, let stand in ice water for 20 minutes; drain well. Combine shrimp and next five ingredients; stir well. Spoon shrimp mixture evenly into tart shells; sprinkle with paprika. Bake at 400 degrees for 8-10 minutes or until bubbly. Garnish with parsley, if desired. These may be frozen and heated in the oven.

Susie Kroencke

Company Rumaki

6 jumbo shrimp
4 water chestnuts, whole
6 slices bacon
Brown sugar
Teriyaki Sauce

Clean and devein shrimp. Cut each in half. Cut each water chestnut into three pieces. Pour Teriyaki Sauce over shrimp and chestnuts in a bowl. Refrigerate about four hours; drain. Cut bacon slices in half. Wrap a piece of shrimp and a piece of water chestnut in each bacon slice. Secure with a toothpick. Roll in brown sugar. Set oven to broil. Broil, turning occasionally, 3-4" from heat 10 minutes, or until bacon is crisp.

Teriyaki Sauce

¼ cup salad oil
¼ cup soy sauce
2 tablespoons catsup
1 tablespoon vinegar
¼ teaspoon pepper
2 cloves garlic, crushed

Mix all ingredients thoroughly.

Virginia Berner

Sautéed Scallops with Mousseline of Champagne

36 sea scallops
Salt and pepper to taste
8 egg yolks
3 tablespoons warm water
1 tablespoon fresh lemon juice
Pinch cayenne
*4 cups clarified butter *see below*
¾ cup heavy cream, whipped
1 cup champagne
36 pink peppercorns

Heat a dry nonstick sauté pan or skillet, and sear the scallops on both sides until well colored, for a total of 3-5 minutes. Season with salt and pepper, set aside, and keep warm. In the top of a double boiler over simmering water, whisk together the egg yolks, water, lemon juice and cayenne until thick and pale. Whisk in the clarified butter and blend thoroughly, then add the cream, champagne and peppercorns. Spoon the sauce onto 12 appetizer plates and place three scallops on top of each. Serves 12

Clarified Butter

Melt butter over low heat. Remove from heat and let stand for a few minutes, allowing the milk solids to settle to the bottom. Skim the white foam from the top and pour the clear butter into a container, being careful to keep the milk at the bottom. One stick of butter produces one-third cup clarified butter.

Betsy Harris

Shrimp Vinaigrette Wrapped in Snow Peas

1 pound of large shrimp (28-30)
1 10 ounce box of frozen snow peas
½ cup olive oil
3 tablespoons white wine vinegar
3 tablespoons Dijon mustard
1 tablespoon chopped shallots
1 teaspoon finely minced ginger
1 clove garlic, minced
1 teaspoon dried dill
Pinch of sugar
Salt and pepper to taste

Boil and peel the shrimp, leave the tails on. Mix all the remaining ingredients, except peas, in a covered jar. Shake well and pour over the shrimp. Coat well, cover the bowl, and refrigerate for 1-2 days, tossing every 12 hours. After the shrimp have marinated, defrost the peas, and if necessary immerse the peas in ice water so they stay very cold. With the tip of a sharp knife, split the chilled pods lengthwise so that you have separate halves. Wrap one of the pea pod halves around the middle of each shrimp, and fasten with a toothpick. Serve cold or at room temperature. Makes 28-30 hors d'oeuvres, but this recipe can be doubled or tripled.

Betsy Harris

Shrimp à la Setz

3 pounds cooked shrimp, peeled
2 red onions, sliced into rings
2 cups Ott's French dressing
½ cup orange juice

Marinate shrimp and onion rings in dressing mixed with orange juice in the refrigerator for six hours or more. Serve cold with your favorite crackers.

Georganne Peel

Celestial Wings

1 cup pineapple juice
1 cup soy sauce
1 clove garlic, minced
2 tablespoons minced onion
1 teaspoon ground ginger
¼ cup brown sugar
1 can beer
¼ cup butter
3 pounds chicken wings, tips removed

In a saucepan, combine first eight ingredients. Cook over medium heat until sugar dissolves. Pour over the chicken wings and marinate for eight hours. Drain and bake chicken in oven on a broiler pan at 325 degrees for about 25 minutes, turn over and bake another 10-15 minutes. Serve on a platter or chafing dish. This was served at Charity Ball 1985.

Kay Stephens

Tortellini with Parmesan Dip

1 cup crème fraîche (recipe follows)
¼ cup Parmesan cheese
Juice of two lemons
Grated peel of two lemons
3 cloves garlic, minced
1½ pounds tortellini (you can use frozen)
40 6" wooden skewers

Combine the first five ingredients to make the dip. Refrigerate until ready to use. Cook the tortellini according to package directions. Drain the pasta and sprinkle with some olive oil to prevent sticking. Put two warm tortellini on each skewer and serve immediately with the dip. Note: you may use whatever type of tortellini you like. Makes 40 servings

Crème Fraîche

2 tablespoons buttermilk
2 cups heavy cream

Heat cream over low heat to just warm. Add buttermilk and stir well. Put in a covered jar and let set at room temperature for 6-8 hours. Refrigerate at least 24 hours before serving. Makes two cups

The Committee

Cold Almond Tea

1 family-sized tea bag
1½ cups sugar
2 tablespoons almond extract
⅔ cup lemon juice
1 bottle ginger ale
1 quart water

Make two cups of strong tea using the tea bag. Stir in the sugar and dissolve. Pour this into a pitcher containing one quart of water. Stir in the almond extract and lemon juice. To each glass pour in ¼ part ginger ale and fill with tea mixture. Serve over ice. May be garnished with a mint leaf.

Linda Bewley

Special Tea

1 quart water
2 cups sugar
7 regular tea bags
Sprig of mint
1 6 ounce can frozen orange juice
1 6 ounce can frozen lemon juice

Bring water to a boil, add sugar, tea bags and mint. Steep for 15-20 minutes covered. Remove bags. Thaw citrus juices and add to the tea. Add water to make one gallon.

Lou Adams

Mexican Hot Chocolate

- 4 *cups milk*
- ½ *cup firmly packed dark brown sugar*
- 2 *ounces unsweetened chocolate, coarsely chopped*
- 2 *egg whites*
- ¾ *teaspoon ground cinnamon*
- ¾ *teaspoon vanilla extract*
- ¾ *teaspoon almond extract*

In a large saucepan over medium heat, cook the milk, sugar and chocolate until smooth, stirring frequently. Increase the heat, bringing the mixture to a gentle boil and remove from heat. Beat the egg whites until frothy. Using a hand mixer gradually beat them into the chocolate mixture. The mixture will be frothy. Stir in the extracts and return to heat for one minute. Serve hot. Serves 4

This makes the best hot chocolate in the world!

Betsy Harris

Mock Champagne Punch

- 1 *6 ounce can frozen lemonade concentrate, thawed*
- 1 *6 ounce can frozen pineapple juice, thawed*
- 2 *cups cold water*
- 14 *ounces chilled ginger ale*
- 14 *ounces chilled sparkling water*
- 1 *bottle chilled white sparkling Catawba grape juice*

Combine in a punch bowl. Makes 20 servings

Annette Holeyfield

White Wine Punch

- 2 *⅘ quarts dry white wine, chilled*
- 2 *quarts apple juice, chilled*
- 6 *tablespoons lemon juice, chilled*
- 1 *8 ounce can pineapple chunks, chilled*
- 1 *6 ounce jar maraschino cherries, chilled*
- 1 *small bunch grapes, stemmed, chilled*

In your punch bowl, combine the first three ingredients. Drain the pineapple and cherries; drop into the bowl along with the grapes. Makes 25 six ounce servings

Kathy Smith

Iced Tea Punch

3 *pints strong tea*
½ *cup sugar*
1 *6 ounce can lemonade, thawed*
1 *6 ounce can orange juice, thawed*
Ginger ale

Mix together the tea and sugar. Stir in the juices. To serve, pour 3 parts tea mixture to 1 part ginger ale into a large pitcher. Serve with mint.

Virginia Berner

Spiced Tea Punch

20 *cups hot water*
8 *rounded teaspoons instant tea*
2½ *cups sugar*
1 *6 ounce can frozen lemonade*
1 *6 ounce can frozen orange juice*
1 *6 ounce can frozen apple juice*
1 *teaspoon cloves*
4 *cinnamon sticks*

Bring water to a boil and dissolve tea and sugar. Add the frozen juices. Stir in the cloves and add the cinnamon sticks. Heat and serve. Serves about 30

Pat Gordon

Strawberry Punch

3 *10 ounce boxes frozen strawberries, partially thawed*
3 *large cans pineapple juice, cold*
3 *1.4 ounce packages unsweetened strawberry fruit flavored drink mix*
3 *cups water*
3 *6 ounce cans frozen orange juice, partially thawed*
1 *1 ounce bottle almond extract*
1 *1 ounce bottle vanilla extract*
1 *1 quart bottle ginger ale, chilled*
3 *pints pineapple sherbet*

Combine first seven ingredients in a large punch bowl. Add enough water to make 2¾ gallons of punch. Add ginger ale and sherbet, broken into chunks just before serving. Makes 100 one cup servings

Marlene Newton

Bailey's Irish Cream

1 cup Irish whiskey
1 cup half and half
1 can sweetened condensed milk
3 whole eggs
2 tablespoons vanilla
2 tablespoons chocolate syrup
½ cup white crème de cacao

Mix all of the ingredients in a blender and refrigerate. Don't worry about the raw eggs, as the liquor "cooks" them. Stir again in the blender before serving.

Toni Weatherford

Freight Train Jane's Margaritas

2 fifths tequila
1 pint triple sec
3½ quarts water
8 6 ounce cans frozen limeade
8 ounces lime juice
½ cup lemon juice
Margarita salt

Mix all ingredients. Freeze; this will take up to 36 hours. Enjoy! This recipe was used by the late Jane Traylor in her catering business "Fabulous Foods" of Little Rock.

Toni Weatherford

Hot Buttered Rum

1 pound butter, softened
1 pound dark brown sugar
1 pound powdered sugar
1 quart vanilla ice cream, softened
Dark rum

Mix first four ingredients together. Store in freezer. For each serving use four parts mixture to one part hot dark rum.

Bonnie Haines

Tennessee Lemonade

1 part whiskey
1 part sweet and sour mix
1 part triple sec
4 parts lemon/lime carbonated beverage

Stir the above together. Add ice and garnish with lemon slices and maraschino cherries.

Connie Neumeier

Whiskey Slush

2 cups strong tea, hot
½ cup sugar, or to taste
2 6 ounce cans frozen orange juice
1 6 ounce can frozen lemonade
3 cups bourbon
7 cups cold water
Fresh mint for garnish

Dissolve the sugar in the tea. Add the remaining ingredients and stir until well mixed. Place in the freezer, stirring occasionally, until it hardens and becomes "slushy". This will take from several hours to overnight. Serve in double old fashion glasses and garnish with a sprig of mint. A summer favorite!

Betsy Harris

Fruit Smoothie

1 6 ounce can frozen orange juice
1 large ripe banana, sliced OR
1½ cups fresh strawberries OR
1½ cups drained canned peaches
1 cup skim milk
1 cup water
2 tablespoons honey
5 ice cubes

Combine orange juice, fruit of your choice, milk, water and honey in the pitcher of an electric blender. Cover, whirl at high speed until thick and smooth, about one minute. Add ice cubes, one at a time, and blend until smooth and frothy. Garnish with a whole strawberry and serve.

Vickie Hale

Tropical Fruit Smoothie

1 8 ounce can pineapple chunks, juice pack
1 large ripe mango
1 large ripe banana
1 8 ounce carton pineapple yogurt

Drain pineapple, reserving juice. Cover and chill the juice. Peel the mango and cut in half, remove seed. Cut mango into chunks. Peel and slice banana. Combine pineapple, mango and banana in freezer-proof bowl. Cover and freeze two hours or until firm. When ready to serve, combine reserved pineapple juice, frozen fruit and pineapple yogurt in blender. Purée until smooth, adding ice gradually until mixture equals four cups. Serve immediately. Makes 4 eight ounce glasses

Patti Nickels

A.C.I. Fruit Fantasy Blender Drink

- 2 *tablespoons red raspberry yogurt*
- *Juice of two oranges*
- 1-2 *cups apple juice*
- 5 *tablespoons pink lemonade concentrate, frozen*
- 5 *frozen strawberries*
- 1 *peach, optional (if in season)*
- 1 *teaspoon vanilla*
- 8 *ice cubes*
- 1 *teaspoon sugar, if needed*
- 1 *egg, optional, for froth*

Put all ingredients into the blender. Touch pulse to blend to desired consistency. Add milk if liquid is needed. Makes 5-6 cups

Jane Barnes

Instant Hot Chocolate Mix

- 8 *quart box of instant milk, powdered*
- 1 *one pound box powdered sugar*
- 1 *16 ounce box Nestle's Quick*
- 1 *6 ounce jar coffee creamer*

Mix thoroughly in a huge bowl or pan. Use ⅓-½ mug or cup of mix and stir in boiling water to fill. This makes a large amount, but you use a lot per cup so it goes fast. I store it in zip lock bags and freeze it.

Jane New

Fireside Mix

- 2 *cups non-dairy powdered creamer*
- 2 *cups hot cocoa mix (5 envelopes equals one cup)*
- 1½ *cups instant coffee granules*
- 1½ *cups sugar (or 1 cup sugar substitute and ½ cup real sugar)*
- 3 *teaspoons cinnamon*
- 2 *teaspoons nutmeg*

Combine all ingredients in a large bowl. Blend 1-1½ cups at a time until fine. Store in an airtight container. To serve: heat a coffee cup full of water to boiling and then stir in three heaping teaspoons and stir until blended. Enjoy by the fireplace!

Tonia Beavers

Coffee Punch

4 quarts strong coffee
5 teaspoons vanilla
5 tablespoons sugar
1 quart whipping cream, whipped and chilled
2 quarts vanilla ice cream

Prepare strong brewed coffee. Add vanilla and sugar and chill thoroughly. When ready to serve, spoon ice cream into punch bowl. Add coffee mixture and fold in whipped cream. Taste before serving, and add more sugar if needed. Best not too sweet. Recipe can be halved for a small group. Serves 50

This is the BEST coffee punch I've ever tasted.

Jackie Gardner

Children's Punch

1 large can apple juice
1 large can pineapple juice
1 large can orange juice
Ginger ale, optional

Mix juices together in a large pitcher, chill. Add chilled ginger ale, if desired, for added flavor.

Connie Neumeier

PASS THE BREAD

Mr. Hampton's Beaten Biscuits

- 6 *cups bleached flour*
- 4 *tablespoons sugar*
- 2 *teaspoons salt*
- 1 *teaspoon baking powder*
- 1 *cup pure lard*
- ⅔ *cup sweet milk*
- ⅓ *cup water*

Heat oven to 350 degrees. Mix flour, sugar, salt and baking powder in a bowl. Cut in lard with a fork or pastry blender until texture resembles cornmeal. Add milk and water. Knead until dough is stiff and elastic. Beat the dough 10-15 minutes with a heavy rolling pin or other instrument or put it through a beaten biscuit machine until smooth. Roll dough to about ¼-inch thickness. Cut out with a 2-inch round biscuit cutter. Prick each biscuit twice with a fork. Place on an ungreased cookie sheet. Bake until slightly golden, about 30 minutes. Biscuits should be crisp throughout and the insides should not be the least bit soggy. Makes 5 dozen

The Committee

Butter Batter Bread

- 3 *cups whole wheat flour*
- 2 *packages active dry yeast*
- 2½ *cups buttermilk*
- ¼ *cup molasses*
- ¼ *cup honey*
- 1 *tablespoon salt*
- ⅓ *cup butter*
- 1½ *cups rolled oats*
- 2 *eggs*
- 2½ *to 3 cups sifted all purpose flour*
- 2 *tablespoons melted butter*

Preheat oven to 375 degrees. Grease two 1½ quart round, 2½" deep casserole dishes. Combine whole-wheat flour and yeast. Heat buttermilk, molasses, honey, salt and butter until warm (105-115 degrees). Pour into 3 quart mixing bowl. Add oats, flour/yeast mixture and eggs. Blend at low speed until moistened. Beat 3 minutes at high speed. Stir in enough flour to make a stiff dough. Brush with melted butter. Cover. Let rise in a warm place until doubled, about 1 hour. Punch down and shape into 2 round loaves. Place in casseroles. Cover and let rise until double, about 45 minutes. Bake for 25-35 minutes or until loaves sound hollow when tapped.

Mary Noel Mabry

Quick Cheese Bread

- 2 *eggs*
- ¾ *cup water*
- 2 *5½ ounce packages biscuit baking mix*
- 2 *teaspoons dry mustard*
- 1½ *cups grated cheese, divided*
- 2 *tablespoons butter*

Heat oven to 350 degrees. Grease an 8½ x 4½ x 2½ loaf pan. Beat eggs in a large bowl. Stir in water. Add biscuit mix and beat. Add mustard and 1 cup cheese. Mix thoroughly. Turn batter into pan. Sprinkle with remaining cheese and dot with butter. Bake 45 minutes. Cool in pan for 15 minutes. Remove and cool on rack before slicing.

Annette Holeyfield

Corn Bread

- 2 *cups buttermilk (room temperature)*
- 1 *egg (room temperature)*
- 1 *tablespoon oil*
- 1½ *cups self-rising cornmeal*
- 3 *tablespoons flour*
- 1 *teaspoon salt*

Combine dry ingredients and mix well. Combine buttermilk, egg and oil. Add to dry ingredients. Mix well. Pour into hot greased 9" iron skillet. Bake 30 minutes at 425 degrees. Serves 6-8

Linda Richardson

Cornlight Bread

- 2 *cups cornmeal*
- 1 *cup flour*
- ½ *cup sugar*
- 1 *teaspoon salt*
- 1 *teaspoon soda*
- 2 *cups buttermilk*
- 3 *tablespoons vegetable oil*

Mix dry ingredients in large mixing bowl. Blend in buttermilk and oil. Pour into greased 9 x 5 loaf pan. Let mixture set 10 minutes then bake at 375 degrees for 35-40 minutes. Let cool 5 minutes before removing from pan.

Susan Dishner

Broccoli Cornbread

- 1 *10 ounce box frozen chopped broccoli*
- 2 *6 ounce packages corn muffin mix*
- 3 *eggs*
- 1 *onion, diced*
- 1 *8 ounce carton cottage cheese*
- 1½ *sticks butter, melted*

Mix all ingredients well. Bake at 425 degrees for 30-35 minutes.

Connie Neumeier

Cream of Wheat Cornbread

½ cup cream of wheat
½ cup sifted flour
¼ cup sugar
1 tablespoon baking powder
Pinch salt
½ cup milk
1 egg
Oil

Oil iron skillet well. Place in oven and preheat to 375 degrees. In medium bowl, mix all ingredients well. When oven and skillet are preheated, pour mixture into skillet and cook 25-30 minutes, until brown.

Susie Nicholson

Nancy's Mexican Cornbread

4 jalapeño peppers, chopped and seeded
1½ cups yellow cornmeal
2 eggs, well beaten
1½ cups milk
½ teaspoon soda
1 teaspoon salt
1 16 ounce can whole kernel corn, drained
1 large onion, chopped
½ cup of bacon drippings, melted and then measured
1 pound hot sausage
1 pound sharp cheddar cheese, grated

Mix together in large bowl the peppers, cornmeal, eggs, milk, soda, salt and corn. Sauté the onion in the bacon drippings and add to the above. Fry the sausage, crumbling it as it cooks, and drain well. Add ⅔ of the sausage to the above mixture. Grease well a 12" iron skillet. Line the bottom with wax paper and grease again. Pour ½ of your batter into the skillet. Top with the grated cheddar cheese. Pour in the rest of your batter and put the remaining ⅓ of the sausage on top. Gently pat into the batter. Bake at 350 degrees for 45 minutes.

The Committee

Helen Richardson's Fried Corn-Meal Patties

1½ cups white cornmeal
2 eggs
¼ cup flour
1½ cups buttermilk

Mix ingredients together (batter should be thicker than for cornbread). Drop in patties in small amount of hot grease. Fry until brown and crispy.

Joyce R. Laws

Refrigerator Bread

2 packages yeast
½ cup warm water
¼ cup sugar
¼ cup shortening
2 cups warm milk
6-7 cups flour
2 teaspoons salt

Dissolve yeast in warm water. Combine remaining ingredients and add yeast mixture. Knead well. Cover and place in refrigerator until double in size (about 2 hours). Punch down and form into cloverleaf rolls. Let rise and bake in 350 degree oven for 20-25 minutes. This dough is also wonderful for making cinnamon rolls. After dough has risen in refrigerator, take half and roll out, brush with melted butter and sprinkle with cinnamon and sugar. Let rise until double and bake at 400 degrees for 20-25 minutes.

Kay Roberts

Spinach Bread

1 10 ounce package chopped spinach
1 6-count package French rolls
¼ cup softened butter
1 medium onion, chopped
¼ cup butter, melted
1 6 ounce roll process cheese food with garlic
1 teaspoon Worcestershire sauce
⅛ teaspoon pepper
2 cups shredded Mozzarella cheese

Drain spinach and squeeze dry with paper towels. Set aside. Cut rolls in half lengthwise. Spread halves with ¼ cup butter. Sauté onion in remaining ¼ cup butter. Add garlic cheese, stirring until cheese melts. Remove from heat. Add spinach, Worcestershire sauce and pepper, stirring well. Spread spinach mixture on bread. Sprinkle with Mozzarella cheese. Bake at 350 degrees for 8 minutes or until cheese melts. Serve immediately. Makes 12 servings

Kathy Smith

Spoon Bread

1 package dry yeast
2 cups warm water
4 tablespoons sugar
1 egg
½ cup powdered milk
¾ cup cooking oil
4 cups flour

Dissolve yeast in water. Add other ingredients in order listed, mix well. Cover and refrigerate until ready to use. Stores well. Drop by tablespoonful into muffin tin. Bake at 425 degrees for 20 minutes.

Jalia Lingle

Applesauce Nut Bread

1 cup sugar
1 cup applesauce
⅓ cup oil
2 eggs
3 tablespoons milk
2 cups flour
1 teaspoon baking soda
½ teaspoon baking powder
½ teaspoon cinnamon
¼ teaspoon salt
¼ teaspoon nutmeg
¾ cup chopped nuts

Combine first five ingredients. Sift together dry ingredients and add to applesauce mixture. Stir in nuts. Pour into a greased loaf pan. Before baking add following topping mixture to top of batter.

Topping

¼ cup brown sugar
½ teaspoon cinnamon
¼ cup chopped pecans or walnuts

Bake at 350 degrees for 1 hour. Cover with foil the last 30 minutes to prevent burning.

Linda Fenech

Old Fashioned Walnut Bread

3 cups sifted flour
1 cup sugar
4 teaspoons baking powder
2 teaspoon salt
1 egg, lightly beaten
¼ cup melted shortening
1½ cups milk
1 teaspoon vanilla
1½ cups chopped walnuts

Resift flour with sugar, baking powder and salt. Add egg, shortening, milk and vanilla to dry mixture. Stir just until all of flour is moistened. Stir in walnuts. Turn into 9 x 5 x 3 greased loaf pan or divide batter between 2 greased 2½ pound cans. Bake at 350 degrees: 1 hour 20 minutes for loaf pan and 1 hour 10 minutes for round cans.

Jalia Lingle

Butter Brickle Bread

1 box butter brickle cake mix
1 small package instant coconut pudding
1 cup hot water
4 eggs
¼ cup Wesson oil
½ cup chopped pecans
⅛ cup poppy seeds

Combine first five ingredients. Beat at medium speed just until combined. Add last two ingredients and stir until moist. Bake at 350 degrees for 15 minutes, then at 325 degrees for 35 minutes.

Patti Nickels

Banana Blueberry Bread

½ *cup shortening*
1 *cup sugar*
2 *eggs*
1 *cup mashed banana*
½ *cup quick cooking oats*
½ *cup chopped pecans or walnuts*
1½ *cups all-purpose flour*
1 *teaspoon soda*
¼ *teaspoon salt*
½ *cup blueberries*

Cream shortening. Gradually add sugar, beating until light and fluffy. Add eggs, one at a time, beating well after each addition. Stir in banana. Combine next 5 ingredients, stirring gently. Add blueberries to creamed mixture and stir until moist. Spoon batter into greased and floured 9 x 5 x 3" loaf pan. Bake at 350 degrees for 50-55 minutes or until wooden pick inserted in center comes out clean. Cool in pan 10 minutes; remove from pan and cool completely on a wire rack.

Judy Thacker

Cream Cheese Banana Nut Bread

1 *cup sugar*
1 *8 ounce package light cream cheese*
3 *ripe bananas*
2 *eggs*
2 *cups biscuit baking mix*
1 *cup chopped pecans*

Preheat oven to 350 degrees. In a bowl, cream together sugar and softened cream cheese. Beat in mashed bananas and eggs. Add biscuit baking mix and pecans. Pour into a greased loaf pan. Bake for 50 minutes, or until done. Cover pan with aluminum foil if it starts getting too brown on top during last 20 minutes of cooking time. Cool before slicing. Spread with butter and warm in microwave.

Tamara Laws

Pear Bread

3 *cups flour*
1 *teaspoon soda*
¼ *teaspoon baking powder*
1 *teaspoon salt*
1 *teaspoon cinnamon*
¾ *cup vegetable oil*
3 *eggs*
2 *cups sugar*
2 *cups peeled and grated pears*
2 *teaspoons vanilla*
1 *cup chopped nuts*

In large mixing bowl combine the flour, soda, baking powder, salt and cinnamon. In another bowl beat the eggs lightly with the vanilla. Mix the vegetable oil into the egg mixture along with the sugar. Add the dry ingredients to the egg mixture and blend well. Stir in the pears and nuts. Pour batter into two greased and lightly floured standard size loaf pans. Bake at 325 degrees for 1 hour and 15 minutes. Makes two loaves

Betsy Harris

Cranberry Bread

2 *cups flour*
1 *cup sugar*
½ *teaspoon soda*
1½ *teaspoons baking powder*
½ *teaspoon salt*
Juice and grated rind of 1 orange
2 *tablespoons of cooking oil*
1 *egg, beaten*
1 *cup chopped pecans*
2 *cups chopped cranberries*

Glaze

½ *cup powdered sugar*
2 *teaspoons melted butter*
Juice of ½ lemon or enough juice to spread

Mix together the flour, sugar, soda, baking powder and salt. To the juice and grated rind, add the cooking oil; add enough boiling water to make ¾ cup liquid. Add beaten egg to dry ingredients; then add the liquid. Last, add pecans and cranberries and mix thoroughly. Pour in greased loaf pan or pans. Bake at 325 degrees for 50-60 minutes. Cool slightly, then glaze.

Jane Fore

Strawberry Cream Cheese Bread

3 *cups flour*
2 *cups sugar*
1 *teaspoon soda*
1 *teaspoon salt*
2 *10 ounce cartons frozen strawberries (reserve ½ cup for filling), thawed*
4 *eggs, beaten*
1 *cup oil*

Spread

1 *8 ounce cream cheese*
½ *cup strawberries*
2 *tablespoons powdered sugar*

Thoroughly mix all dry ingredients. Make a hole in the center of the mixture and add liquid ingredients and strawberries. Mix by hand. Pour mixture into two greased and slightly floured loaf pans. Bake at 325 degrees for 45 minutes. Cool, slice and serve with spread.

Gaye Croom

Sweet Potato Bread

1½ cups sugar
½ cup vegetable oil
2 eggs
½ cup water
1¾ cups all purpose flour
½ teaspoon cinnamon
1 teaspoon nutmeg
1 teaspoon baking soda
½ teaspoon salt
1 cup cooked mashed sweet potatoes
½ cup chopped pecans
½ cup raisins, optional

Combine sugar, oil, eggs and water. Beat at medium speed just until combined. Mix next five ingredients in separate bowl. Pour into egg mixture and stir until moist. Add sweet potatoes, raisins and pecans. Pour mixture into two greased loaf pans. Bake at 350 degrees for one hour. Cool 10 minutes in pan. Remove and allow to cool completely.

Patti Nickels

Zucchini Bread

3 eggs
1 cup oil
2 cups sugar
2 cups peeled and grated zucchini
1 teaspoon vanilla
3 cups flour
1 teaspoon salt
1 teaspoon soda
3 teaspoons cinnamon
¼ teaspoon baking powder
½ cup pecans, optional
½ cup raisins, optional

Beat eggs until light. Mix oil, sugar, zucchini and vanilla in a separate bowl and set aside. Mix flour, salt, soda, cinnamon, baking powder, raisins and pecans. Blend wet and dry ingredients together and pour into two greased loaf pans. Bake at 325 degrees for 60 minutes or until toothpick inserted comes out clean.

Judy Murphy

Coffee Cake

1 package frozen Parker House dinner rolls
½ cup sugar
1½ teaspoons cinnamon
½ cup chopped pecans
½ cup brown sugar
1 small package butterscotch pudding (not instant)
1¼ sticks butter or oleo

Lightly grease bundt pan. Layer rolls in pan. Mix cinnamon and sugar and pour over rolls. Layer nuts, pudding and brown sugar. Slice butter and put on top. Cover and set in warm place (top of refrigerator) 8-12 hours (overnight). Bake the next morning at 350 degrees for 35-40 minutes.

Jane Fore

Crumb Coffee Cake

2½ cups flour
1 cup brown sugar
1 cup white sugar
1 teaspoon salt
1 teaspoon nutmeg
1 teaspoon cinnamon
¾ cup vegetable oil
1 egg
1 cup milk
1 teaspoon soda

Mix flour, sugars, salt, cinnamon, nutmeg and oil together. Set aside ⅔-1 cup for topping. Add remaining ingredients to first mixture. Pour into 9 x 13 pan. Sprinkle with crumbs that were set aside. Bake at 350 degrees for 30-45 minutes.

Ruth Narveson

Jewish Coffee Cake

2⅓ cups flour
¾ cup brown sugar
1 cup white sugar
¾ cup salad oil
1 cup buttermilk
6 tablespoons margarine
1 teaspoon nutmeg
1 teaspoon soda
1 teaspoon salt
1 teaspoon baking powder
1 cup chopped nuts
2 teaspoons cinnamon

Stir flour and sugars together. Take out one cup after mixing and into this cup stir cinnamon and nuts. Set aside for topping. Into remaining flour mixture, stir nutmeg, soda, salt and baking powder. Beat in oil and buttermilk. Pour into greased and floured 9 x 12 pan. Sprinkle with topping mixture and drizzle with melted butter. Bake 30 minutes at 350 degrees.

Kay Roberts

True Blueberry Buttermilk Muffins

2½ cups all purpose flour
2½ teaspoons baking powder
1 cup sugar
¼ teaspoon salt
1 cup buttermilk
2 eggs, beaten
½ cup butter, melted and slightly browned
1½ cups fresh blueberries, rinsed and drained

Grease 24 small muffin cups. In a large bowl sift together the dry ingredients. Make a well in the center and add the buttermilk, eggs and butter. Mix well. Fold in the blueberries. Pour into the prepared muffin cups. Bake at 400 degrees for 20 minutes.

Vickie Hale

Easy Cinnamon Muffins

⅔ cup butter
1 cup sugar
3 cups flour
3 teaspoons baking powder
1 teaspoon salt
½ teaspoon nutmeg
2 eggs
1 cup milk
⅔ cup melted butter
1 cup sugar
1 teaspoon cinnamon

Cream butter and sugar. Add eggs to the creamed mixture. Sift flour, baking powder, salt and nutmeg together. Add dry ingredients to creamed mixture, alternating with milk. Mix thoroughly after each addition. In lightly greased small muffin tins place dough to fill about ¾ full. Bake for 20 minutes at 350 degrees. Cool slightly. Combine other sugar and cinnamon. Roll muffins in melted butter and then in the sugar/cinnamon mixture.

Debbie Bell

Breakfast Raisin Muffins

1½ cups water
1 cup golden raisins
1 teaspoon baking soda
1½ cups all purpose flour
¾ cup sugar
1 teaspoon ground nutmeg
1 teaspoon ground cinnamon
¼ cup vegetable oil
1 egg, beaten

Bring water to a boil. Add raisins and return to a boil. Cover, reduce heat and simmer 20 minutes, stirring occasionally. Drain, reserving liquid; add water to measure ½ cup, if necessary. Dissolve soda in liquid. Combine next 4 ingredients; stir in raisins and make a well in center of mixture. Combine oil, egg and soda mixture. Add to dry ingredients, stirring just until moistened. Spoon batter into greased muffin pans, filling ⅔ full. Bake at 350 degrees for 20-25 minutes. Yields 1 dozen

Carol Shoptaw

Chocolate Muffins

1¾ cups sugar
1 cup flour
4 eggs
2 sticks oleo
¾ cup chocolate chips
2 cups chopped pecans

Mix sugar, flour and eggs. Melt oleo and chocolate chips. (Do not heat too long for this tends to make muffins fall.) Add melted ingredients to eggs, flour and sugar. Pour into paper lined muffin tins and bake 20-25 minutes at 325 degrees.

Connie Neumeier

Robbin's Peach Muffins

1 large egg
1 cup milk
¼ cup melted butter
⅔ cup sugar
½ teaspoon salt
¼ teaspoon cinnamon
1 teaspoon lemon juice
¼ teaspoon vanilla
2 cups flour
3 teaspoons baking powder
1 cup unpeeled, chopped ripe peaches

Beat egg. Stir in next seven ingredients. In separate bowl mix the flour and baking powder. Fold flour mixture into egg mixture. Do not overmix. Fold just until blended. Lightly fold in chopped peaches. Grease a standard size muffin pan with solid vegetable shortening. Fill tins about ¾ full. Bake in a preheated 425 degree oven for 20-25 minutes. Makes 12 muffins

The Committee

Blue Corn Muffins

1½ cups blue cornmeal (from health food stores)
1 cup all purpose flour
⅓ cup sugar
1 teaspoon salt
1 tablespoon baking powder
2 eggs
6 tablespoons butter
½ cup vegetable shortening
1 cup milk
½ cup cream
½ red bell pepper, diced
½ yellow bell pepper, diced
4 tablespoons diced onion
¾ cup diced cooked ham

Preheat oven to 375 degrees. In saucepan, melt butter and shortening. Set aside to cool. In clarified butter or oil, sauté peppers and onion. Set aside. In mixing bowl, sift together dry ingredients and set aside. Beat eggs lightly and add melted shortening and butter. Stir in milk, peppers, onions and ham. Add liquid mixture to dry ingredients and stir to blend. Do not overmix. Pour mixture into buttered muffin tins and bake in preheated oven for 12-15 minutes or until lightly browned.

Betsy Harris

Sausage-Corn Muffins

1 6 ounce package cornbread mix
¾ pound mild or hot sausage
1 cup grated sharp cheddar cheese

Prepare mix as directed. Add sausage which has been fried, drained and crumbled. Stir in grated cheese. Spray muffin tins with non-stick spray. Makes about a dozen if using regular muffin pan. Have oven preheated at 400 degrees and bake for 8-10 minutes.

Jackie Gardner

Cornmeal Muffins

1 cup flour
1 cup yellow cornmeal
⅓ cup sugar
1 teaspoon baking powder
1 teaspoon salt
2 teaspoons finely chopped onions
1 cup cream style corn
½ cup mayonnaise
3 teaspoons vegetable oil
1 egg

In large mixing bowl combine dry ingredients. Make a well in center and add all remaining ingredients. Stir just until mixed. Spoon into muffin tins. Bake at 400 degrees for 20 minutes. Yields 12 large or 36 small muffins

Marie Biggers

Hush Puppy Muffins

1 6 ounce box corn muffin mix
2 eggs, beaten
1 cup sour cream
3 teaspoons melted margarine
1 can whole-kernel corn, drained
⅓ cup onions, green or white
½ cup grated cheese

Blend ingredients. Fill muffin cups ⅔ full. Bake at 375 degrees for 25 minutes or until done.

Susie Kroencke

Variety Muffins

1 cup flour
1 cup variable
1 teaspoon baking powder
½ teaspoon salt
¼ cup sugar
1 egg, beaten
⅓ cup oil
1 cup milk

Variables

1 cup bran buds
1 cup oats
1 cup graham crumbs plus 1 teaspoon cinnamon
1 cup whole wheat
1 cup flour plus 1 teaspoon vanilla

Mix together dry ingredients. Make a well in center. If using bran or oats, soak in milk for 15 minutes before mixing. Mix together liquids and pour into flour. Mix until moistened. Spoon into greased muffin cups. Bake 15-20 minutes in 400 degree oven. Good additions are: raisins in bran or oatmeal muffins; 1 cup cranberries or blueberries to plain flour muffins; reduce milk to ¼ cup and add 1 cup mashed bananas to bran muffins; reduce milk to ¼ cup and add 1 cup pumpkin and 1 teaspoon cinnamon or pumpkin spice at Thanksgiving; chocolate lovers reduce milk to ¾ cup, increase oil to ½ cup and stir in ⅔ cup semi-sweet chocolate chips to vanilla muffins.

Virginia Berner

Old Fashioned Sour Milk Pancakes

1 cup sour milk (or fresh milk plus 1½ teaspoons lemon juice)
1 cup sifted flour
1 teaspoon sugar
½ teaspoon salt
¼ teaspoon baking powder
1½ teaspoons soda
4 egg whites
1 teaspoon cream of tartar
2 egg yolks
2 teaspoons melted butter

Sift flour, sugar, salt, baking powder and soda together. Add egg yolks and butter to sour milk. Beat egg whites till fluffy then whisk in cream of tartar. Stir liquid mixture into flour mixture. Fold in egg white mixture and blend. Cook on electric skillet at 365 degrees.

Maysel Teeter

Blueberry Pancakes

1 cup flour
1 teaspoon baking powder
½ teaspoon salt
1 egg
1 cup buttermilk
1 teaspoon sour cream
1 teaspoon molasses
½ cup blueberries

Combine first three ingredients in a medium bowl. In another bowl combine buttermilk, egg, sour cream and molasses. Stir into the dry ingredients. Fold in blueberries. For each pancake, pour about ½ cup batter onto a hot, lightly greased skillet or griddle. Turn pancakes when tops are bubbly. Serve with syrup.

Tonia Beavers

Whole Wheat Pancakes

1 cup whole wheat
1 cup white flour
½ cup wheat germ
4 teaspoons baking powder
2 cups milk
2 eggs
½ cup oil

Mix above ingredients and cook on a hot griddle. Great with blueberry syrup.

Pat Gordon

Waffles

- 2 *eggs*
- 1 *teaspoon salt*
- 1 *tablespoon sugar*
- 1 *package dry yeast*
- ¼ *cup warm water*
- 2 *cups warm milk*
- ½ *cup vegetable oil*
- 3¼ *cups flour, sifted*

Beat eggs thoroughly in a large bowl. Add salt and sugar, blending well. Dissolve yeast in warm water and add it to the egg mixture. Combine the milk and oil. Add them to the egg mixture alternately with sifted flour, ending with a portion of the flour. Cover the bowl and refrigerate it overnight or longer. Bake the waffles according to the directions for your waffle iron. Serve with syrup and melted butter. Serves 6

Betsy Harris

Apple Waffles

- 1¼ *cups flour, sifted*
- 2 *teaspoons baking powder*
- ½ *teaspoon salt*
- 1 *teaspoon cinnamon*
- 3 *tablespoons sugar*
- 2 *tablespoons shortening*
- 2 *eggs, separated*
- 1 *cup milk*
- 1½ *cups grated apples*

Sift together first five ingredients. Cut in shortening. Blend egg yolks and milk. Add to dry ingredients and blend just until moistened. Stir in apples. Beat egg whites until stiff, but not dry. Fold into apple mixture. Cook on your favorite waffle iron.

Kay Roberts

Easy Oatmeal Nut Waffles

- 2 *cups milk*
- 2 *egg yolks*
- 1½ *cups pastry flour*
- 2 *tablespoons cornmeal*
- 4 *tablespoons melted butter or oil*
- 2 *teaspoons baking powder*
- 2 *tablespoons honey or sugar*
- 1 *cup rolled oats*
- 1 *cup chopped pecans or walnuts*
- 2 *egg whites, beaten stiff*

In blender, mix first seven ingredients. Add oats and nuts. Blend until mixed only. Beat egg whites and fold in by hand. Bake in hot greased waffle iron.

Janes Barnes

Brown Sugar Syrup

⅔ cup butter
1½ cups dark brown sugar
1 cup water
1 teaspoon vanilla
½ teaspoon almond extract

Melt butter in saucepan over low heat. Add sugar and water. Bring to boil stirring constantly until sugar is dissolved. Stir in extracts. Makes two cups

Maysel Teeter

Cinnamon Cream Syrup

1 cup sugar
½ cup light corn syrup
¼ cup water
½-¾ teaspoon cinnamon
½ cup evaporated milk

Combine the first four ingredients and bring to a boil over medium heat, stirring constantly. Cook and stir for 2 minutes more. Let the mixture cool for 5 minutes and then stir in the evaporated milk. Makes 1⅔ cups

Betsy Harris

Irish Freckle Bread

2 packages yeast
1 cup warm potato water or water
¼ cup lukewarm mashed potatoes
8 tablespoons sugar
5¼ cups unsifted flour
1 teaspoon salt
2 eggs
½ cup shortening or margarine, melted
1 cup seedless raisins

Dissolve yeast in water. Add mashed potatoes, 2 tablespoons sugar and 1 cup of flour. Beat until smooth. Cover and let set until bubbly (about ½ hour). Stir down and add remaining sugar, salt and 1 cup flour. Beat until smooth. Stir in beaten eggs, then melted and cooled shortening. Add raisins. Stir in flour to make a soft dough. Turn out onto lightly floured board. Knead until smooth and elastic, about five minutes, and place in oiled bowl turning to grease top. Cover and let rise in warm place until double in size. Punch down, divide into 4 equal parts, let rise five minutes, shape each part into a slender loaf about 9" long. Put 2 loaves side by side in two well greased loaf pans. Let rise in warm place one hour or until doubled. Bake at 350 degrees or until done. Makes two loaves

Karen Dunn

The Staff of Life

- 2 *cups milk*
- ½ *cup sugar*
- ½ *cup margarine*
- 1 *teaspoon salt*
- 2 *eggs, well beaten*
- 2 *packages yeast*
- ½ *cup lukewarm water*
- 5 *cups flour*

Put milk, sugar, margarine, salt and eggs in pan and scald. Let cool. Dissolve yeast in water and add to the cooled mixture. Add 3 cups of flour. Beat well then add remaining flour and knead well. Put in oiled bowl and let it rise to double. Knead down well. Can be made into rolls or put in refrigerator. Keeps well for several days. Knead down daily.

Karen Dunn

Bonnie's Homemade Rolls

- 1 *cup water*
- ¾ *cup sugar*
- 1 *cup shortening*
- 1 *teaspoon salt*
- 2 *packages dry yeast*
- 1 *cup warm water*
- 2 *eggs, beaten*
- 7 *cups sifted flour, in large bowl*

Melt shortening and sugar in 1 cup water over low heat. Add salt. When mixture is cool, add eggs. Beat, then add yeast. Pour over flour and mix well. Set aside until double in bulk (1-2 hours) or place in refrigerator over night with damp cloth covering top. When dough has risen, roll out as you would biscuit dough. Melt 1 stick butter. Cut dough with biscuit cutter. Dip each roll in melted butter. Fold roll in half and place in buttered pans. Allow to rise until double or place in refrigerator with wax paper loosely over top. One hour before baking remove from refrigerator and allow to rise. Bake rolls at 350 degrees for 20 minutes, or until brown. This recipe can be easily doubled and you will be glad you did.

Ann Ray

Crescent Rolls

- 2 *packages dry yeast*
- 1 *tablespoon sugar*
- 1 *cup warm water*
- 3 *eggs*
- 1 *teaspoon salt*
- ½ *cup sugar*
- ½ *cup oil*
- 5 *cups sifted flour*

Dissolve yeast and 1 tablespoon sugar in warm water. Add eggs, mix. Add salt, sugar and oil. Stir in flour. Refrigerate overnight. Divide into 2 parts and roll out as thin as pie crust in round shape. Cut into 16 pie shaped wedges, brush with butter and roll from widest point. Let rise on greased sheet 3-4 hours. Bake at 350 degrees for 15 minutes.

Kay Armstrong

Encore Cinnamon Rolls

1½ cups scalded milk
½ cup sugar
2 teaspoons salt
1 package dry yeast
½ cup warm water
2 eggs
½ cup oil
7 cups sifted flour
1 stick butter
Sugar
Cinnamon

Dissolve sugar and salt in scaled milk. Let cool. Place yeast in the warm water for 5 minutes. Do not stir! Add to milk mixture. Stir in eggs and oil. Gradually add flour. Let rise 2 hours at 80 degrees with damp cloth covering bowl. Punch down and knead. Roll out ½ dough at a time into large rectangle. Spread melted margarine on rectangle and sprinkle generously with a sugar and cinnamon mixture. Roll up and cut ½-¾" slices and place into greased pans. Bake at 375 degrees for 15-20 minutes.

Powdered Sugar Glaze

1 cup powdered sugar
2 tablespoons milk
½ teaspoon vanilla

Blend above ingredients together to desired consistency. Pour over warm rolls.

Ann Ray

Big Mama's Doughnuts

1 cup sugar
2 tablespoons shortening
1 cup buttermilk
1 egg, beaten
1 teaspoon baking powder
¼ teaspoon soda
½ teaspoon salt
1 teaspoon vanilla
4 cups flour
Nutmeg and granulated sugar

Cream sugar and shortening. Add rest of ingredients, except the flour, and mix well. Add flour slowly until it's incorporated. Roll out on lightly floured board to about ¼" thick. Cut with a doughnut cutter which has been lightly dipped in flour, and fry in at least 3" of very hot bacon drippings. If you do not have bacon drippings use solid shortening or vegetable oil. While the doughnuts are hot, roll them in sugar spiked with nutmeg until heavily coated. After they have cooled, put any remaining sugar mixture over them and seal in airtight container.

Betsy Harris

Teacakes

2 tablespoons butter
4 tablespoon sugar
1 cup milk
1¼ tablespoons dried yeast
2 eggs, beaten
2½ cups plain flour
½ teaspoon salt

Grease a baking sheet or 2 round cake tins and leave in warm place. Dissolve the butter and 1 teaspoon of the sugar in the milk, heating gently. Do not boil. Remove from heat. Mix the yeast and remainder of sugar together and add to the warm milk. Add the beaten eggs. Let stand 1 hour. Sift flour and salt in large bowl. Make a well in center. Strain liquid and add to flour. Mix well to form soft dough. Knead lightly for 2 minutes on floured surface. Cut dough into equal pieces and shape round. Put on greased tin. Cover with warm cloth and let stand 35 minutes. Bake at 425 degrees for 20-25 minutes. Brush the top with a tablespoon sugar mixed with 1 tablespoon milk and pop back into oven for a few minutes to dry the glaze.

Cathy Andrasik

Keenan's Hush Puppies

2 cups yellow cornmeal
¾ cup flour
2 tablespoons sugar
1 teaspoon salt
1 teaspoon chopped parsley
¼ teaspoon soda
2 tablespoons baking powder
¼ teaspoon cayenne pepper
¼ teaspoon garlic powder
4 green onions, chopped
1 egg
1 cup evaporated milk
1 cup water

Mix dry ingredients. Add liquids and egg and blend well. Make into small rolls or drop by spoonful into hot vegetable oil. Cook until golden brown. Drain on paper. Raw dough can be frozen.

The Committee

Seasoned Bread Crumbs

4-5 slices bread
1 tablespoon crushed oregano leaves
½ teaspoon ground thyme
½ teaspoon onion salt
½ teaspoon salt
¼ teaspoon pepper

Dry bread slices at 250 degrees until crisp and golden. Put in blender on medium speed a few seconds. Mix in seasonings. Store covered in dry place. Makes 1 cup. Adds just that different gourmet taste to casseroles and salads calling for bread crumb toppings.

Susan Barefield

Granola

6 cups old-fashioned rolled oats
1 cup chopped almonds, pecans or cashews
1 cup unsalted sunflower seeds
1 cup unsweetened shredded coconut
1 cup wheat germ
½ cup sesame seeds (optional)
1 cup honey
1 cup oil
1 tablespoon vanilla
1 teaspoon salt

Mix dry ingredients in a large roasting pan or a big Dutch oven-like pan. In a quart jar mix the oil, honey, salt and vanilla. Put a tight lid on the jar and shake vigorously until the honey and oil are mixed. Pour the honey-oil mixture over oatmeal mixture and stir until dry ingredients are moist and well mixed. Bake about 45 minutes in a 275-300 degree oven. Set timer to stir mixture every 10 minutes. It will brown around the edges first. Store in the refrigerator when cooled.

Suzanne Singleton

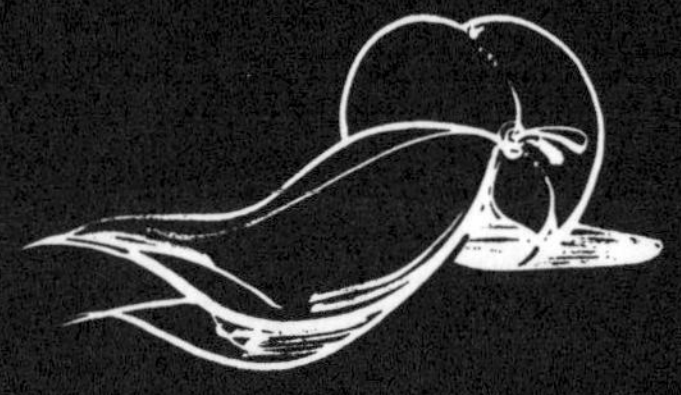

SOUP'S ON, SANDWICHES, TOO

Artichoke-Sausage Soup

- 12 *ounces Italian sausage*
- 2 *14 ounce cans artichoke hearts, drained*
- 3 *14 ounce cans Italian plum tomatoes*
- 1 *envelope onion soup mix*
- 3 *or 4 cups water*
- ½ *teaspoon Italian seasoning*
- ½ *teaspoon oregano*
- ½ *teaspoon basil*

Crumble sausage into pieces in a soup pot. Brown and drain off fat. Cut artichoke hearts and tomatoes into bite-sized pieces. Add to sausage. Add remaining ingredients. Heat thoroughly. Can be made several days in advance. Serves 8

Terri Knight

Black Bean Soup

- 1 *cup black beans, rinsed and soaked overnight*
- 1 *onion, chopped*
- 3 *cloves garlic, minced*
- 1 *jalapeño pepper, seeded and chopped*
- 1 *stalk celery, chopped*
- *Salt and pepper to taste*
- 1 *quart chicken stock*
- 1 *quart beef stock*
- 1 *pound bacon*
- 2 *tablespoons balsamic vinegar*
- 1 *lemon, juiced*
- 1 *carton sour cream or plain yogurt*

Place beans, onion, garlic, jalapeño pepper, celery, chicken and beef stocks, and bacon in large stock pot. Bring to a boil over high heat. Lower heat and simmer for about 2 hours or until beans are soft, skimming off foam frequently. Purée soup in food processor until smooth. Add vinegar, lemon juice, salt and pepper. Serve with a dollop of sour cream or yogurt.

Maysel Teeter

Cold Berry Soup

- 1 *quart fresh orange juice*
- 4 *cups combined yogurt, buttermilk and sour cream (equal amounts of 1⅓ cups each)*
- 1 *tablespoon honey*
- 2 *tablespoons fresh lemon juice*
- *Dash cinnamon*
- *Dash nutmeg*
- 1½ *pints fresh strawberries*

Whisk together all ingredients except berries and chill thoroughly. Wash and drain berries. At serving time, divide berries into serving bowls and ladle soup on top. Garnish with mint. Serves 6-8

Susan Barefield

Mexican Pinto Bean Soup

1 pound dried pinto beans
2 medium onions, chopped
2 tablespoons olive oil
4 cups water
2 cloves garlic, minced
1 teaspoon chili powder
1 sweet red pepper, sliced in ¼" strips
¼ pound Monterey Jack cheese, grated
2 teaspoons salt
1 4 ounce can chili peppers
3 whole chicken breasts, skinned, boned and cut into 1" pieces

Put beans in large bowl. Cover 3" above bean-level with water. Soak overnight. Drain. In large pot, sauté onion in olive oil until golden. Add beans, water, garlic, chili powder and salt. Simmer 1½ hours. Add chili pepper and simmer 30 minutes longer. Add chicken and red pepper. Simmer another 30 minutes or until beans are tender. Add cheese. Remove from heat and serve. Serves 6

Connie Neumeier

Broccoli Soup

1 cup chopped carrots
¼ cup chopped onions
½ cup chopped celery
2 cups chicken broth
1 10 ounce package frozen broccoli
2 cups milk
¼ cup cornstarch
2 cups shredded cheddar cheese

Cook carrots, celery, onion for 10 minutes in broth. Add frozen broccoli, cooking just until tender. Combine cornstarch and milk. Stir into vegetables and cook until thick. Add cheese and stir until melted. Substitute diced potatoes for broccoli for creamy potato soup. Serves 6-8

Georganne Peel

Cabbage Soup

1 pound turkey kielbasa
1 onion, chopped
½ head cabbage, chopped
1-2 cups water
1 can red beans
1 10 ounce can diced tomatoes and green chilies
1 28 ounce can tomatoes, chopped
1 8 ounce can tomato sauce
Garlic powder to taste
Salt and pepper to taste

In a stockpot brown sausage and onion. Add cabbage and water. Cook 10 minutes. Add remaining ingredients. Simmer over low to medium heat for 30 minutes. Gets better and better after it sets awhile. Serves 8

Susie Nicholson

Creamy Cauliflower Soup

1 medium head cauliflower, cut into florets
¼ cup butter or margarine
⅔ cup chopped onion
2 tablespoons flour
1 can chicken broth
1 half pint whipping cream
1 teaspoon Worcestershire sauce
¾ teaspoon salt
1 cup grated cheddar cheese
Chopped chives or parsley

Cook cauliflower in boiling salted water (do not overcook, you don't want it mushy). Drain, reserving liquid. Melt butter. Add onion and cook until soft. Blend in flour; add broth and cook, stirring constantly, until the mixture comes to a boil. Stir in 1 cup liquid drained from the cooked cauliflower, cream, Worcestershire sauce and salt. Add cauliflower. Heat to boiling, stir in cheese. Serve sprinkled with chives or parsley. Makes 2 quarts

Pat Gordon

Chunky Cheese Soup

4 cups frozen hash brown potatoes
1 teaspoon salt
¼ teaspoon pepper
1 cup chopped onion
1 16 ounce package frozen mixed vegetables
6 cups canned chicken broth
2 10 ounce cans cream of chicken soup
1½ pounds processed cheese spread

Add salt and pepper to hash browns. Combine hash brown potatoes, onion, mixed vegetables and broth in a 6 quart saucepan. Bring to a boil over medium-high heat. Cover and reduce heat. Simmer for 15 minutes. Add soup and mix well. Bring to a simmer, stirring frequently. Cut cheese into 1-inch cubes; add several at a time to hot soup. Cook until cheese melts, stirring constantly. Serves 8

Becky Ellison

Chili

3 pounds hamburger meat
3 onions, chopped
2 bell peppers, chopped
5 tablespoons chili powder
3 cloves garlic
3 tablespoons vinegar
2 28 ounce cans of tomatoes, mashed
3 teaspoons salt
¼ teaspoon cayenne pepper
2 teaspoons cumin
Pepper to taste
3 teaspoons Worcestershire sauce
Drained mushrooms, to taste
Drained kidney beans, to taste

Brown hamburger meat; drain. Add remaining ingredients and bring to a boil. Turn to low and simmer 3-4 hours. Serves 10-12

Linda Richardson

Cheddar Chowder

- 2 *cups boiling water*
- 2 *cups diced potatoes*
- ½ *cup sliced carrots*
- ½ *cup diced celery*
- ¼ *cup chopped onion*
- 1½ *teaspoons salt*
- ¼ *teaspoon pepper*
- ¼ *cup margarine*
- ¼ *cup flour*
- 2 *cups milk*
- 2 *cups shredded sharp cheddar cheese*
- 1 *cup cubed cooked ham*

Add water to potatoes, carrots, celery, onion, salt and pepper. Cover; simmer 10 minutes. Do not drain. Make white sauce with margarine, flour and milk. Add cheese; stirring until melted. Add cheese sauce and ham to undrained vegetables. Heat but do not boil. Serves 6-8

Cathy Andrasik

Chicken Corn Chowder

- 4 *slices bacon*
- ½ *cup chopped onion*
- ½ *teaspoon thyme leaves*
- 3 *tablespoons flour*
- 3 *cups milk*
- 1½ *cups cubed cooked chicken*
- 1 *10 ounce package frozen whole kernel corn*
- 1 *medium potato, diced*
- 2 *cups water*
- 2 *tablespoons chicken flavor instant bouillon*
- *Salt and pepper to taste*

Cook bacon until crisp in a large saucepan or kettle. Remove, crumble and reserve bacon. In bacon drippings, sauté onion and thyme until tender. Stir in flour until smooth. Add remaining ingredients except bacon and bring to a boil. Reduce heat and simmer 30 minutes or until vegetables are tender, stirring occasionally. When serving, garnish with bacon. Substitute half and half for milk for a richer soup.

Jackie Gardner

Chicken-Sausage Gumbo

4 split fryer breasts, skinned
2 celery ribs, chopped
1 carrot, cut into fourths
1 onion, cut into fourths
2 bay leaves
1 teaspoon salt
⅓ cup oil
½ cup flour
1 pound frozen okra
1 cup chopped onion
1 cup chopped celery
1 cup chopped green pepper
3 green onions, chopped
2 teaspoons minced garlic
2 bay leaves
1 tablespoon poultry seasoning
1 can tomatoes, undrained
1 pound smoked sausage, sliced
2 tablespoons Worcestershire sauce
1 tablespoon each, salt and pepper
Hot pepper sauce to taste
Steamed rice

In stock pot, bring 3 quarts water to a boil. Add chicken, celery, carrot, onion, bay leaves and salt. Simmer for 25 minutes. Remove chicken and bone. Set meat aside and return bones to broth, continuing to simmer. In another large heavy pot, heat oil and flour, stirring constantly on medium-medium high heat, cooking until you have reached a chocolate color. Add okra, onions, celery, green onions and green pepper. Cook 5-10 minutes. Add seasonings, tomatoes and chicken meat. Strain stock and add to gumbo. Fry sausage and drain on paper towels. Add to gumbo. Simmer 1½ hours. Add Worcestershire sauce, salt and pepper. Add hot pepper sauce to taste. Serve over steamed rice. Serves 12

Tamara Laws

Italian Chicken Soup

2 teaspoons oil
2 whole chicken breasts, cut into 1" pieces
½ cup chopped onion
¼ cup chopped celery
2 garlic cloves, minced
1 teaspoon basil
¼ teaspoon pepper
1 cup water
1 can chicken broth
1 14 ounce can stewed tomatoes
1 cup frozen corn
1 ounce vermicelli, broken into 2" lengths
2 tablespoons Parmesan cheese

Heat oil in 6 quart stock pot. Add chicken and sauté until brown. Add onion, celery and garlic. Cook until tender. Stir in basil, pepper, water, broth and tomatoes. Simmer 1-1½ hours. Stir in corn and noodles and simmer until noodles are al dente. Remove from heat and stir in the Parmesan cheese. Serves 6-8

Tonia Beavers

Ham Bone Soup

- 1 *ham hock, one ham bone, or 1 pound chopped ham*
- 3 *quarts water*
- ¼ *teaspoon black pepper*
- 3 *onions, chopped*
- 4 *medium potatoes, peeled and cubed*
- 1 *small head cabbage, chopped*
- 1 *quart fresh or canned tomatoes*
- *Cayenne pepper, to taste*
- *Salt, to taste*

Boil ham in water with pepper and onion. If ham has been previously cooked, two hours will be sufficient; if not, cook three hours. Remove meat pieces from bone, discard bone. Return meat to water with potatoes, cabbage and tomatoes. Simmer one hour. Taste and adjust seasonings. Let soup cool slightly and remove grease.

Pam Huggins

Ham and Northern Bean Soup

- 2 *16 ounce cans Northern beans*
- 1 *pound ham, diced*
- 4 *medium carrots, diced*
- 1 *onion, diced*
- ½ *green pepper, diced*
- 4 *ribs celery, diced*
- 3 *tablespoons oil*
- 4 *tablespoons flour*
- 2 *tablespoons parsley*
- 2 *teaspoons salt*
- ½ *teaspoon pepper*
- 1 *tablespoon catsup*

In a large pot pour in the cans of Northern beans, ham and carrots. Cover with water and bring to a boil. Turn heat down to simmer. While simmering, in another pan fry onion, celery, green pepper in oil until golden. Place vegetables in soup, reserving oil. Put flour into oil and fry over medium heat until flour mixture turns golden brown. Keep stirring soup and add hot flour mixture by spoonfuls until it dissolves and thickens soup. Add parsley, salt, pepper, catsup to season. Simmer until ready to serve, being sure the carrots are cooked through. Serves 6

Linda Fenech

Hamburger-Vegetable Soup

- 1 *pound ground round*
- 1 *cup diced onions*
- 1 *cup diced potatoes*
- 1 *cup diced carrots*
- 1 *cup diced celery*
- 4 *cups canned tomatoes*
- ¼ *cup uncooked rice or ½ cup uncooked macaroni*
- 3 *cups water*
- 3 *teaspoons salt*
- ¼ *teaspoon basil*
- ¼ *teaspoon thyme*
- 1 *bay leaf*

Brown ground round and drain. Transfer to a stock pot and add remaining ingredients. Simmer 1 hour. May be easily doubled. Serves 6

Linda Bewley

Fogmoor Soup

2 quarts water
8 new potatoes
1 pound smoked sausage, sliced
6 small ears of corn, may use frozen
1 box shrimp and crab boil
1 large onion, quartered
2 pounds shrimp, washed and unshelled
1 can peeled wedge tomatoes
Butter
1 loaf French bread

Boil water, potatoes, onion, shrimp and crab boil. When potatoes are almost tender, add corn, sausage, shrimp and tomatoes. Cook until shrimp is pink (about 10 minutes). Pour into a big bowl. Cover with butter. Serve with sliced French bread for dipping. To make shrimp sauce, mix ½ cup catsup, 1½ teaspoons horseradish and lemon juice. Combine together and chill. Serves 6

Tamara Laws

Lobster-Apple Bisque

1 medium yellow onion, minced
4 green onions (include tops), minced
2 Granny Smith apples
1 stick of margarine
1 tablespoon flour
1 can cream of tomato soup
4 cups half and half
1 teaspoon salt
¼ teaspoon white pepper
1 pound of frozen, minced lobster meat, cooked
¼ cup sherry

Peel, core and dice apples. Sauté onions and apples in butter until soft. Stir in flour and cook, stirring constantly for about 3 minutes. Stir in soup. Stir in half and half, salt and pepper. Let simmer for a few minutes. Add lobster and let simmer a few minutes more. Add sherry.

Betsy Harris

Swiss Onion Soup

1 can cream of chicken soup
1 can chicken broth
1 can French onion soup
¾ can whole milk
¼ can white wine
1 cup shredded Mozzarella cheese

Blend canned soups together. Add milk and wine. Heat thoroughly on range top until all soups, milk and wine are creamed together. Simmer until hot. Divide cheese evenly into 4 soup bowls. Pour blended soup mixture on top and serve immediately. Serves 4

Sue Streett

Oyster Rockefeller Soup

5 *tablespoons flour*
5 *tablespoons butter*
2 *cloves garlic, minced*
1 *onion, chopped*
1½ *cups chicken broth*
3 *cups half and half, scalded*
20 *ounces chopped spinach, drained*
1 *bay leaf*
White wine, salt, pepper, hot pepper sauce to taste
2½ *cups oysters*

Melt butter, add onion and garlic. Cook over medium heat until onions are transparent. Stir in flour, cook and blend. Add chicken stock and cream. Stir until thickened. Add spinach, bay leaf, white wine, salt and pepper. Bring to a boil. Reduce heat and simmer 1 hour. Add oysters and hot pepper sauce. Let soup simmer another hour and adjust seasonings if needed.

Kay Roberts

Baked Potato Soup

4-6 *slices bacon*
½ *small onion, chopped*
5-6 *potatoes, diced*
Water
Milk
Salt and pepper to taste
1 *cup grated cheddar cheese*
1 *bunch green onions, chopped*

Cook bacon in stock pot, removing when crisp. Sauté onion in bacon grease. Add potatoes and just cover with water. Cook over medium heat until potatoes are cooked. Pour off water into measuring cup. Add back that same amount of milk. Simmer over low heat. Add salt and pepper to taste. Garnish servings with cheese and green onions. Serves 6-8

Susie Nicholson

Golden Cream of Potato Soup

6 *cups cubed, peeled potatoes*
2 *cups water*
1 *cup sliced celery*
1 *cup thinly sliced carrots*
½ *cup finely chopped onion*
2 *teaspoons dried parsley flakes*
2 *chicken flavored bouillon cubes*
1 *teaspoon salt*
⅛ *teaspoon pepper*
3 *cups milk, divided*
¼ *cup flour*
¾ *pound processed cheese spread, cubed*

Combine first 9 ingredients in a Dutch oven. Bring to a boil. Cover, reduce heat and simmer 7-8 minutes or until vegetables are tender. Gradually stir ¼ cup milk into flour making a smooth paste. Stir into soup. Add remaining 2¾ cups milk and cheese. Cook over medium heat until soup is thickened. Makes 9 cups

Annette Holeyfield

Spring Vegetable Soup

2 cups water
2 pounds asparagus
4 cups chicken broth
1 cup thinly sliced carrots
1 cup chopped onion
½ cup thinly sliced celery
1 teaspoon minced garlic
1 teaspoon dried tarragon
½ teaspoon salt
¾ cup milk
¾ cup half and half
2 tablespoons fresh lemon juice

Bring water to a boil in large sauce pan. Meanwhile, cut asparagus in 2-inch lengths and reserve tips. Add tips to water and boil until bright green and crisp tender. Drain, rinse in cold water and drain again. Wrap and refrigerate for garnish. Put chicken broth, asparagus pieces, carrots, onion, celery, garlic, tarragon and salt into same saucepan. Bring to a boil, reduce heat, cover and simmer 30-35 minutes until vegetables are very tender. Remove from heat. When cool enough to handle, process batches in food processor or blender until smooth. Return to saucepan, stir in milk and half and half. Heat until simmering. Remove from heat and stir in lemon juice. Garnish with reserved asparagus tips. Makes 7 cups

Sue McCoy

Cold Peach Soup

5 large, very ripe peaches, peeled and quartered
¼ cup sugar (more if needed)
1 cup sour cream
¼ cup fresh lemon juice
¼ cup sherry or white wine
1 tablespoon orange juice concentrate
Sliced, peeled fresh peaches for garnish

Purée peaches and sugar in blender. Mix in sour cream. Add lemon juice, sherry and orange juice, blending until smooth. Refrigerate until well chilled. Serves 6-8

The Committee

Tuna Cheese Buns

⅛ pound sharp American cheese, cubed
2 boiled eggs, chopped
1 can chunk style tuna
1 teaspoon minced green pepper
2 teaspoons minced onion
¾ teaspoon salt
3 teaspoons chopped stuffed olives
2 teaspoons pickle relish
½ cup mayonnaise
6 hamburger buns, buttered

Combine all ingredients and mix. Spoon between split buns. Wrap each bun in foil. Refrigerate. To serve, bake in foil at 350 degrees for 20 minutes. Makes 6 servings

Betsy Harris

BLT Soufflé

4 slices bread
2 eggs
1½ cups grated sharp cheddar cheese
1 teaspoon prepared mustard
Dash Worcestershire sauce
Salt and pepper to taste
4 slices of tomato
4 slices onion
12 half-strips bacon

Place bread on a greased cookie sheet. Combine eggs, cheese, mustard, Worcestershire sauce, salt and pepper in a bowl. Spread mixture onto each slice of bread. Place 2 slices of tomato on each slice of bread. Place onion slice on top of tomato. Crisscross 3 strips of bacon over each. Bake at 300 degrees for 30 minutes. Serves 4

Joyce R. Laws

Cheese and Bacon Spread

1 pound extra sharp cheddar cheese, softened
16 slices crisp bacon, crumbled
1 teaspoon salt
12 green onions, chopped, include part of the tops
1 cup slivered almonds, toasted
2 cups mayonnaise

Grate cheese. Mix all ingredients in order given. Cover and refrigerate. This will keep for days.

Betsy Harris

Crab Soufflé Sandwiches

18 slices bread, trimmed and buttered
2 6½ ounce cans crabmeat, drained
4 tablespoons chopped onion
⅔ cup mayonnaise
4 tablespoons mustard
½ teaspoon salt
Dash pepper
Dash paprika
Dash celery salt
8 slices American cheese
4 eggs
2 cups milk
½ teaspoon salt
½ teaspoon dry mustard

Place 8 slices of bread, buttered side up in a buttered 2 quart casserole dish. Combine crabmeat, onion, mayonnaise, mustard, salt, pepper, paprika and celery salt. Spread crabmeat mixture over bread in casserole. Top each piece of bread with a slice of cheese. Add other 8 slices of bread. Over the sandwiches, pour mixture of eggs, milk, salt and mustard. Bake at 325 degrees for 45-50 minutes. Serve 8

Kathy Smith

Grilled Cheese and Pear Sandwich

½ stick butter, room temperature
⅛ teaspoon grated nutmeg
⅛ teaspoon cinnamon
⅛ teaspoon ground coriander
⅛ teaspoon ginger
Pinch of salt
4 slices firm white bread, crust removed
1 large pear, peeled
2 ¼" thick slices Gruyère cheese
2 ¼" thick slices Fontina cheese

Cream butter and all the seasonings in a small bowl. Spread on both sides of the bread. Cut pear lengthwise into four ¼" thick slices, discarding core. Layer 1 Gruyère slice, 1 pear slice, 1 Fontina slice and another pear slice on each of 2 slices of bread. Cover each with second bread slice. Press down on sandwiches to hold shape. Heat heavy large skillet over medium heat. Add sandwiches and weight with pan lid or plate. Cook until golden brown, turning once, about 4 minutes per side. For variation add 2 paper thin slices of Prosciutto to each of the sandwiches. Serves 2

Betsy Harris

Jack Lowrey's Pimiento Cheese

1 pound pasteurized process cheese spread, softened
1 pound sharp old English cheese, softened
1 pound American cheese, softened
1 large onion, minced
2 medium potatoes, boiled and peeled
10 ounces chopped pimientos with juice
Chopped green olives, optional
Toasted pecans, optional

Put each cheese through a food processor. Add remaining ingredients and process until well mixed.

Betsy Harris

Yocco's Famous Hot Dog Sauce

5 slices bacon
1 pound lean ground beef
½ onion, chopped finely
2 1½ ounce cans of chili powder
Salt and pepper to taste

Fry the bacon in a medium skillet. When done, remove bacon and set aside for another use. In the bacon grease remaining in the skillet, brown the ground beef and onion. Stir in the chili powder and mix. Cover the meat with water, mix well and simmer, covered, for one hour. Let cool in the pan and freeze in small styrofoam cups. When ready to serve, simply reheat. Watch out, this stuff is really potent.

Toni Bachman

TOSS THE SALAD

Ambrosia

1 15 ounce can crushed pineapple, undrained
1 can Mandarin oranges, drained
1 cup seedless green grapes, halved
1 3½ ounce can coconut
1-2 cups tiny marshmallows
½-1 cup sour cream
¼ teaspoon salt

Mix together and chill overnight. Serve in a cut glass bowl.

Tonia Beavers

Hot Apple-Cranberry Salad

3 cups chopped apples
2 cups washed cranberries
1 cup sugar
1 cup quick oats
½ cup brown sugar
½ cup chopped pecans
¼ cup margarine

Combine first 3 ingredients and place in a slightly greased 8 x 12 baking dish. Combine remaining ingredients and process in a food processor. Pour over apples and cranberries. Bake 1 hour at 325 degrees. Watch so it doesn't get too dry.

Susie Kroncke

Orange Almond Salad

2 cups chopped celery
4 green onions, chopped
2 cups Mandarin oranges
12 cups of lettuce or spinach
¾ cup frozen peas

Toss ingredients and set aside.

Dressing

2 teaspoons salt
Dash pepper
4 tablespoons sugar
4 tablespoons red wine vinegar
½ cup oil
2 teaspoons parsley
Dash hot pepper sauce

Mix together all ingredients. Set aside.

Almonds

½ cup slivered almonds
2 tablespoons plus 2 teaspoons sugar

Cook the almonds and sugar over low heat until sugar melts and almonds are coated. Pour out on wax paper to cool. To serve, toss salad, top with almonds. Pour dressing on top just before serving.

Pat Gordon

Blueberry Salad

- 2 *3 ounce packages black cherry gelatin*
- 2 *cups boiling water*
- 1 *8¼ ounce can crushed pineapple*
- 1 *16 ounce can blueberries, partially drained*
- 1 *8 ounce package cream cheese*
- ½ *cup sour cream*
- ½ *cup sugar*
- ¾ *cup chopped pecans*

Add hot water to gelatin to dissolve. Add pineapple juice and blueberries with juice. Pour into 2 quart rectangular casserole dish and chill until set. Combine remaining ingredients and spread over firm gelatin mixture. Serves 8-10

Jalia Lingle

Cranberry Salad

- 1 *cup raw cranberries, ground*
- 1 *cup sugar*
- 1 *3 ounce package lemon gelatin*
- 1 *orange, peeled and sectioned*
- 1 *apple, chopped*
- 1 *cup pecans*

Combine cranberries with sugar and let stand 2 hours or more. Dissolve gelatin as directed on the box. Chill until partially set. Add all other ingredients. Refrigerate until firm. Serves 8

Linda Bewley

Apricot Salad

- 2 *3 ounce packages apricot gelatin*
- 2 *cups boiling water*
- 2 *cups cold water*
- 1 *20 ounce can crushed pineapple, drain (reserve juice)*
- 1 *cup miniature marshmallows*
- 6 *large bananas, sliced*
- 1 *cup chopped pecans*

Dissolve gelatin in 2 cups boiling water. Add cold water. Place in the refrigerator until it starts to thicken. Meanwhile, combine remaining ingredients. Add to gelatin mixture. Pour into large glass casserole dish and refrigerate until set.

Icing

- 3 *tablespoons butter*
- 3 *tablespoons flour*
- 1 *cup reserved pineapple juice*
- ¾ *cup sugar*
- 6 *ounces cream cheese*

Melt butter in a non-stick skillet. Add flour and mix well. Add pineapple juice and sugar. Mix well. Cook until mixture thickens. Pour over cream cheese and blend well. Spread over chilled gelatin.

Bonita Church

Pear-Pomegranate Salad

3 medium soft-ripe pears
1 tablespoon lemon juice
2 cups lightly packed spinach leaves, washed and crisped
½ cup pomegranate seeds
⅓ cup cheddar cheese, shredded
Madeira dressing
Salt and pepper

Halve and core pears. Place in bowl with lemon juice; turn gently to coat. Place a pear half and equal portion of spinach on each of 6 salad plates. Sprinkle with pomegranate seeds and cheese.

Madeira Dressing

1½ tablespoons lemon juice
1½ tablespoons minced Major Grey chutney
2 tablespoons salad oil
2 tablespoons Madeira wine

In a small bowl, whisk together all ingredients. Serve over above salad. Serves 6

Betsy Harris

Peach Salad Supreme

½ cup crushed pineapple, drained
½ cup shredded coconut
½ cup cottage cheese
½ cup sour cream
4 fresh peaches, peeled, seeded and halved

Combine first four ingredients in a medium bowl. Stir well. Chill. Fill peach halves with mixture and serve immediately. Yields 8 servings

Tonia Beavers

Zeta House Salad

3 tablespoons sugar
¾ cup butter
2⅔ cups coarsely crushed large pretzels
1 8 ounce cream cheese
1 cup sugar
1 8 ounce carton frozen whipped topping, thawed
1 6 ounce strawberry gelatin
2 cups boiling water
1 16 ounce package frozen strawberries, thawed

To make crust, cream sugar and butter. Add pretzels and press into a 9 x 13 pan. Bake at 350 degrees for 10 minutes. To make filling, cream sugar and cheese together. Add frozen whipped topping. Spread on cooled crust. To make topping, dissolve gelatin in boiling water; add berries. Allow to partially set. Pour over filling and refrigerate. Note: When I was at college, our house mother served this before every football game. It was a hit.

Susie Nicholson

Pimiento Cheese Salad

- 2 *5 ounce jars pimiento cheese spread*
- 1 *large carton frozen whipped topping*
- 1 *15 ounce can crushed pineapple, drained*
- 1 *cup chopped pecans*

Mix together and chill.

Marlene Newton

Luncheon Chicken Salad

- ½ *cup sour cream*
- ½ *cup mayonnaise*
- ½ *teaspoon soy sauce*
- 1 *small onion, finely chopped*
- 4 *cups cooked chicken breast, cubed*
- 1 *apple, unpeeled and chopped*
- 2 *ribs celery, chopped*
- 2 *tablespoons finely chopped cucumber*
- 1 *cup raisins*
- 1 *cup chopped pecans*

Mix all ingredients together in order given. Chill overnight. Serve either on a bed of lettuce or in pita bread with lettuce and tomatoes. This recipe doubles easily. Serves 8

Teresa Wilkins

Chicken Salad

- 2½ *cups diced, cooked chicken*
- 1 *cup finely cut celery*
- 1 *cup seedless grapes*
- 1 *cup finely chopped nuts*
- 1 *teaspoon minced onion*
- 1 *teaspoon salt*
- ¾-1 *cup mayonnaise or salad dressing*
- ½ *cup heavy cream, whipped*
- *Crisp lettuce*
- *Olives*
- *Sweet pickles*

In a large bowl, combine the chicken, celery, grapes, nuts, onion, salt, mayonnaise and cream. Chill. Serve on lettuce and garnish with sweet pickles and olives. Serves 6

Vickie Hale

Chicken and Carrot Salad

2 cups diced, cooked chicken
1 cup shredded carrots
¾ cup diced celery
½ cup slivered, blanched almonds
2 tablespoons chopped onion
Salt to taste
1 tablespoon lemon juice
1 cup mayonnaise
Lettuce

Combine first six ingredients. Combine lemon juice and mayonnaise and add to chicken mixture. Toss lightly. Chill. Serve on lettuce. Makes 4 servings

Kathy Smith

Chicken Salad

2 2 pound chickens
1 hard cooked egg, chopped
½ cup diced pineapple
Mayonnaise to moisten
½ bunch celery, diced
½ cup chopped nuts
2 apples, diced
½ cup chopped sweet pickles
Salt and pepper to taste

Cook chicken over low heat in salted water until meat is tender (about 1 hour). Remove chicken from stock, cool, remove bones and dice. Combine chicken with remaining ingredients. Chill before serving. Serves 8-10

Linda Richardson

Wild and Brown Rice Chicken Salad

1 chicken
1 6 ounce box long grain brown & wild rice with seasonings
½ cup chicken broth
¼ cup fresh lemon juice
½ teaspoon salt
¼ teaspoon pepper
½ cup pimiento
½ cup chopped celery
½ cup chopped green onion
½ cup sliced almonds
1 10 ounce package frozen peas, thawed

Boil, skin, bone and chop chicken. Cook rice according to package directions, omitting all butter. Set aside to cool. Place warm chicken in medium bowl and pour over broth and lemon juice. Sprinkle with salt and pepper. In large bowl, mix together pimiento and chopped celery. Add chopped green onions. Add rice, stirring gently. Add chicken with juice and broth. Finally, add almonds and green peas. Mix well, cover and refrigerate until completely chilled. Serve on dark green lettuce leaves.

Becky Ellison

Crabmeat Salad

2 6 ounce cans crabmeat, drained
2 4.25 ounce cans shrimp, drained
1 cup chopped celery
1 medium onion, chopped
2 boiled eggs, diced
2 cups mayonnaise
18 slices of bread, cubed

Combine all ingredients and mix. Great on crackers or a bed of lettuce.

Susan Barefield

Crab and Avocado Salad

3 tablespoons olive oil
1 tablespoon tarragon vinegar
½ pound fresh crabmeat
½ cup thinly sliced celery
1 tablespoon chives
2 avocados, peeled and seeded
Lemon juice
Salad greens

With fork, beat together oil and vinegar. Add crabmeat, celery and chives. Mash avocados and add lemon juice to prevent browning.

Dressing

½ cup mayonnaise
1 hard cooked egg, finely chopped
1 tablespoon minced green pepper
1 tablespoon minced stuffed olives
1 teaspoon minced parsley
½ teaspoon grated onion

In a separate bowl, mix ingredients together. Toss with crabmeat mixture. Stir in avocados. Chill. Serve on salad greens.

Laurie Bibler

San Francisco Salad

1 package chicken flavored rice vermicelli mix
2 jars marinated artichoke hearts, drained and chopped (reserve half the oil from one jar)
1 small jar green olives, drained and chopped
3 green onions, chopped
Mayonnaise to taste

Cook chicken flavored rice vermicelli mix as directed. Cool. Add chopped artichoke hearts, olives and green onions. Mix mayonnaise with remaining oil and add to rice mixture. Serve cool. Serves 6

Maysel Teeter

Wild Rice Salad

- 1 *13¾ ounce can beef or chicken broth*
- 1 *16 ounce package long grain and wild rice*
- 1 *11 ounce can Mandarin oranges, drained*
- 1 *8 ounce can sliced water chestnuts, drained*
- ¼ *cup sliced scallions*
- ½ *cup mayonnaise*
- *Lettuce leaves*

Reserve 2 tablespoons broth. Add enough water to remaining broth to substitute for water in the rice package directions. Cook rice according to package directions omitting butter or margarine. Cool. Stir in oranges, reserving some for garnish, water chestnuts and scallions. Blend reserved broth and mayonnaise. Stir into rice mixture. Cover and refrigerate 2-3 hours. Serve on lettuce leaves. Garnish with reserved oranges. Serves 6-8

Ruth Narveson

Tortellini with Sun-dried Tomato Pesto

Sun-Dried Tomato Pesto

- ½ *stick pepperoni cut into small pieces*
- 3 *tablespoons Dijon mustard*
- 4 *cloves garlic, minced*
- 1 *tablespoon fennel seeds*
- 1 *7 ounce jar sun-dried tomatoes packed in oil*
- 1½ *cups olive oil*
- 2 *tablespoons fresh lemon juice*
- *Salt and freshly ground pepper to taste*

Salad

- 2 *pounds of cheese or meat-filled tortellini, cooked and drained*
- 2 *ripe medium tomatoes, seeded and chopped*
- 1 *yellow bell pepper, seeded and diced*
- 1 *stick pepperoni, thinly sliced*
- ½ *cup chopped fresh parsley*
- 3 *tablespoons chopped fresh basil*

Prepare the pesto by placing the pepperoni, mustard, garlic, fennel seeds and sun-dried tomatoes with oil in a food processor fitted with the steel blade. Process until smooth. With the machine running, pour the olive oil in a thin steady stream through the feed tube and continue processing until the mixture is smooth. Season with the lemon juice and salt and pepper to taste. Set aside. Combine the tortellini, tomatoes, yellow pepper and pepperoni in a large bowl. Add the pesto and toss to coat. Sprinkle with the parsley and basil. Serve warm or at room temperature.

Joyce R. Laws

Steak Salad

2 *pounds boneless sirloin (2" thick)*
Salt and freshly ground pepper to taste
½ *pound mushrooms, sliced*
6 *scallions, sliced*
1 *14 ounce can hearts of palm, drained and sliced*
2 *tablespoons chives, chopped*
2 *tablespoons parsley, chopped*
2 *tablespoons dill, chopped*

Season steak with salt and pepper. Broil to medium rare. Cool and slice thinly into bite sized pieces. Combine steak, mushrooms, scallions, hearts of palm and herbs. Toss and pour mustard vinaigrette over salad and refrigerate overnight. The marinade will continue to cook the meat.

Mustard Vinaigrette

1 *egg, beaten*
⅓ *cup olive oil*
2 *teaspoons Dijon mustard*
1½ *tablespoons tarragon vinegar*
1 *teaspoon salt*
¼ *teaspoon fresh ground black pepper*
Dash hot pepper sauce

Combine all ingredients together and pour over above salad. Serves 8-10

Kay Ewing

Surprising Broccoli Salad

3 *cups broccoli florets*
6 *slices bacon, fried crisp, drained and crumbled*
1 *cup chopped red onion*
1 *cup shredded cheddar cheese*

Dressing

1 *cup mayonnaise*
2 *tablespoons white vinegar*
¼ *cup sugar*

Toss together broccoli florets, bacon, onion and cheese. In a small bowl, combine dressing ingredients and mix well. Pour dressing over salad and toss thoroughly. Cover and refrigerate until ready to serve. Will keep several days if kept in a tightly sealed container in the refrigerator. Serves 6

Terri Knight

Kraut Salad

1 *cup chopped kraut*
½ *cup chopped onion*
¼ *cup chopped carrots*
½ *cup chopped bell pepper*
½ *cup chopped celery*
¼ *cup sugar*

Mix all ingredients together and store in refrigerator. Better if made a day ahead.

Jalia Lingle

Cabbage Salad

1 large head cabbage, shredded
½ cup chopped celery
½ cup sliced radishes
½ cup chopped green pepper
½ cup chopped green onions
½ cup grated or sliced carrots
½ cup sliced cucumbers
½ cup sliced cauliflower
½ cup chopped broccoli

Mix ingredients together in large bowl with cover.

Dressing

¾ cup oil
¾ cup sugar
½ cup vinegar

Mix together and pour over vegetables. Salt and pepper to taste. Refrigerate one hour or overnight. Keeps well in refrigerator for several days.

Marlene Newton

Betty's Cauliflower Salad

2 cups mayonnaise
⅓ cup sugar
1 small purple onion, chopped
Salt and pepper to taste
¼ cup Parmesan cheese
1 head cauliflower, cut into florets
8 slices crisp bacon, crumbled
1 large head of lettuce

Combine all ingredients except lettuce. Store in jar in refrigerator overnight. Add to broken lettuce when ready to serve. Serves 8

Susie Nicholson

Greek Salad

1 head leaf lettuce
½ red onion
1 large tomato
1 can whole black olives
½ pound feta cheese, crumbled
¼ cup olive oil
½ teaspoon lemon juice
2 tablespoons oregano

Wash vegetables. Tear lettuce into bite size pieces and put in bowl. Slice onion and tomato. Add rest of the ingredients and toss. Serves 4

Linda Fenech

Corn Salad

2 cans shoe peg corn, drained
8 ounces bottled Italian dressing
2 ounces chopped pimiento
1 bunch green onions, chopped
2 stalks celery, chopped
½ bell pepper, chopped
2 tomatoes, chopped
Hot pepper sauce to taste

Mix all ingredients together. Refrigerate at least 2 hours before serving.

Patti Blackmon

Marinated Cucumbers

1½ cups mayonnaise
½ cup sugar
Vinegar
Water
Onions, cut into rings
Cucumbers, cut into slices
Salt

Mix mayonnaise and sugar. Add enough vinegar and water to make ½ quart. Add onions and cucumbers to make 1 quart. Salt to taste. Let set overnight.

Marlene Newton

Korean Salad

½ cup corn oil
¼ cup vinegar
¼ cup catsup
⅓ cup sugar
½ medium onion, grated
Salt to taste
1 16 ounce can bean sprouts, drained
1 pound spinach, torn
1 5 ounce can water chestnuts, thinly sliced
2 hard cooked eggs, chopped
6 slices crisp bacon, crumbled

Combine first 6 ingredients in jar; shake well. Mix bean sprouts, spinach and water chestnuts in salad bowl. Add dressing; toss to mix. Top with eggs and bacon. Serves 4-6

Joy Mason

Potato Salad

8 potatoes, boiled
1 2 ounce jar pimientos
1 onion, minced
8 hard-boiled eggs, chopped
3 sweet pickles, chopped
1 cup salad dressing
½ cup sugar
1 tablespoon prepared mustard
1 teaspoon celery seed
Salt and pepper to taste

Peel and dice potatoes, drain pimientos reserving juice. Place potatoes, onions, eggs, pickles and pimientos in salad bowl. Combine reserved juice and remaining ingredients. Mix well. Pour over potato mixture; toss to coat evenly. Chill several hours before serving. Serves 10-12

Annette Holeyfield

Hot Potato Salad

8 medium potatoes
1 onion, chopped
4 strips bacon, chopped
¼ pound processed cheese spread
1 cup salad dressing
¼ teaspoon dry mustard

Cook potatoes in jackets. Peel and chop. Pour into a 3 quart casserole. Add onion, bacon and cubed cheese. Stir remaining ingredients with potatoes and bake at 350 degrees for 45 minutes or until bubbly.

Marcia Godown

Pennsylvania Dutch Potato Salad

4 extra large potatoes
4 slices bacon
2 eggs, beaten lightly
¼ cup sugar, or to taste
½ teaspoon salt
¼ cup vinegar
½ cup milk or cream
Chopped onions
2 tablespoons of mayonnaise

Boil the potatoes in the jackets until they are tender. Peel and cut them into large chunks. Keep warm. Fry the bacon until crisp, remove from skillet and reserve drippings. To the beaten eggs add the next four ingredients, mixing well. Add egg mixture to bacon drippings and cook over low heat, stirring constantly, until this is a custard consistency. Crumble bacon and stir into dressing. Pour dressing over warm potatoes and toss gently. When cool, add plenty of chopped onions and mayonnaise. Serves 6-8

Betsy Harris

Coleslaw with Bacon

5 slices bacon, diced
2 eggs
1 teaspoon salt
5 tablespoons sugar
½ cup vinegar
½ cup water
½ cup whipping cream
1 head cabbage, finely chopped

Fry bacon until crisp in a medium skillet. Set aside half the pieces. Beat the eggs, add salt, sugar, vinegar and water. Stir into bacon and drippings in the pan. Heat over low heat and stir until thick. Do not boil. Remove from heat and stir in the cream. Pour over chopped cabbage. Toss lightly. Top with remaining bacon. This recipe is easy to half. Serves 10-12

Tonia Beavers

My Favorite Slaw

1 *cabbage, shredded*
3 *green onions, chopped*
4 *tablespoons sesame seeds, toasted*
4 *tablespoons sliced almonds*
2 *packages Ramen noodles, uncooked, crushed slightly*
2 *chicken breasts, boned, skinned, cooked, drained, and chopped*

Combine above ingredients.

Dressing

1 *cup salad oil*
4 *tablespoons sugar*
6 *tablespoons wine vinegar*
Salt and pepper to taste

Combine ingredients and pour over slaw mixture. Refrigerate for several hours before serving.

Toni Weatherford

Sweet and Sour Coleslaw

1 *16 ounce bag coleslaw*
1 *medium onion, chopped*
½ *cup white vinegar*
¾ *teaspoon salt*
½ *teaspoon dry mustard*
½ *teaspoon celery seed*
⅓ *cup salad oil*
¼ *cup sugar*

Combine coleslaw and chopped onions in a bowl. Set aside. In a saucepan, combine vinegar, salt, dry mustard, celery seed, salad oil and sugar. Bring to a boil for one minute. Cool. Pour cooled dressing over slaw and onion mixture. Refrigerate before serving.

Patti Nickels

Spinach Salad

1 *pound fresh spinach, washed and dried*
1 *can bean sprouts, drained*
4 *hard boiled eggs, sliced*
¼ *cup chopped green onions*
1 *can sliced mushrooms, drained*
Bacon, crumbled

Dressing

¾ *cup sugar*
¼ *cup vinegar*
¼ *cup salad oil*
⅓ *cup catsup*
2 *teaspoons salt*
1 *teaspoon Worcestershire sauce*

Toss salad together. Shake dressing ingredients together. Pour dressing on salad just before serving.

Bonnie Haines

Squash Salad

4-6 small yellow crookneck squash
⅓ cup salt
1 cup finely chopped purple onion
1 cup finely chopped bell pepper
1 2 ounce jar pimiento, chopped
1¼ cups sugar
1 cup vinegar
1 tablespoon mustard seed

Slice squash into 1½ quarts cold water into which the salt has been added. Refrigerate overnight. Drain. Add onion, bell pepper and pimiento to squash. Boil sugar, vinegar and mustard seed. Pour over vegetables. Refrigerate covered, overnight.

Betsy Harris

Tomato Aspic

4 cups tomato juice
2 envelopes unflavored gelatin
¼ cup cold water
1 teaspoon salt
1 teaspoon sugar
1 teaspoon dried green onion
1 teaspoon dried parsley
1 tablespoon Worcestershire sauce
1 tablespoon onion juice
5 drops hot pepper sauce
1 tablespoon lemon juice
1 tablespoon horseradish
¾ cup chopped celery
¾ cup sliced black olives
1 14 ounce jar artichoke hearts, drained

Spray a 9 x 13 pan with cooking spray. Heat tomato juice until it begins to boil. Dissolve gelatin in cold water. Add to tomato juice with salt, sugar, dried onion and parsley. Allow mixture to cool. Add Worcestershire, onion juice, hot pepper sauce, lemon juice and horseradish. Taste to see if more salt is needed. Add celery, olives and artichoke hearts. Spoon into pan. Chill. To serve, add a dollop of mayonnaise and a shrimp. Can be spooned into individual molds for a luncheon. Serves 12

Kay Ewing

Ellen's Special Vegetable Salad

1 can French green beans
1 can shoe peg corn
1 can English peas
1 green pepper, finely chopped
1 cup celery, finely chopped
1 small onion, finely chopped
1 cup sugar
¾ cup vinegar
½ cup salad oil
1 2 ounce jar pimiento

Drain liquid from beans, corn and peas. Combine vegetables and set aside. Bring sugar, vinegar and oil to a boil. Pour over vegetables. Refrigerate three hours or overnight before serving. Serves 8-10

Debbie Bell

Marinated Vegetable Salad

1 pound carrots, sliced and cooked until crisp
1 cucumber, sliced
1 cup cauliflower florets
2 onions, cut into rings
2 celery ribs, chopped
1 can tomato soup
1 cup sugar
¾ cup vinegar
¼ cup oil
1 tablespoon Worcestershire sauce
1 teaspoon black pepper
1 teaspoon mustard
¼ teaspoon salt

Combine all vegetables together. Toss in large bowl. Mix tomato soup, sugar, vinegar, oil, Worcestershire sauce and spices. Pour over vegetables and chill overnight. Serves 6-8

Georganne Peel

Vegetable Rice Salad

1 large can mixed vegetables, drained
1 can Mexican corn, drained
2 cups cooked rice
2 cups chopped celery
2 cups chopped green onions
2 cups chopped green pepper
¼ cup vinegar
½ cup oil
1 cup mayonnaise

Combine first six ingredients. Mix vinegar, oil and mayonnaise and pour over vegetable mixture. Refrigerate until chilled.

Sue McCoy

Blue Cheese Salad Dressing

1 egg
1½ cups oil
3 tablespoons cornstarch
½ cup water
½ teaspoon salt
½ teaspoon garlic powder
¼ cup stuffed olives, chopped fine
¼ cup blue cheese

Beat egg until light and fluffy. Add oil very slowly until creamy and thick. In a small pan, cook cornstarch in water until thick and clear, stirring constantly over low heat. Add starch mixture to egg/oil mixture slowly. Add remaining ingredients and beat well. Keep refrigerated. Makes 1 pint

Bobbie Moore

Dieters Special Dressing

Dash lemon juice
1 cup corn oil
1 cup apple cider vinegar
1 tablespoon celery salt
4 packages sugar substitute
1 teaspoon oregano
1 teaspoon paprika
Garlic powder to taste
2 eggs

Combine all ingredients in a blender and blend well. Dressing will be light and foamy. Keep refrigerated.

Mary Noel Mabry

Fruit Salad Dressing

1 cup mayonnaise
1 cup marshmallow creme
¼ teaspoon ginger

Mix mayonnaise and marshmallow creme together. Add the ginger and mix well. Serve over fresh fruit. This will keep for up to 30 days in refrigerator. Makes 2 cups

Shirley Leonard

Italian Salad Dressing

½ cup olive oil
¼ cup cider vinegar
1 teaspoon garlic powder
1 tablespoon minced dried onion
1 tablespoon bell pepper flakes
1 teaspoon sugar
¾ teaspoon salt
⅛ teaspoon basil
⅛ teaspoon black pepper
⅛ teaspoon oregano
⅛ teaspoon thyme

Place all ingredients in a jar with a tight fitting lid. Shake well. Let stand one hour before serving to allow herbs to soften and flavors to blend. Makes 1 cup

Patti Nickels

Mustard Vinaigrette Salad Dressing

2 tablespoons Dijon mustard
¾ cup olive oil
3 teaspoons fresh lemon juice
3 teaspoons vinegar
1 clove pressed garlic
¼ teaspoon salt
Pinch sugar

Combine all ingredients together. Makes 1 cup

Virginia Berner

Poppy Seed Dressing

1 *cup frozen apple juice concentrate, thawed*
6 *tablespoons lemon juice*
6 *tablespoons balsamic or red wine vinegar*
4 *tablespoons Dijon mustard*
2 *tablespoons honey*
2 *tablespoons olive oil*
1 *tablespoon pepper*
1 *tablespoon poppy seeds*

In a bowl, whisk together ingredients. Serve over mixed greens. This dressing contains 12 calories and 1 gram of fat per tablespoon.

Patti Nickles

"Almost Ranch" Low Cal Blender Dressing

1 *cup low fat cottage cheese*
½ *cup buttermilk or yogurt*
2 *tablespoons vinegar*
½ *teaspoon garlic powder*
½ *teaspoon celery seed*
½ *teaspoon paprika*
¼ *teaspoon pepper*
¼ *teaspoon salt*
½ *teaspoon onion powder*
¼ *cup mayonnaise (can use up to ½ cup)*
1-2 *teaspoons dill weed*

Put all ingredients in blender and blend until smooth. Best if made a few hours ahead and refrigerated.

Jane Barnes

Soy Dressing for Spinach Salad

¾ *cup corn oil*
¼ *cup vinegar*
2 *tablespoons white wine*
2 *tablespoons soy sauce*
½ *teaspoon seasoned pepper*
½ *teaspoon seasoned salt*
1 *teaspoon regular salt*
1 *teaspoon dry mustard*
½ *teaspoon curry powder*
Dash garlic powder

Mix all ingredients and chill for several hours. Serve over fresh spinach. Makes 1½ cups

Susie Kroencke

Betty Jane's Lemon Mayonnaise

2 *large egg yolks*
2 *tablespoons white vinegar*
1 *heaping teaspoon mustard*
1 *teaspoon salt*
½ *teaspoon sugar*
2 *teaspoons fresh lemon juice*

Combine all ingredients in a food processor or blender, then slowly add 1¾ cups oil. Beat for several minutes. Makes two cups. Great for lobster or shrimp salads.

Betsy Harris

DINNER'S READY

New Beef Brisket

1 tablespoon Worcestershire sauce
1 tablespoon garlic powder
1½ teaspoons celery salt
1 tablespoon bottled brown bouquet gravy
1 5 pound brisket, trimmed

Make a paste with the first four ingredients. Rub into brisket and place in a pan with a lid or cover with foil. Refrigerate overnight. Bake at 225 degrees for 6-8 hours.

Jane New

Beef Brisket LeHigh

1 tablespoon meat tenderizer
4 tablespoons liquid smoke
2 teaspoons salt
½ teaspoon pepper
1 teaspoon celery salt
1 teaspoon onion salt or powder
1 teaspoon garlic salt or powder
½ teaspoon nutmeg
1 teaspoon paprika
¼ cup brown sugar
Worcestershire sauce
1 5 pound beef brisket, trimmed

Combine first 7 ingredients. Pour over brisket. Marinate overnight. Before cooking, add last four ingredients. Wrap well in foil. Cook 5 hours at 275 degrees. Let cool slightly before slicing across grain.

Toni Weatherford *Cathy Andrasik*

Bar-B-Que Brisket

4 tablespoons paprika
2 teaspoons salt
2 teaspoons onion powder
2 teaspoons black pepper
1 teaspoon cayenne pepper
2 teaspoons chili powder
1 5 pound brisket

Mix all spices thoroughly. Sprinkle on brisket. Let stand 20-30 minutes until it appears wet. Cook brisket very slowly 4-5 hours at 300 degrees.

Bonnie Johnson

Best Ever Easy Roast

1 tablespoon oil
1 4 pound roast
1 envelope onion soup mix

Sear roast on all sides in oil in a large Dutch oven. Place roast fat side down and cover with onion soup mix. Cover and cook over low heat until tender. It makes its own juice which can be used for gravy. If you are using chuck roast, you may want to add vegetables near the end of cooking time. Allow enough time for vegetables to be tender.

Bobbie Moore

Stuffed Filet of Beef tied with Leek Ribbons

1 six pound untrimmed filet
1 red pepper, seeded and cut into 2" strips
1 leek, cleaned and julienned into 2" lengths
2 cloves garlic, minced
4 tablespoons butter
1 teaspoon fresh rosemary, chopped or fresh thyme
⅓ cup finely chopped parsley
Salt and freshly ground pepper
Kitchen string and scissors
1 whole leek with plenty of green top
Bowl of ice water
4 tablespoons melted butter

Turn filet so that it's bottom up. Using a sharp knife, carefully slice it lengthwise about ¾ of the way through being careful not to slice all the way through. Sauté red pepper, leek and garlic in butter until just tender. Add rosemary or thyme and parsley. Place this mixture in the incision made in filet. Roll filet back together again and tie every 2" with pieces of string. Roast in a preheated 500 degree oven for 15 minutes. Meanwhile, bring a large pot of water to a boil. Carefully separate long leaves of whole leek using a small sharp knife to slit the bottoms. Wash off all dirt. Place long leaves into boiling water for about 20 seconds. Quickly remove and plunge into ice water. Drain. Slice each leaf in half lengthwise. After filet has cooked for 15 minutes, remove from oven. Tie leek "ribbons" around filet between string ties, securing each with a knot. Trim ends neatly with scissors. Brush with melted butter and return to oven for another 7 minutes. When ready to carve, cut strings off with scissors and slice in between the leek "ribbons".

Betsy Harris

Oven Swiss Steak

1½ pounds boneless beef round steak
¼ cup flour
1 teaspoon salt
1 16 ounce can stewed tomatoes
½ cup chopped celery
½ cup sliced carrots
2 tablespoons chopped onions
½ teaspoon Worcestershire sauce
½ cup grated cheddar cheese

Cut meat into serving pieces. Combine flour and salt. Pound into meat. Set aside remaining flour. Brown meat in small amount of oil. Place meat in 9 x 12 baking pan. Blend remaining flour with drippings in skillet. Add tomatoes, celery, carrots, onions and Worcestershire sauce. Cook, stirring constantly until mixture boils. Pour over meat. Cover and bake in 350 degree oven for 1½-2 hours. Sprinkle cheese on top when done, returning to oven to melt. Serves 4

Linda Bewley

Vineyard Beef Roast

1 3-4 pound beef roast
1 teaspoon salt
Black pepper to taste
1 clove garlic, finely chopped
1 carrot, cut into thin strips
1 large onion, sliced
¾ cup burgundy wine
¾ cup sour cream
½ cup water
2-3 tablespoons flour
1 teaspoon lemon juice

Rub meat with salt and pepper. Brown meat on all sides over high heat in a heavy Dutch oven. Add garlic, carrot and onion. Combine wine and sour cream with a wire whisk to blend well. Pour over roast. Cover with a tight lid and bake until tender. Remove meat and vegetables and skim off any fat. Mix water and flour to a smooth paste. Add to pan juices and cook on top of stove until thickened. Add a little more boiling water if gravy is too thick. Stir in lemon juice. Serves 4-6

Susie Kroncke

Martha's Roast

1 4 pound English cut roast
¼ cup oil
Liquid from 4 ounce jar of pepper sauce
¼ cup brown sugar
1 teaspoon prepared mustard
Garlic powder to taste
Worcestershire sauce to taste
1 small jar apple jelly
¼ cup flour

Roll roast in flour and lightly brown in oil. Mix liquid from pepper sauce jar, brown sugar, mustard, garlic powder, Worcestershire sauce and apple jelly. Pour over roast and bake, covered, until done. Pour sauce off and cool. When cool, skim fat off. Add a tablespoon of bottled brown bouquet sauce if desired. Heat and thicken with a little cornstarch if desired.

Joyce R. Laws

Marinated Flank Steak

3 pounds flank steak
Garlic powder
½ cup soy sauce
¼ cup cooking oil
¼ cup Worcestershire sauce
2 tablespoons honey
2 tablespoons vinegar
1 teaspoon ginger
1 chopped green onion (optional)

Pierce flank steak liberally with fork and sprinkle with garlic powder. Mix all remaining ingredients together. Place meat in shallow glass dish and pour marinade over. Marinate 4-6 hours at room temperature, turning frequently. Can also marinate overnight in refrigerator. Grill meat over hot coals 6-7 minutes per side. Slice across the grain to serve. Serves 8-10

Jackie Gardner

Husky Beef Kabobs

1 pound lean beef round, cut in cubes
1 cup salad oil
¾ cup soy sauce
½ cup lemon juice
¼ cup Worcestershire sauce
¼ cup prepared mustard
1 teaspoon coarsely cracked pepper
2 cloves garlic, minced
Mushroom caps
Boiled whole potatoes

Combine oil, soy sauce, lemon juice, Worcestershire sauce, mustard, cracked pepper and garlic. Add beef cubes, turning to coat. Refrigerate 24-36 hours to give marinade time to tenderize the beef. Turn the meat occasionally. Fill skewers, alternating meat cubes with mushroom caps or small whole boiled potatoes. Broil, turning frequently until all sides are brown. Serves 3-4

Lou Adams

Beef Stroganoff

3 tablespoons oil
2-3 onions, sliced
2 pounds round steak, sliced in strips
1 pound mushrooms, sliced
Salt and pepper to taste
Garlic to taste
2-3 tablespoons flour
2 cubes beef bouillon
1 cup water
1 can cream of mushroom soup
½ pint sour cream
1 teaspoon bottled brown bouquet sauce

In a large frying pan, fry onions and round steak strips in oil until brown. Add salt, pepper and garlic powder to taste. Add mushrooms and simmer until tender. Remove from pan and set aside. In the same pan make gravy by adding 2-3 tablespoons flour to oil from meat. Brown until golden. Add water and crushed bouillon. Return meat mixture to pan. When it starts to thicken, add mushroom soup, sour cream and bottled brown bouquet sauce. Serve on cooked noodles. Serves 4

Linda Fenech

Round Steak Dinner

Several strips bacon
1½ pounds round steak, cut into pieces
4 medium potatoes, pared and sliced
2 large onions, peeled and sliced
Salt and pepper

Place bacon strips in electric skillet. Place steak over bacon. Place potatoes over steak and then onions. Season to taste. Turn heat to high for 1-2 minutes. Reduce heat and simmer, covered for 1½ hours.

Marlene Newton

Overnight Barbecue Beef

4-6 pound chuck roast
5 ounces Worcestershire
5 ounces liquid smoke
1 cup ketchup
2-3 cups reserved liquid
1 cup ketchup
1 cup brown sugar

Place roast and next 3 ingredients in crockpot on low setting for 10-12 hours. Remove meat, reserving liquid. Tear cooked meat into small pieces and return to crockpot. Mix last three ingredients and pour over meat. If needed, add additional liquid. If you really want to make it delicious, serve on lightly buttered buns topped with cheddar and Mozzarella cheese. Place under the broiler until melted. Serves 10-12

Ann Ray

Beef Enchiladas

1 pound ground beef
1 medium onion, chopped
2 tablespoons flour
1 tablespoon chili powder
1-2 dashes cumin
¼ cup water
Salt and pepper to taste
1 can enchilada sauce
1 can chili
1 chili can of water
1 package corn tortillas
Chopped onion
Grated cheddar cheese

Brown meat and onions. Add spices, flour and water. Season with salt and pepper. Combine enchilada sauce, chili and water. Heat thoroughly. Warm tortillas in ungreased skillet. Place an even amount of the meat mixture in center of each tortilla with some of the chopped onion and grated cheese and roll up. Place fold side down in glass baking dish. Cover with heated enchilada sauce, chopped onion and cheese. Bake at 350 degrees for 15-20 minutes.

Connie Neumeier

Beefy Jalapeño Corn Bread

1 cup cornmeal
1 teaspoon salt
1 teaspoon baking soda
1 teaspoon baking powder
½ cup bacon drippings or oil
2 eggs
1 cup milk
1 can cream style corn
1 pound ground beef
1 large onion, chopped
2 or 3 jalapeño peppers, chopped
½ pound grated cheddar cheese

Mix first 8 ingredients. Brown hamburger meat and onion. Drain and set aside. Grease 13 x 9 casserole dish. Pour half corn bread mixture into pan, sprinkle ground beef, onions and peppers, then cheese. Pour remaining corn bread mixture on top of meat. Bake in 350 degree oven for 50 minutes or until done.

Susan Lewis

Beef and Green Chili Enchiladas

1 pound ground beef
1 medium onion, chopped
Salt and pepper to taste
1 cup grated cheddar cheese
1 dozen corn tortillas
Vegetable oil

Sauce

¼ cup butter
3 tablespoons flour
2 cups milk
½ teaspoon salt
½ pound pasteurized process cheese spread
1 4 ounce can chopped green chilies, drained

Preheat oven to 350 degrees. Brown ground beef with onion. Drain, add salt, pepper and cheddar cheese. Heat oil in skillet over medium heat. Quickly dip each tortilla in hot oil to soften, then drain on paper towel. Place 2 tablespoons of beef mixture in each shell, then roll up. Place each enchilada seam side down in baking dish. (Try not to touch). To make sauce, melt butter in saucepan. Add flour, stirring constantly until mixture bubbles. Stir in salt and milk. When sauce begins to thicken, add cheese spread and green chilies. Stir until cheese melts. Pour over enchiladas and bake for 30 minutes until hot and bubbly. Sauce can easily be made in microwave. Serves 6

Marie Biggers

Mexican Manicotti

8 manicotti shells
½ pound lean ground beef, browned
1 cup refried beans
1 teaspoon oregano, crushed
½ teaspoon ground cumin
1 8 ounce jar picante sauce or taco sauce
1 8 ounce carton sour cream
¼ cup chopped green onion
¼ cup sliced ripe olives
½ cup shredded Monterey Jack cheese

Cook manicotti shells according to package directions, set aside. Combine ground beef, refried beans, oregano and cumin. Mix well. Fill cooked manicotti shells with meat mixture. Arrange in 10 x 6 x 2 baking dish. Pour picante sauce over manicotti shells. Cover with vented plastic wrap. Microwave on medium high for 10 minutes, giving dish a half turn after 5 minutes. Combine sour cream, green onion and olives. Spoon down center of manicotti. Top with cheese. Microwave on high until cheese melts, about 2 minutes. Serves 4

Patti Nickels

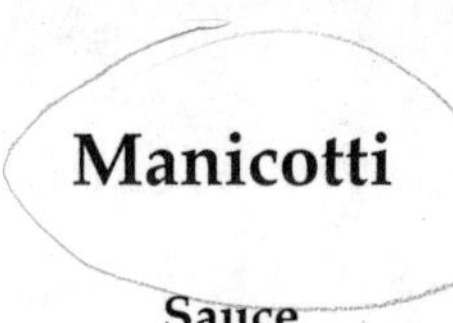

Manicotti

Sauce

- 1 *medium onion, chopped*
- 1 *clove garlic, chopped*
- 4 *tablespoons olive oil*
- 1 *28 ounce can tomatoes*
- 1 *6 ounce can tomato paste*
- ½ *cup chopped parsley (or flakes)*
- 1 *teaspoon salt*
- ¼ *teaspoon pepper*
- 1 *teaspoon basil*
- 1 *bay leaf*

Filling

- 1 *pound ground beef*
- 1 *clove garlic, crushed*
- 1 *cup cream style cottage cheese*
- 4 *ounces Mozzarella cheese, grated*
- ½ *teaspoon salt*
- ½ *cup mayonnaise*
- 1 *package manicotti noodles, cooked*

To make sauce, brown onion and garlic in olive oil. Add remaining ingredients and simmer 45 minutes or longer until slightly thickened. To make filling, brown meat and garlic. Add remaining ingredients, except noodles. Fill shells with the meat filling. Grease a 9 x 13 baking dish and fill with stuffed shells. Cover with most of the sauce. Bake 25-30 minutes at 350 degrees. Heat remaining sauce and pour over manicotti before serving. Serves 8

Susie Kroencke

Sweet and Sour Meatballs

- 1 *pound lean ground beef*
- 3 *tablespoons steak sauce*
- 1 *egg, beaten*
- ½ *cup soft bread crumbs*
- 1 *medium clove garlic, crushed*
- 1 *teaspoon salt*
- 1 *teaspoon oil*
- 1 *8 ounce can pineapple chunks, undrained*
- 1 *cup sliced carrots*
- 1 *cup sliced onion*
- ¾ *cup beef broth*
- 2 *tablespoons steak sauce*
- 2 *tablespoons cider vinegar*
- ¼ *teaspoon ground ginger*
- 1 *tablespoon cornstarch*
- 1 *large green pepper, cut in strips*

Combine beef, 3 tablespoons steak sauce, egg, bread crumbs, garlic and salt. Form into 24 meatballs. In large skillet, brown meatballs well in oil; drain. Add remaining ingredients except cornstarch. Cover and simmer until vegetables are tender. Dissolve cornstarch in 1 tablespoon warm water and stir into mixture. Simmer, uncovered, for 5 minutes. Serve over white rice.

Kathy Soto

Cranberry Meat Loaves

1 pound ground beef
1 cup cooked rice
½ cup tomato juice
1 slightly beaten egg
¼ cup minced onion
1½ tablespoons salt
1 tablespoon bottled brown bouquet sauce
2 cups cranberry sauce
⅓ cup brown sugar
1 tablespoon lemon juice

Combine first seven ingredients. Shape into 5 individual loaves. Leave a depression in the top of each one. Place in a baking dish. Combine remaining ingredients and pour over loaves. Bake at 350 degrees for 40 minutes or until done.

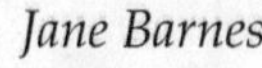

Jane Barnes

Everyday Meat Loaf

1½ pounds ground beef
2 eggs
¾ cup milk
⅔ cup fine, dry bread crumbs
2 tablespoons chopped onions
¾ teaspoon salt
½ teaspoon dried sage, crushed
Dash pepper
¼ cup ketchup
2 tablespoons brown sugar
1 teaspoon dry mustard
1 teaspoon lemon juice

In mixing bowl, stir together eggs, milk, bread crumbs, onion, salt, sage and pepper. Add ground beef and mix well. Shape into loaf in shallow 9 x 13 baking pan. Bake at 350 degrees for 1 hour. Combine ketchup, brown sugar, mustard and lemon juice. Spoon over meat loaf. Bake an additional 15 minutes.

Pam Huggins

Microwave Meat Loaf

1½ pounds ground round
1 egg
¼ cup Italian bread crumbs
¼ cup chopped onion
¼ cup milk
½ teaspoon salt
½ teaspoon garlic powder
¼ teaspoon pepper
¼ cup chopped bell pepper (optional)
1 tablespoon Worcestershire
Ketchup to cover top

In a large bowl combine all ingredients. Mix well. Press into a 1½ quart loaf pan. If desired, top with ketchup. Cook in microwave on high, covered with wax paper, for 8-9 minutes. Let stand 5 minutes before serving. Serves 6

Tonia Beavers

Big Noise's Spaghetti and Meatballs

Sauce

- *5 14 ounce cans tomatoes*
- *1 tablespoon basil*
- *1½ teaspoons salt*
- *½ teaspoon pepper*
- *¼ cup sugar*
- *5 14 ounce cans water*

Meatballs

- *2 pounds ground beef*
- *1 pound sausage*
- *½ cup bread crumbs*
- *2 eggs, slightly beaten*
- *2 tablespoons chopped parsley*
- *⅔ cup Parmesan cheese*
- *1 clove garlic, minced*
- *1 6 ounce can tomato paste*
- *1 teaspoon salt*
- *½ teaspoon pepper*
- *1 stalk celery, chopped*
- *⅔ cup chopped onion*

To make sauce, stir tomatoes in blender or processor long enough to break them up. Bring all ingredients for sauce to a boil and reduce heat. Simmer while making meatballs. To make meatballs, mix all ingredients except onions, garlic, sausage and celery. Form meat balls. (Retain 1 cup ground beef). Brown sausage in pan and add to sauce. In the reserved sausage grease, add onions, garlic, celery, cup of ground beef and tomato paste. Brown meat balls in this mixture, rolling them to pick up paste color. When browned, add to sauce. When all meatballs are browned, add contents of frying pan to sauce and simmer for at least 5 hours, uncovered, stirring frequently. Ladle off excess grease. Serve over spaghetti. Serves 6

Maysel Teeter

Spaghetti Sauce

- *2 pounds ground beef*
- *3 onions, chopped*
- *2 bell peppers, chopped*
- *4 15 ounce cans tomatoes*
- *½ large head of garlic*
- *4 6 ounce cans tomato paste*
- *1 tablespoon oregano*
- *1 tablespoon salt*
- *2 small cans mushrooms*
- *3 tablespoons black pepper*
- *1½ tablespoons crushed red pepper*
- *½ cup vegetable oil*
- *½ gallon red wine*
- *2 tablespoons parsley flakes*
- *1 tablespoon basil leaves*
- *Jalapeño peppers to taste*

Brown ground beef, add onions and bell peppers; sauté. Put 3 cans of tomatoes into blender. Blend slightly. Mix with meat along with the other can of tomatoes. Peel and dice garlic cloves and add to meat. Add tomato paste, oregano, mushrooms, salt, peppers and vegetable oil. Add wine a little at a time. Add remaining ingredients and simmer, stirring frequently. The longer you simmer the sauce, the more enhanced the flavor. Serves 15

Becky Ellison

Creamed Tacos

- 2 *pounds hamburger*
- 1 *10 ounce can tomatoes with chilies*
- 1 *pound brick of chili*
- 1 *can chili beans*
- 1 *pound pasteurized process cheese spread*
- 1 *pint whipping cream*

Brown hamburger and add next four ingredients. Add whipping cream when mixture is well blended and almost ready to serve. Serve over tortilla chips and garnish with lettuce, tomatoes, onion and grated cheddar cheese. Serves 8-10

Mary Smith *Jane Fore*

Easy Skillet Beef and Noodles

- 1 *pound ground beef*
- 1 *envelope dry onion soup mix*
- 1 *28 ounce can tomatoes*
- 4 *ounces egg noodles*

In a large skillet, cook and stir ground beef until brown. Stir in remaining ingredients. Heat to boiling. Reduce heat, cover and simmer, stirring occasionally, about 20 minutes or until noodles are tender. Serves 6-8

Susan Barefield

Brian's Hot Tamales

- 2 *pounds hamburger meat*
- 2 *medium onions, chopped*
- 3 *cloves garlic, chopped or garlic powder to taste*
- 2 *tablespoons salt*
- 2 *teaspoons red pepper*
- ½ *cup cornmeal*
- ½ *cup water*
- 1 *cup tomato sauce*
- 3 *tablespoons chili powder*
- 1 *teaspoon cumin*
- 2 *cups cornmeal*
- 2 *teaspoons salt*
- 1 *teaspoon red pepper*
- *Tamale papers*
- ½ *small can tomato sauce*
- 2 *tablespoons chili powder*
- *Pinch salt*

In a large bowl, combine first 10 ingredients; set aside. In a small bowl, combine the next three ingredients; set aside. Wet papers and spread out six at a time. Drop ½ teaspoon cornmeal mixture on each paper. Add a small roll of meat and top with ½ teaspoon cornmeal mixture. Fold and roll paper. Place tightly rolled tamales in a heavy pot. Cover with mixture of the last three ingredients. Weigh down tamales with a heavy plate. Let come to a boil. Turn heat down and simmer. Cook for 1 hour 15 minutes. Makes 6 dozen

Nancy Burns

Pasta with Hot Tomato and Bacon Sauce

½ pound thickly sliced bacon
3 tablespoons olive oil
2½ large onions, coarsely chopped
3 large garlic cloves, minced
1 28 ounce AND 1 16 ounce can tomatoes, chopped, with liquid
1 tablespoon tarragon or 2 teaspoons sugar
2 teaspoons salt, or to taste
¼ teaspoon red pepper flakes or cayenne
¼ cup minced fresh parsley
1½ pounds pasta
Unsalted butter, as needed
Parmesan cheese, optional

Fry bacon until crisp. Drain. Pour all grease except one tablespoon from skillet. Add olive oil and onions to skillet. Sauté onions until wilted, about five minutes. Stir in garlic, tomatoes, salt, tarragon and pepper. Simmer 30 minutes to reduce liquid. Crumble bacon and add along with parsley. Remove sauce from heat. (If you like a smoother sauce, give it a whirl in a blender, but don't overdo it.) Toss cooked pasta with a bit of butter and then some of the sauce. Top each serving with additional sauce and cheese. Serves 6

Betsy Harris

Jean's Lasagna

1 pound sausage
1 teaspoon sweet basil
1 teaspoon parsley
1 clove garlic, minced
1 teaspoon fennel seeds
2 6 ounce cans tomato paste
1 32 ounce can tomatoes
8-10 lasagna noodles
1 pound Mozzarella, shredded
3 cups small curd cottage cheese
½ cup Parmesan cheese
2 beaten eggs
2 tablespoons parsley

Brown sausage, drain in colander (reserve 1 tablespoon fat). Put 1 tablespoon fat in pan with spices. Cook on medium-low for 5 minutes. Add tomato paste, tomatoes and sausage. Simmer, uncovered, 30 minutes. Cook lasagna noodles according to package directions, drain and set aside. In a large bowl, mix cottage cheese, Parmesan cheese, eggs and parsley. Spray two 13 x 13 x 2 pans with non stick cooking spray. Layer lasagna in the following order: noodles, cottage cheese mixture, Mozzarella, sausage mixture; repeat ending with sausage mixture. Bake at 350 degrees for 45-55 minutes or until bubbly. Serves 12-16

Maysel Teeter

Cheryl's Cajun Jambalaya

- ¾ *cup chopped onion*
- ½ *cup chopped celery*
- ¼ *cup chopped bell pepper*
- 1 *clove garlic, minced*
- 2 *tablespoons butter*
- *Several small pieces of salt pork*
- 1 *28 ounce can tomatoes*
- 1 *10 ounce can tomatoes with green chilies*
- 1 *teaspoon sugar*
- ½ *teaspoon cayenne pepper*
- ½ *teaspoon chili powder*
- ½ *teaspoon thyme*
- 1 *can beef broth*
- 1¼ *cups water*
- *Dry Creole seasoning to taste*
- *Several shakes of hot sauce*
- 2 *cups chopped ham*
- 1 *pound pork sausage, sliced*
- 1 *cup raw rice*

Brown first six ingredients together. Drain. Add next 12 ingredients. Cook on simmer for 1 hour. Add rice and cook until rice is done, about 30 minutes.

Maysel Teeter

Egg Rolls

- 2 *cups finely chopped cooked pork*
- 1 *4.5 ounce can shrimp, drained*
- 2 *cups finely chopped celery*
- 1 *cup finely chopped green onions*
- 1 *cup finely chopped water chestnuts*
- 1 *teaspoon seasoned salt flavor enhancer*
- 1 *teaspoon soy sauce*
- 2 *tablespoons sugar*
- 1 *teaspoon salt*
- 1 *small egg*
- 2 *cans bean sprouts, drained*
- ½ *cup shortening*
- *Egg roll wrappers*

Mix all ingredients except shortening and wrappers. Melt shortening in skillet. Place even amount of mixture in each egg roll wrapper. Roll up tightly, tucking in ends. Deep fry until golden. Drain. Makes 15-20

Linda Bewley

Pork Loin with Mustard Sauce

- 1 *tablespoon fresh crushed sage*
- ¼ *teaspoon whole marjoram*
- 2 *tablespoons fresh garlic*
- ¼ *cup soy sauce*
- ½ *cup Dijon mustard*
- *Fresh ground pepper*
- 1 *5 pound pork loin*

Combine all ingredients. Pour over pork loin and marinate overnight. Bake at 325 degrees for 2-2½ hours or until meat thermometer registers 160 degrees.

Maysel Teeter

Porc à l'Orange

1 6-7 pound pork loin roast
1 clove garlic, sliced
1 teaspoon rosemary
½ teaspoon salt
¼ teaspoon pepper
2 tablespoons Dijon mustard
2 tablespoons orange marmalade
1 tablespoon light brown sugar
⅓ cup orange juice, divided
2 oranges, thinly sliced
Fresh parsley
1-2 tablespoons orange flavored liqueur

When buying roast, ask the butcher to saw across the ribs at the base of the backbone of the roast to separate ribs from backbone. Cut small slits in fat of loin and insert garlic slices. Rub with rosemary, salt and pepper. Place meat, fat side up, on rack in open shallow roasting pan. Roast at 325 degrees until done, allowing 30-35 minutes per pound. Combine mustard, marmalade, brown sugar, and 2 tablespoons orange juice, mixing well. About 15 minutes before roast is done, brush with mustard mixture to glaze. Continue roasting 15 minutes. Remove roast to serving platter. Garnish with orange slices and parsley. Skim fat from roasting pan. Add remaining orange juice and orange liqueur to pan drippings, mixing well. Serve with roast.

Annette Holeyfield

Apple Cider Pork Roast

1 5 pound smoked pork loin
1 cup apple cider
½ cup brown sugar

Mix together apple cider and brown sugar. Place pork loin in baking pan wrapped in foil. Pour apple cider mixture over top and fold foil over top to create a tent. Bake at 350 degrees until hot (25-30 minutes).

Tamara Laws

Pork Chops on Rice

4 pork chops
Salt and pepper
2 cups cooked rice
¼ cup chopped onion
¼ cup chopped celery (optional)
1 can cream of chicken soup
1 cup milk

Grease skillet, brown chops on both sides, season with salt and pepper. Mix together rice, onion, celery, soup and milk. Add more salt and pepper, if desired. Place mixture in greased casserole. Lay chops on top. Add drippings from skillet. Cover and bake 30-45 minutes at 350 degrees or until pork chops are no longer pink.

Carolyn Srygley

Country Pork Ribs

8-10 pork ribs
2-3 tablespoons shortening
Onion flakes
2 tablespoons Worcestershire sauce
2-3 shakes of hot pepper sauce
Seasoned salt to taste
1 can tomato soup
1¼ cups water
2 teaspoons butter
⅓-½ cup brown sugar
Salt and pepper
½ cup ketchup
¼ cup vinegar

Brown floured ribs in shortening. Mix above ingredients and pour over ribs. Cook, covered, in 325 degree oven for 3 hours.

Ann Ray

French Pork Chops

6 lean pork chops
1 cup flour
1 teaspoon pepper
1 cup cooking oil
1 can French onion soup
1 8 ounce carton sour cream

Dredge chops with flour to which pepper has been added. Brown chops in small amount of oil. Mix French onion soup and sour cream together. Pour over chops. Cover skillet and simmer about 30-45 minutes until tender. A small amount of water or more French onion soup may be added to provide more sauce.

Sue Streett

Ham Meat Loaf

1½ pounds cured ham, ground
1 pound ground pork
1 teaspoon pepper
1 tablespoon Worcestershire sauce
2 eggs
½ cup tomato juice
¼ cup milk
1½ cups cracker crumbs

Sauce

1 cup brown sugar
2 teaspoons mustard
⅓ cup vinegar
½ cup water

When buying meat, ask for the ham and pork to be ground together. Mix all meat loaf ingredients together and shape into loaf. Place in large baking dish. In a saucepan, mix all sauce ingredients together and boil. Pour over meat loaf. Bake at 350 degrees for 2 hours. Baste every 15 minutes. The sauce will get thick and will glaze the ham loaf. Serves 6-8

Shirley Leonard

Apricot Chicken

8 ounces apricot preserves
1 8 ounce bottle Russian dressing
1 envelope onion soup mix
6 chicken breasts

Preheat oven to 300 degrees. In a bowl, mix apricot preserves, dressing and soup mix. Place the chicken breasts in a large, greased baking dish and pour apricot mixture over chicken. Bake uncovered for two hours. Serve 6

Joyce R. Laws

Chicken Alfredo

¼ cup oil
¼ cup lemon juice
¼ cup Parmesan cheese
2 teaspoons oregano
4 teaspoons salt
1 teaspoon pepper
2 chicken fryers, halved
1 cup flour
4 teaspoons paprika
2 teaspoons salt
½ teaspoon pepper
2 teaspoons Parmesan cheese
½ cup oleo

Combine oil, lemon juice, cheese, oregano, 2 teaspoons salt and 1 teaspoon pepper. Beat well. Pour over chicken halves, cover and refrigerate overnight. Combine remaining ingredients, except oleo. Remove chicken from marinade and roll in flour mixture. Sauté chicken in oleo until browned on both sides. Place each chicken half, skin side up, in the center of a double thick square of heavy foil. Bring up sides and seal with tight folds. Place packets on baking sheet and bake at 425 degrees for 1 hour. Serve 4

Tonia Beavers

Crab Stuffed Chicken Breasts

1 7½ ounce can crabmeat or ½ pound frozen
1 egg, slightly beaten
½ teaspoon salt
3 whole chicken breasts, boned and split
¼ cup butter, melted
¼ cup soy sauce
¼ teaspoon Worcestershire sauce

Break canned crabmeat into smaller pieces or remove any pieces of shell from frozen crabmeat. Combine crab with egg and salt. Lift chicken skin from flesh, being careful to leave it attached to longest edge. Place 2-3 tablespoons of crabmeat mixture under skin. Secure with toothpicks which have been soaked in water. Place chicken skin side down on broiler pan (with tray removed). Combine butter, soy sauce and Worcestershire sauce. Brush chicken with this mixture. Preheat broiler for 5 minutes. Place broiler pan on bottom rack position. Broil 20 minutes; turn and broil for 15 minutes longer. Baste occasionally. Serves 6

Lou Adams

Chicken Cheesecake

Crust

2 cups crushed pretzels
¼ cup margarine, melted
1 envelope unflavored gelatin

Filling

2 8 ounce packages cream cheese, softened
3 eggs
2 chicken bouillon cubes
2 tablespoons very hot water
1 envelope unflavored gelatin
1 8 ounce carton French onion dip
5 green onions, chopped
2 ribs celery, chopped
3 tablespoons green pepper, chopped
2 tablespoons pimiento, chopped
¼ teaspoon salt (omit if using canned chicken)
2 cups cooked chicken, chopped

To make crust, combine crushed pretzels with melted margarine and gelatin. Press on bottom and up sides of a 9" springform pan. To make filling, beat cream cheese with mixer until light and fluffy. Add eggs one at a time, beating well after each. Mix bouillon cubes with hot water and gelatin. Add to cream cheese, mixing well. Add onion dip, green onions, celery, green pepper, pimiento, salt, and blend well. Add chicken and stir until well blended. Pour mixture over pretzel crust. Bake at 300 degrees for 45 minutes. Turn oven off, partially open door and leave for one hour. Remove from oven, cool, cover and chill. Serve plain or top with melted red pepper jelly. Assorted accompaniments, such as almonds and crumbled bacon may be added.

Susie Kroencke

Chili-Chicken

16 ounces medium noodles
½ cup chopped onion
2 tablespoons butter or margarine
3 cans cream of mushroom soup
1 2 ounce jar pimiento, chopped
2 tablespoons finely chopped pickled hot green chili pepper (remove seeds and stems)
3-4 cups cut-up cooked chicken or turkey
Salt and pepper to taste
2-3 cups shredded sharp cheddar cheese

Heat oven to 350 degrees. Cook noodles as directed on package; drain. In large skillet, cook onion in butter until tender. Stir in soup, pimiento and chili pepper. In greased 4 quart casserole, layer half the noodles and half the chicken, season with salt and pepper. Top with half the soup mixture and half the cheese. Repeat layers. Bake uncovered about 45 minutes. Serves 8-12

Mary Noel Mabry

Creamed Chicken

- *4 tablespoons butter*
- *½ cup flour*
- *1½ teaspoons salt*
- *¼ teaspoon pepper*
- *2 cups half and half*
- *1 cup whipping cream*
- *1 cup chicken broth*
- *2½ cups cooked chicken*
- *¼ cup pimiento*
- *½ cup diced green pepper*
- *¼ pound mushrooms, sliced*

Melt butter, blend in flour, salt and pepper. Add half and half, whipping cream and broth. Cook, stirring constantly until sauce is medium consistency. Add remaining ingredients, blend and heat. Serve over toast. Serves 6

Becky Ellison

Favorite Chicken Casserole

- *1 6 ounce box long grained wild rice*
- *6 chicken breasts, cooked and boned*
- *1 can cream of celery soup*
- *1 onion, minced*
- *1 2 ounce jar pimientos*
- *2 cups mayonnaise*
- *8 ounce can water chestnuts, sliced thin (optional)*
- *2 16 ounce cans French style green beans, drained*
- *Paprika*
- *Grated Parmesan cheese*

Cook rice as directed on box. Add all ingredients except paprika and Parmesan cheese. Mix thoroughly. Pour into greased 9 x 13 baking dish. Sprinkle with paprika and Parmesan cheese. Bake at 350 degrees for 30-40 minutes. Freezes well. Thaw before cooking.

Judy Taylor

Chicken Dorothy

- *4 chicken breast halves*
- *Salt and pepper*
- *¼ cup butter*
- *1 cup sour cream*
- *1 can cream of mushroom soup*
- *1 small can mushrooms, sliced*
- *½ cup white wine*

Salt and pepper chicken. Brown in butter. Remove to casserole dish. In pan where chicken was browned, combine sour cream, soup, mushrooms and wine. Pour over chicken. Cover casserole and bake at 350 degrees for one hour. Serves 4

Connie Neumeier

Chicken and Dumplings

1 *4-5 pound chicken*
3 *carrots, sliced thinly*
3 *ribs celery, with leaves, sliced finely*
1 *large yellow onion, chopped*
1½ *teaspoons thyme*
½ *teaspoon rosemary*
2 *teaspoons salt*
½ *teaspoon freshly ground pepper*

Rinse chicken, cut into pieces and place in a large pot, covering with water. Cook 45 minutes. Remove chicken, bone and return meat to stock. Add carrots, celery, onion and spices. Bring to a boil. Reduce to simmer and cook while making dumplings.

Dumplings

1½ *cups flour*
½ *teaspoon salt*
3 *tablespoons shortening*
1 *egg, beaten*

To make dumplings, mix flour, salt and shortening. Add egg and make a soft dough. Roll thin, about ¼". Dry 20 minutes. Cut into strips 1-1½" square. Drop into boiling broth and cook until done. Serves 6-8

Maysel Teeter

Chicken Enchiladas

1 *cup chopped onion*
¼ *cup butter*
¼ *cup flour*
2½ *cups water*
1 *tablespoon instant chicken bouillon*
1 *8 ounce carton low fat yogurt*
3 *cups cooked chicken*
2 *cups lowfat cheese*
1 *4 ounce can green chilies*
1 *ounce pimiento, chopped*
1 *teaspoon chili powder*
1 *teaspoon cilantro*
10 *8" corn tortillas*

Sauté onion in butter. Stir in flour and water; add bouillon and dissolve. Remove from heat. Stir in yogurt. In bowl, combine 1 cup sauce, chicken, 1 cup cheese, chilies, pimiento, chili powder and cilantro. Mix well. Dip each tortilla into remaining sauce to soften. Fill and arrange in 9 x 13 dish. Spoon remaining sauce over enchiladas. Sprinkle with cheese. Bake at 350 degrees for 25 minutes.

Gravy

4 *tablespoons flour*
¼ *cup cooking oil*
2 *tablespoons chili powder*
2 *tablespoons cumin*
1 *teaspoon salt*
2 *cloves garlic, crushed*

Brown flour in oil in saucepan. Add remaining ingredients. Simmer one hour. Pour over enchiladas. Serves 8-10

Bonnie Johnson

Chicken Fajitas

- ½ *cup vegetable oil*
- 2 *tablespoons tarragon vinegar*
- ½ *cup lime juice*
- ⅓ *cup finely chopped green onion*
- 1 *teaspoon sugar*
- ⅛ *teaspoon black pepper*
- ¼ *teaspoon cumin*
- 2 *cloves garlic, chopped*
- 2 *pounds boneless, skinless chicken breast*
- 10 *flour tortillas*

Combine the first 8 ingredients in a shallow glass container. Mix well. Cut chicken into strips ¼" wide. Add chicken strips to sauce and toss to coat. Cover and refrigerate 8 hours or overnight. Remove from sauce and drain. Grill over medium coals 6-8 minutes, turning once. Heat tortillas according to package directions. Place 1/10 of chicken in each tortilla and top with choice of toppings: picante sauce, guacamole salad, chopped tomatoes, finely chopped onion and sour cream. Serves 10

Becky Ellison

Greek Phyllo Chicken

- 1 *cup whole almonds*
- 3 *cups chopped cooked chicken*
- 1 *8 ounce package feta cheese, crumbled*
- ½ *cup sliced green onion*
- ¾ *cup heavy cream*
- 2 *tablespoons Dijon mustard*
- 1 *clove garlic, minced*
- 1½ *teaspoons basil*
- 1 *teaspoon herb pepper*
- ½ *pound phyllo dough*
- ½ *cup butter, melted*

Spread almonds in shallow pan. Toast at 350 degrees, 15 minutes, stirring once or twice. Cool. Coarsely chop almonds. In a large bowl, combine almonds with chicken, feta cheese, green onions, heavy cream, mustard, garlic, basil and herb pepper seasoning. Divide phyllo dough in half, cover with plastic wrap to keep from drying. Brush bottom of 9 x 13 x 2 pan with butter. Layer with 1 sheet phyllo, folding excess edges down to fit pan; brush with melted butter. Repeat using half a sheet of phyllo. Spoon chicken mixture over phyllo. Top with remaining half of phyllo, brushing each sheet with butter and fitting edges into pan. Bake at 375 degrees, 30 minutes or until golden brown. Cool slightly before serving. Serves 8

Bonnie Haines

Honey of Chicken Breast

3 whole chicken breasts, skinned, split and boned
Salt and pepper
1 cup bread crumbs
½ teaspoon thyme
1 teaspoon salt
¼ teaspoon pepper
½ teaspoon oregano
½ cup white wine
½ cup oil

Sauce

1 cup honey
¼ cup prepared mustard
¼ cup prepared horseradish, mild

Season chicken with salt and pepper. Combine crumbs and herbs. Brush chicken with oil, then roll lightly in crumbs. Make sauce by combining honey, mustard and horseradish. Spread sauce on each piece and roll into ball. Place in baking dish. Pour wine over chicken. Then cover with more sauce. Bake until golden brown. Freezes well. Yields 6

Virginia Berner

Chicken Kabobs

Marinade

⅓ cup oil
1 clove garlic, minced
⅔ cup dry white wine
1 small onion, chopped
1 teaspoon salt
¼ teaspoon pepper
½ teaspoon tarragon

Chicken

8 chicken breasts cut into chunks
2 medium green peppers, cut into 1" chunks
4 medium onions, cut each into 6 wedges
2 medium zucchini, cut into 1" slices
4 medium tomatoes, cut each into 6 wedges
24 mushrooms

Make marinade by combining all ingredients. Place chicken in casserole dish. Cover chicken with marinade and refrigerate overnight. When ready to cook kabobs, alternate vegetables and chicken on skewers. Broil 6" from heat on grill. Turn several times, until chicken and vegetables are done.

Linda Fenech

King Ranch Chicken

4 cups cooked, chopped chicken
1 large bell pepper, chopped
1 large onion, chopped
1 stick margarine
1 package corn tortillas, torn into pieces
1 10 ounce can tomatoes with green chilies
1 cup grated Monterey Jack cheese
1 teaspoon chili powder
8 ounces chicken broth
1 can cream of mushroom soup

Sauté pepper and onion in margarine. Add chicken and set aside. Line a 9 x 13 casserole dish with tortilla pieces and spread half the chicken mixture over them. Put in another layer of tortillas and cover with remaining chicken mixture then top with another layer of tortillas. Place tomatoes, including juice, in blender with soup, broth and chili powder. Blend well and pour over casserole. Bake at 350 degrees for 30 minutes. Remove from oven and cover with cheese. Return to oven for another 30 minutes. Let set 10 minutes before serving. Serves 8-10

Debbie Bell

Chicken Monterey

¼ cup flour
1 envelope taco seasoning mix
4 chicken breasts, boned
¼ cup butter
1 cup crushed tortilla chips

Sauce

1 tablespoon butter
2 tablespoons finely chopped onion
2 tablespoons flour
¼ teaspoon salt
1 cup milk
¼ teaspoon bottled hot sauce
1 cup grated Monterey Jack cheese
¼ cup sliced ripe olives

Combine flour and taco seasoning in plastic bag. Add chicken and shake to coat. Melt butter in baking dish and turn chicken over in butter. Roll chicken in crushed chips and return to baking dish. Bake at 275 degrees for 45-50 minutes. Meanwhile, make sauce by melting butter in a sauce-pan and cook onion until soft. Blend in flour and salt and add milk. Cook and stir until mixture thickens. Add hot sauce, cheese and olives and stir until cheese melts. Do not boil. Serve sauce over chicken. Serves 4

Judy Thacker

Summertime Chicken Mousse

2 cups chicken
1 envelope unflavored gelatin
¼ cup cold water
1½ cups boiling chicken stock
¼ cup chopped celery
¼ cup sweet pickle relish
1 teaspoon Worcestershire sauce
¼ teaspoon paprika
1 tablespoon lemon juice
⅛ teaspoon nutmeg
¼ teaspoon pepper
½ teaspoon onion purée
½ teaspoon salt
½ cup mayonnaise

Cook chicken and save broth. Cut chicken into small pieces. Dissolve gelatin in cold water. Add this to boiling chicken stock. Add remaining ingredients except mayonnaise. Taste to see if more salt is needed. Cool. Add mayonnaise. Pour into a 9 x 5 x 3 greased pan. Chill 2 hours before serving. Serves 6-8

Kay Ewing

Nutmeg Chicken

4 chicken breasts, boned
Salt
Ground nutmeg
4 tablespoons melted butter
4 tablespoons minced onion
4-6 mushrooms, sliced
⅔ cup dry white wine
¼ cup cashews
1 teaspoon cornstarch
2 teaspoons dry white wine

Sprinkle chicken with salt and nutmeg (coat chicken well with nutmeg). Brown each side in butter in a heavy skillet. Add onion, mushrooms and ⅔ cup wine. Bring to a boil, reduce heat, cover and simmer 20 to 25 minutes. Add cashews. Remove chicken. Combine cornstarch and 2 teaspoons wine. Mix well and stir into skillet. Cook, stirring constantly until thickened. Serve chicken and sauce over hot cooked rice. Serves 4

Judy Thacker

Oven Fried Chicken

3 pound fryer
½ cup melted butter
2 cups crushed potato chips, plain or barbecued
¼ teaspoon garlic salt
Dash pepper

Cut up chicken. Dip chicken pieces in melted butter. Roll in mixture of potato chips, salt and pepper. Place pieces skin side up, not touching, in a greased shallow baking pan. Sprinkle with remaining butter and chips. Bake at 375 degrees about 1 hour or until done. Serves 4

Vickie Hale

Chicken Parmesan

- 4 *chicken breasts, boned and pounded to ½" thick*
- 2 *eggs, beaten*
- 1 *teaspoon salt*
- ½ *teaspoon pepper*
- ¾ *cup bread crumbs*
- ½ *cup vegetable oil*
- 1 *15 ounce can tomato sauce*
- ¼ *teaspoon basil*
- ⅛ *teaspoon garlic powder*
- 1 *tablespoon butter*
- ½ *cup grated Parmesan cheese*
- 8 *ounces Mozzarella cheese*

Dip chicken into egg, salt, pepper, basil, garlic, and grated Parmesan mixture. Roll chicken in bread crumbs until covered. Heat oil in heavy skillet. Brown chicken lightly. Place browned chicken in buttered baking dish. Dribble tomato sauce over chicken. Sprinkle additional basil and garlic powder over sauce. Bake at 350 degrees for 30 minutes. Top with Parmesan and Mozzarella cheese and bake an additional 10 minutes. Serves 4

Georganne Peel

Good and Easy Chicken Pie

- 3 *whole chicken breasts*
- 1 *teaspoon celery salt*
- 1 *teaspoon tarragon*
- 2 *tablespoons lemon juice*
- 2 *cans cream of chicken soup*
- 1 *can mixed vegetables*
- *Salt and pepper*
- *Crescent dinner rolls*

Simmer chicken breasts about 1 hour in a covered pan with celery salt, tarragon, lemon juice and about 1½ cups water. When tender, drain (reserving broth), remove skin and bone from meat. Chop into large pieces. In 11 x 7 baking dish, pour soup, and thin with ½ cup of the broth. Add drained mixed vegetables, season with salt and pepper and stir in chicken pieces. Top with crescent rolls (unroll, but do not separate). Dough need not meet exactly in center or on sides. Bake at 375 degrees until crust is brown and filling is bubbling. About 30 minutes. Serves 6

Marilyn Moores

Chicken with Raspberry Sauce

- 1 *pound chicken tenderloins*
- *Cayenne pepper to taste*
- 1 *tablespoon oil*
- 6 *tablespoons raspberry preserves*
- 2 *tablespoons red wine vinegar*
- ½ *teaspoon horseradish*
- ½ *teaspoon garlic, minced*
- *Fresh raspberries (optional)*

Lightly sprinkle chicken with pepper. Heat oil in skillet over medium high heat. Brown chicken in oil, turning once, 3 to 4 minutes per side. Do not overcook. Combine remaining ingredients except fruit in small saucepan. Simmer 3 minutes. Serve chicken garnished with sauce and fruit. Serves 4

Patti Nickels

Chicken and Rice Casserole

1 can cream of mushroom soup
1 can cream of celery soup
1 can cream of chicken soup
1¼ cups of water
1 small can mushrooms, drained
¾ stick butter
1¼ cups uncooked instant precooked rice
8 boneless chicken breasts

Combine soups, water, mushrooms and butter in saucepan. Heat and stir over moderate heat. When warm and thoroughly mixed, remove 1 cup of mixture and set aside. Add rice to saucepan and stir. Pour mixture of rice and soup in baking dish. Place chicken on top. Pour remaining soup over chicken pieces. Bake at 350 degrees for 30 minutes or until chicken is done. Serves 8

Kay Armstrong

Chicken Roberto

6 whole, boned, skinless chicken breasts
1 teaspoon salt
¼ teaspoon garlic salt
1 teaspoon pepper
1 teaspoon Greek seasoning
¾ pound sausage
6 slices process cheese
3 slices bacon, cut in half
5 tablespoons barbecue sauce
Non stick cooking spray

Pound each unsplit breast with meat mallet to flatten to about ¼" thick. Sprinkle with salt, pepper, garlic salt and Greek seasoning and pound into breast meat. In frying pan, crumble and fry sausage until done. Drain excess fat. Add processed cheese and heat until cheese melts. Evenly spoon sausage mixture onto one side of each chicken breast. Fold other breast over sausage topped breast. Pound edges with a mallet to seal. Top each roll with ½ strip of bacon. Place rolls on cookie sheet sprayed with non stick cooking spray. Bake uncovered at 450 degrees for 30 minutes. Brush with barbecue sauce. Turn off oven and let set in oven for 5 minutes until sauce sets. Serves 6

Annette Holeyfield

Baked Chicken Salad

1½ cups cooked diced chicken
1 cup cream of chicken soup
1 cup finely diced celery
½ teaspoon salt
2 tablespoons chopped green onions
½ cup slivered almonds
1 cup cooked rice
3 teaspoons lemon juice
¾ cup mayonnaise
3 hard boiled eggs
2 ounces chopped pimiento
1 cup bread crumbs, or crushed butter flavored crackers

Mix all ingredients and place in a casserole. Top with bread crumbs. Bake at 350 degrees for 30 minutes.

Connie Neumeier

Every Event Chicken Shells

4 cups chicken
2 cups sliced mushrooms
1 8 ounce package cream cheese
1 can cream of mushroom soup
1 tablespoon sherry
Salt and pepper to taste
12 pastry shells

Boil chicken and cut into bite sized pieces. Sauté sliced mushrooms. Add chicken, cream cheese, soup and sherry. Heat until cheese and soup melts. Add salt and pepper to taste. Serve in pastry shells. Serves 10-12

Kay Ewing

Chicken Tarragon

4 boneless, skinless chicken breasts
Salt and pepper
¾ cup flour
Butter
Tarragon
½ pint cream

Salt and pepper chicken and coat lightly with flour. Sauté in butter in frying pan until each side is browned. Sprinkle lightly with tarragon. Add cream and simmer until chicken is completely done. Serves 4

Lynda Hill

Spectacular Chicken Spaghetti

4 large chicken breasts, boned
1 green pepper, chopped
1 large onion, chopped
1 cup chopped celery
½ cup margarine
1 16 ounce can tomatoes
1 can cream of mushroom soup
2½ tablespoons lemon juice
2 tablespoons Worcestershire sauce
2 tablespoons chili powder
1 bay leaf
1 teaspoon paprika
1 teaspoon minced garlic
1 teaspoon salt
1 tablespoon pepper
1 4 ounce can mushrooms, undrained
2 cups chicken broth
1 small can sliced black olives
1 small package sliced almonds
12 ounces thin spaghetti, cooked and drained
16 ounces sliced sharp cheddar cheese

Boil chicken and reserve broth. Sauté green pepper, onions and celery in margarine. Add next 10 ingredients. Stir. Add juice of mushrooms and 2 cups chicken broth. Cook for 45 minutes. Add mushrooms, olives, almonds and boned, cut up chicken. Stir in cooked spaghetti and place in casserole. Cover with grated cheese. Bake, covered at 350 degrees for 30 minutes. Serves 10-12

Tamara Laws

Chicken Stir Fry

1 pound boneless, skinless chicken breast chunks
1½ teaspoons cornstarch
1 egg white, lightly beaten
8 ounces broccoli
1 cup chicken stock
4 teaspoons soy sauce
½ teaspoon hot red pepper flakes
1½ cups sliced onion
3-4 cloves garlic, finely chopped
1 tablespoon peeled freshly grated ginger

Mix the chicken chunks with 1 teaspoon of the cornstarch and the lightly beaten egg white. Cut the florets from the broccoli stalks and separate them into smaller pieces. Peel the stalks and slice them into long, narrow strips. Mix together chicken stock, remaining ½ teaspoon cornstarch, soy sauce and pepper flakes. Set aside. Heat 2 tablespoons oil in a large skillet. When hot, add the chicken and cook 2 minutes, turning the pieces as they brown. Remove the chicken from the skillet. Add the onions and sauté for about 30 seconds. Add the broccoli, cover the pan and cook for 2 minutes, stirring occasionally. Return the chicken to the pan and add the garlic and ginger. Stir the reserved chicken stock mixture into the pan and simmer for 2-3 minutes, until the chicken is heated through and the sauce is thickened. Serve immediately.

Bonnie Haines

Chicken Tetrazzini

4 chicken breasts
4 chicken thighs
3 chicken flavored bouillon cubes
4 ounces cheddar cheese
1 bell pepper, diced
1 bunch green onions, diced
1 2 ounce jar pimientos
1 can cream of mushroom soup
3 cloves garlic, minced
8 ounces fresh mushrooms, sliced
1 cup heavy cream
1 stick butter
4 ounces processed cheese spread, cubed
2 eggs, beaten
Cayenne pepper
Salt and pepper
8 ounces fettuccine, cooked and drained

Cover chicken with water and add bouillon cubes. Boil slowly until chicken is done. Remove chicken and cut into bite-size pieces. Reserve 1 cup broth. Sauté bell pepper, onion, garlic and mushrooms in butter. Add soup, pimientos, cream, processed cheese and spices. Cook on low until cheese melts. Stir in eggs. Mix with fettuccine and pour into a greased 9 x 13 casserole dish. Bake at 350 degrees for 45 minutes. Top with cheddar cheese and cook 5 minutes.

Sue McCoy

Sesame Seed Chicken

3 chicken breasts
1 can cream of mushroom soup
1 can cream of celery soup
1 8 ounce carton sour cream
1 small package slivered almonds

Topping

1 stick margarine
Butter flavored crackers
2-3 tablespoons sesame seeds

Cook and bone chicken. Mix with soups, almonds and sour cream. Pour into a large glass casserole dish. Melt butter. Crumble crackers to take up butter and put on top of chicken mixture. Sprinkle sesame seeds on top. Bake at 350 degrees for 1 hour. Serve over rice.

Carol Shoptaw

Turkey Elegante with Rice

1½ cups uncooked rice
3 cups hot turkey or chicken broth
1 cup chopped green onion
¼ cup butter, melted
4 cups cubed cooked turkey
1 8 ounce can water chestnuts, drained and sliced
1 tablespoon sliced fresh ginger
1 16 ounce carton sour cream
Salt to taste

Cook rice according to package directions using broth instead of water. Set aside and keep warm. Sauté onion in butter until tender. Add turkey, water chestnuts and ginger. Cook, stirring constantly, until heated thoroughly. Stir in sour cream and salt. Cook over low heat until heated thoroughly. Serve over rice. Serves 8

Annette Holeyfield

Picnic Cornish Hens

8 Cornish hens (about 10-12 ounces each)
Salt and pepper
½ cup Dijon mustard
⅔ cup white bread crumbs
3 tablespoons minced shallots
½ cup butter
White wine

Rub each bird with salt, pepper and 1 tablespoon of the mustard. Sprinkle with bread crumbs. Place in square of foil and fold to center. Add 1 teaspoon shallots, 1 tablespoon butter and 3 tablespoons white wine to each package. Fold over the foil tightly and bake at 400 degrees for 45 minutes. Open foil, baste hens and bake about 15 minutes more, until browned. Re-seal and carry to picnic in foil. Good cold, too! If you are serving at home, remove from foil, stuff cavity with fresh parsley and serve juices separately. Serves 8

Laurie Bibler

Crabmeat au Gratin

1½ cups canned crabmeat
1 cup soft bread crumbs
1 cup mayonnaise
¾ cup milk
6 hard boiled eggs, finely chopped
⅓ cup onion, chopped
¾ teaspoon salt
Dash pepper
½ cup buttered soft bread crumbs
Paprika

Combine all ingredients, except buttered bread crumbs and paprika. Place mixture in greased individual scallop shells. Top with crumbs and sprinkle on paprika. Bake at 350 degrees for 20-25 minutes or until bubbly and browned. Serves 6-8

Kathy Smith

Swiss and Crab Pie

4 ounces natural Swiss cheese, shredded
1 9" unbaked pastry shell
1 7½ ounce can crabmeat, drained, flaked, and cartilage removed
2 green onions, sliced (with tops)
3 beaten eggs
1 cup light cream
½ teaspoon salt
½ teaspoon grated lemon peel
¼ teaspoon dry mustard
Dash ground mace
¼ cup sliced almonds

Arrange cheese evenly over bottom of pastry shell. Top with crabmeat; sprinkle with green onions. Combine eggs, cream, salt, lemon peel, mustard and mace. Pour evenly over crabmeat. Top with sliced almonds. Bake at 325 degree oven for about 45 minutes or until set. Remove from oven and let stand 10 minutes before serving. Serves 6

Vickie Hale

Crawfish Fettuccine

2 onions, chopped
3 ribs celery, chopped
1 bell pepper, chopped
2-3 cloves garlic, chopped
1 cup butter
3 tablespoons flour
1 pint half and half
4 tablespoons parsley
Creole seasoning, to taste
1 8 ounce jar processed cheese spread
1 4 ounce roll jalapeño cheese
2 pounds crawfish, peeled
12 ounces fettuccine

Sauté vegetables in butter for 10 minutes. Add flour and blend. Pour in half and half, stirring constantly. Add parsley and seasonings. When mixture is bubbly, add cheeses and stir well. Add crawfish and cook 20 minutes. Boil fettuccine (break into thirds). Add crawfish mixture to drained noodles. Pour into a greased 9 x 12 casserole dish and bake uncovered for 20 minutes at 350 degrees. Serves 6

Kay Roberts

Sacrey's Catfish — Cajun Style

- *1 can beer*
- *3 tablespoons Worcestershire sauce*
- *½ cup brewed coffee*
- *24 catfish fillets*
- *2 cups cornmeal*
- *1 teaspoon salt*
- *1 tablespoon garlic powder*

Marinate catfish in first three ingredients for 15 minutes. Drain fillets. Roll in cornmeal, salt, and garlic. Deep fry until golden.

The Committee

Halibut with Piquant Sauce

- *¼ cup butter*
- *½ teaspoon dry mustard*
- *1½ teaspoons dried parsley flakes*
- *⅛ teaspoon garlic powder*
- *1½ teaspoons lemon juice*
- *1 pound halibut fillets*

Place butter in 1½ quart (10 x 6) baking dish. Microwave until melted. Add mustard, parsley, garlic and lemon juice. Dip halibut in seasoned butter, put in dish with thick edges toward the outside of the dish. Cover with plastic wrap. Microwave on high for 6-7 minutes or until fish flakes easily. Let stand, covered, for five minutes before serving. Serves 4-6

Camille Thurlby

Orange Roughy Parmesan

- *2 pounds orange roughy fillets*
- *2 tablespoons fresh lemon juice*
- *½ cup grated Parmesan cheese*
- *4 tablespoons butter, softened*
- *3 tablespoons mayonnaise*
- *3 tablespoons chopped green onions*
- *¼ teaspoon salt*
- *Black pepper to taste*

In buttered baking dish, place fillets in a single layer. Brush with lemon juice. Let stand 10 minutes. In a small bowl, combine cheese, butter, mayonnaise, onion, salt and pepper. Broil fillets 3-4" from broiler for five minutes. Spread with cheese mixture and broil for another 2-3 minutes, watching closely. Serves 6-8

Camille Thurlby

Baked Salmon Croquettes

1 7¾ ounce can salmon, reserve liquid, flake
1½ cups cooked rice
2 tablespoons chopped green onion
2 teaspoons grated lemon peel
½ teaspoon salt
2 eggs
1 tablespoons water
Buttered cracker crumbs
1 recipe Cheese Sauce

Combine salmon with liquid, rice, onion, lemon peel, salt and one egg. Shape into 8 croquettes. Beat remaining egg with water. Roll croquettes in egg and then in cracker crumbs. Chill for 30 minutes. Bake at 375 degrees for 25-30 minutes on greased cookie sheet. Make Cheese Sauce.

Cheese Sauce

2 tablespoons butter
1 tablespoon flour
¼ teaspoon salt
Dash white pepper
1 cup milk
¾ cup grated cheddar cheese

Melt butter in saucepan. Blend in flour, salt and pepper. Cook and stir one minute. Pour in milk and continue stirring. Add cheese, stirring until it melts. Pour over individual croquettes. Serves 8

Connie Neumeier

Simple Scallops

1 pound scallops
½ cup butter
1 bay leaf
¼ pound fresh mushrooms, washed and sliced
1 cup white wine

Sauté desired amount of scallops in butter. Add bay leaf, mushrooms and white wine. Cover and let steam for a few minutes. Remove lid and simmer to reduce liquid. Serves 2

Joyce R. Laws

Shrimp and Asparagus Stir Fry

¼ cup sesame seeds
1 tablespoon butter
1 onion, finely sliced
2 tablespoons soy sauce
1 pound fresh shrimp, peeled and deveined
1 pound fresh asparagus

Heat sesame seeds in a 9" skillet until toasted. Set aside. Sauté onion in butter until clear. Add soy sauce, shrimp and asparagus. Stir fry until shrimp is pink and the asparagus is tender crisp. Place on a serving platter and sprinkle with sesame seeds. Serves 2-3

Shirley Leonard

"Miss Patsy's" Shrimp Creole

- *¾ cup salad oil*
- *3 tablespoons flour (heaping)*
- *1 bunch shallots or one large onion, chopped*
- *1 bell pepper, chopped*
- *4 pounds shrimp, cleaned*
- *2 10 ounce cans tomatoes with chilies*
- *Salt to taste*
- *Hot cooked rice*

Make a roux by heating oil and flour, stirring constantly, on medium heat, until the color of chocolate. Add onion and bell pepper, cooking until soft. Add shrimp. Stir until shrimp are coated with roux and none of roux or onions stick to the pan. Add tomatoes. Cook slowly about 45 minutes to one hour. Serve over rice. Serves 4-6

Connie Neumeier

Cajun Shrimp Etouffée

- *½ cup butter*
- *1 medium onion, chopped*
- *1 bell pepper, chopped*
- *3 ounces tomato paste, optional*
- *½ teaspoon black pepper*
- *½ teaspoon cayenne pepper*
- *1 pound shrimp, peeled and deveined*

In a large frying pan, melt butter; add vegetables and sauté until tender. Stir in seasonings and tomato paste. Add shrimp and cook 10 minutes. Serve over hot cooked rice. Serves 2-4

Connie Austin

Shrimp Victoria

- *1 pound shrimp, peeled and cleaned*
- *1 small onion, finely chopped*
- *¼ cup butter*
- *1 small can mushrooms*
- *1 tablespoon flour*
- *Salt and cayenne pepper, to taste*
- *1 cup sour cream*
- *5 cups cooked rice*

Sauté shrimp and onions in butter 10 minutes or until tender. Add mushrooms and cook 5 minutes or more. Sprinkle in flour, salt and pepper. Stir in sour cream and cook gently 10 minutes. Do not boil. Serve over rice. Makes 4-6 servings

Pam Rushing

Shrimp Pesto on Linguine

Cooked linguine
2 teaspoons minced garlic
2 tablespoons vegetable oil
1 tablespoon chopped fresh basil
12 shrimp, peeled
Splash white wine, optional
2 tablespoons pesto (see recipe below)
½ cup clam juice
½ cup tomato sauce OR marinara sauce
Salt and pepper to taste
Pinch oregano

Cook linguine according to package directions; hold warm. Brown garlic in oil. Add basil, shrimp, wine, pesto, clam juice and sauce. Salt and pepper. Simmer long enough for shrimp to turn pink. Add oregano. Serve sauce over linguine. Serves 2

Pesto

1 teaspoon minced garlic
2 cups fresh basil leaves OR 2 cups fresh parsley plus 1 tablespoons dried basil
¼ cup Parmesan cheese
½ cup pine nuts (or English walnuts)
Olive oil to moisten

In a blender mix first four ingredients. Drizzle in enough olive oil to make a paste. Blend briefly. Keep in refrigerator.

Jane Barnes

Shrimp Pierre

1 tablespoon garlic powder or 3-4 cloves, minced
1 yellow onion, diced
½ cup fresh parsley or ¼ cup dried flakes
1 teaspoon dry mustard
1 teaspoon salt
⅓ cup olive oil
½ cup white wine, optional (increase oil to ½ cup if you do not use wine)
1 teaspoon lemon juice
1 pound shrimp, peeled and deveined
4 cups hot cooked rice

Combine first eight ingredients in a plastic lidded container and mix well. Add shrimp and marinate in the refrigerator for at least five hours to overnight. Pour marinated shrimp mixture into an electric skillet or frying pan and sauté over medium heat for about 10-15 minutes, or until shrimp are done. Serve over the rice. Serves 4

Tonia Beavers

Seafood Fettuccine

1 large onion
6-7 cloves garlic
1 cup butter
3 tablespoons flour
1 pint half and half
1 12 ounce jar marinated artichoke hearts, drained
½-1 cup Parmesan cheese
1½ cups chopped fresh parsley
1-2 pounds shrimp, peeled and cleaned
3 3-4 ounce cans clams
Salt and pepper, to taste
1 pound fettuccine, cooked

Using blender, chop onion and garlic; sauté in a large skillet with ½ cup butter. Sprinkle in flour and stir well. Add the remaining butter and half and half and stir until smooth and thick. Chop the artichokes and add to the sauce. Add Parmesan and parsley. This can be done ahead and refrigerated. When ready to serve: add shrimp and clams, salt and pepper to taste, and heat through. Serve over hot fettuccine. Serves 6

Linda Fenech

Seafood Gumbo

6 tablespoons lard, shortening or oil
6 tablespoons flour
1 large onion, chopped
2-3 cloves garlic, chopped
½ bell pepper, chopped
3 quarts water
Salt, red and black pepper to taste
1 can fresh claw crabmeat
Several whole crabs
1 pound shrimp, peeled
1 pint oysters and liquid
½ cup parsley
3-4 green onions, chopped

Cook grease and flour in a large black iron pot to make a roux, stirring constantly until the color of chocolate. Add onion, garlic and bell pepper, stirring well. Slowly, pour in about three quarts of water. Add salt and peppers to taste. Add can of crabmeat and whole crabs, cooking about one hour. Add shrimp and liquid from a pint of oysters, cooking until shrimp are done. About 30 minutes before serving, add the chopped parsley and green onions. About 15 minutes before serving, add the oysters. Serve over rice. Be sure to have a bottle of fresh filé on hand so each person can add their own. This freezes well; however, add fresh oysters at the time of serving rather than freeze them in the gumbo.

Patti Blackmon

Seafood Pasta

1 9 ounce package fresh soft linguine
1 tablespoon olive oil
1 pound shrimp, peeled, deveined and rinsed
1 pound scallops
1 cup flour
½ teaspoon salt
½ teaspoon pepper
¼ pound butter
2½ tablespoons minced garlic
2 tablespoons dried, flaked, hot red pepper
Parsley for garnish

Boil water. Add pasta and olive oil to water. Mix flour, salt and pepper; dredge scallops in flour mixture. Melt butter in large skillet, adding garlic and red pepper flakes. Stir in shrimp and scallops. Cook for 5-6 minutes. Drain pasta while cooking seafood and put on serving platter. Top with seafood. Serves 6-8

Patti Nickels

Shellfish Casserole

3 cups chicken broth
1 large onion, chopped
1 carrot
1 teaspoon parsley flakes
1 tablespoon lemon juice
1½ teaspoons salt
1 bay leaf
8 peppercorns
¼ teaspoon thyme
⅛ teaspoon marjoram
1 cup water
1 16 ounce container frozen lobster tails
1 16 ounce container frozen crabmeat
2 pounds cooked shrimp, peeled
⅓ cup minced onion
4 tablespoons minced green pepper
2 tablespoons tomato sauce
½ clove garlic, crushed
2 teaspoons lemon juice
¼ teaspoon hot pepper sauce
1 cup raw rice
¼ cup butter
¼ cup flour
¾ teaspoon salt
¼ teaspoon pepper
1 cup light cream
½ cup milk
⅜ cup fish broth
½ cup slivered almonds

Combine first 10 ingredients and simmer 10 minutes. To this mixture, add the lobster tails and cook until tender. Strain broth; measure out ⅜ cup and reserve. Shell and cut lobster; drain and shred crab. Return remaining broth to pan, add water, ⅓ cup onion, green pepper, tomato sauce, garlic, lemon juice, and pepper sauce and bring to a boil. Add rice. Cover and cook for 20-25 minutes. Melt butter in a skillet over medium heat; stir in flour, salt and pepper. Cook three minutes. Add cream, milk, and reserved fish broth slowly to mixture and cook until smooth. To cream sauce, add lobster, crab, shrimp and rice. Place in a greased 1½ quart casserole. Cover top with almonds. Bake at 325 degrees for 30 minutes or until mixture bubbles. Serves 4-6

Lou Adams

Whitey's Grilled Dove

Dove breasts
Bacon
Butter
Vegetable oil
Lemon juice

Wrap each dove breast in one slice of bacon, and secure the bacon with a toothpick. Mix equal parts of butter and oil to make basting sauce, adding lemon juice to taste. Place the breasts on a grill and cook slowly, basting frequently. Takes about 30-40 minutes to grill.

The Committee

Duck and Wild Rice Casserole

2 *medium ducks (3 cups cubed meat)*
3 *ribs celery*
1 *onion, halved*
Salt and pepper to taste
1 *6 ounce package seasoned wild and long grain rice*
½ *cup margarine*
½ *cup chopped onion*
¼ *cup flour*
1 *4 ounce jar sliced mushrooms*
1½ *cups half and half*
1 *tablespoon chopped parsley*
1½ *teaspoons salt*
¼ *teaspoon pepper*
Slivered almonds

Boil ducks for one hour (or until tender) in water to cover, with celery, onion, salt and pepper; remove ducks and cube meat. Reserve broth. Cook rice according to package directions. Melt margarine, sauté onion; stir in flour. Drain mushrooms, reserving juice, and add mushrooms to the onions. Add enough duck broth to the mushroom juice to make 1½ cups liquid; stir this into the onion mixture. Add the remaining ingredients, except almonds. Pat into a greased 9 x 13 casserole. Sprinkle with almonds. Bake covered at 350 degrees for 15-20 minutes. Uncover and bake for 5-10 minutes more, or until very hot. Serves 6

Susan Lewis

Toni's Easy and Delicious Duck

1 *duck*
½ *cup cooking sherry*
½ *envelope dry onion soup mix*
¾ *can mushroom soup*
Seasoning salt to taste

Place each duck on a large piece of heavy duty aluminum foil. Combine the remaining ingredients and pour over duck. Close foil, making a tent 2" above the duck breast. Place in a baking pan. Do not cover. Bake at 350 degrees for two hours. Do not open tent during cooking. The stock makes wonderful gravy for rice. Do not cook more than one duck in a tent. Serves 2

Toni Weatherford

Duck and Sausage Gumbo

1 cup oil
1 cup flour
3 cups chopped onion
1 cup chopped celery
1 cup chopped green pepper
2 pounds smoked sausage links, sliced
3 ducks, parboiled until tender, boned, reserving stock
Salt and pepper to taste
1 cup minced green onions
⅔ cup parsley, minced

Make a dark roux by heating oil in a large pot, add flour and stir continuously until flour is chocolate brown. Stir in onions, celery and green pepper. Cook until vegetables are tender. Add duck stock (plus enough water to make about three quarts) to roux mixture and simmer 30 minutes to one hour. Add duck and season to taste. Simmer another hour. Taste and season. Brown sausage and drain; add with green onions and parsley to the gumbo. Cover and simmer another 30-45 minutes. Serve over rice with hot pepper sauce. Serves 8-10

Tonia Beavers

Jim's Duck Stir Fry

3 duck breasts, filleted
1 onion, chopped
1 bell pepper, chopped
1 bunch broccoli, chopped
8 carrots, chopped
Teriyaki sauce
Cooked wild rice

Boil breasts 1-2 minutes, drain, slice and marinate in teriyaki sauce while preparing vegetables. Stir fry vegetables in a heated wok until tender crisp. Add duck and cook until done, about 7-10 minutes. Serve with wild rice. Serves 4

Bonnie Johnson

Buddy Lew's Pheasant

2 pheasants, cut into pieces
Salt, pepper, and paprika to taste
1 cup chopped yellow onion
1 cup chopped celery
1 cup fresh mushrooms, sliced
1 tablespoon parsley, fresh, chopped
2 cans cream of mushroom soup
½ cup sherry
1 pint heavy cream

Season pheasants with salt, pepper and paprika. Dust with flour and brown in oil (not butter). Remove and drain on paper towels. In oil, sauté the onions, celery, mushrooms, and parsley. In a large roasting pan, place pheasant pieces, vegetables, sherry, and soup and bake at 300 degrees for one hour. Remove from oven and add heavy cream, stir well. Return to oven and continue baking 1-1½ hours. Great when served with wild rice casserole. Serves 6-8

Maysel Teeter

Pheasant in Horseradish Cream

½ cup margarine
½ cup flour
8-10 pheasant breasts (or chicken)
¼ cup margarine
2 tablespoons bacon drippings
¼ cup brandy
1½ cups chicken stock
1 cup horseradish, or to taste
¾ teaspoon salt
Pepper, to taste
3 cups heavy cream
½ pound bacon, crisp-fried, crumbled

Melt ½ cup margarine in skillet. Stir in flour. Cook until medium brown; set aside. Pat breasts dry. Brown in ¼ cup margarine and bacon drippings in skillet. Remove to 9 x 13 baking dish. Stir brandy into skillet; bring to a boil; reduce heat. Simmer for several minutes. Add stock, horseradish, salt and pepper. Stir in cream. Bring to a simmer. Stir in browned flour. Cook until thick, stirring constantly. Pour over pheasant breasts. Bake, covered at 350 degrees for one hour. Sprinkle with crumbled bacon. Serves 8

Tonia Beavers

Quail in Wine

6-8 quail
Salt and pepper to taste
Flour
6 tablespoons butter
2 cups sliced mushrooms
1 cup Madeira wine
1 cup consommé
1 rib celery, quartered
1 slice lemon per bird
Chopped parsley

Salt, pepper and flour each bird. Brown until golden in butter. Place birds in large baking dish. Sauté mushrooms in butter; add wine and consommé and bring to a boil. Pour over birds. Add celery and lemon slices and sprinkle with parsley. Cover and bake 350 degrees for one hour or until tender. Serve sauce with wild rice and birds. (Discard lemon and celery pieces). Serves 6-8

Kay Ewing

Squirrel and Dumplings

3 dressed squirrels, cut into serving pieces
Water
Salt and pepper
2 cups biscuit baking mix
¼ cup milk

Place squirrels in a large soup pot with enough water to cover. Let simmer slowly until tender, several hours. Season with salt and plenty of black pepper. When squirrels are done, combine biscuit mix and milk in a bowl, and mix thoroughly with a fork. Bring the water with squirrel to a rolling boil. Drop in spoonfuls of the dumpling mix. Cook 10 minutes covered and 10 minutes uncovered. Serves 3-6

Pam Huggins

Dr. Robertson's Country Fried Venison Steak

2 pounds ½" thick venison steaks
2 teaspoons Worcestershire sauce
1 quart sweet milk
Salt and pepper to taste
¾ cup flour
Vegetable oil
1 medium onion, chopped
2 tablespoons flour
1 10 ounce can cream of mushroom soup, undiluted
Hot cooked rice

Prepare venison by removing all fat and removing connective tissues. Cut meat into serving pieces, pound each piece into ¼" thickness. Sprinkle with Worcestershire sauce. Place meat in a shallow two quart container, pour milk over meat, refrigerate for two hours. Remove meat from milk, reserving the milk. Salt and pepper meat, dredge in ¾ cup flour. Cook venison in ½" hot oil in an extra large skillet or two large skillets, until lightly browned on both sides. Remove from skillet and set aside. Drain oil, reserving two tablespoons in one skillet. Add onion and sauté until tender. Stir in flour and cook until lightly browned. Add milk to flour, mix and stir until smooth. Add soup, stir well. Place venison in soup mix and cook over low heat one hour. (Water may be added to gravy to prevent scorching if necessary.) Serve over cooked rice. Serves 6

Marilyn Moores

Great Northern Bean Italian Casserole

2 cups dry great Northern beans
6 cups water
1 cup chopped onion
1 cup chopped celery
2 cloves garlic, minced
¼ cup olive oil
½ pound Italian sausage, sliced
½ teaspoon thyme
¼ teaspoon basil
¼ teaspoon oregano
1 teaspoon salt
1 6 ounce can tomato paste
2 cups reserved bean liquid

Soak and cook beans in water; drain, reserve liquid. Cook onion, celery and garlic in oil until tender. Brown sausage and drain. Combine beans, vegetables, sausage and remaining six ingredients in a large bowl. Pour into greased 9 x 13 pan. Bake at 350 degrees for one hour. Add more liquid if needed. Serves 6

Joyce R. Laws

Artichoke Chicken-Rice

- 1 *whole chicken, cooked, boned and chopped*
- 1 *package chicken flavored rice vermicelli mix*
- 2 *cups hot water*
- 4 *green onions, chopped*
- ½ *green pepper, chopped*
- 12 *pimiento stuffed olives*
- 1 *12 ounce jar marinated artichokes*
- ¾ *teaspoon curry powder*
- ⅓ *cup mayonnaise*

Bring rice, water, and seasonings package to a boil. Cover, reduce heat to low and simmer 15-20 minutes. Set aside and cool. Drain artichokes, reserve liquid. Combine artichoke liquid with curry powder and mayonnaise. Mix rice, artichokes and mayonnaise mixture together. Toss lightly with chickens, olives and peppers. Serve chilled.

Sue McCoy

Chicken and Wild Rice Casserole

- 1 *6 ounce package long grain and wild rice mix*
- ¼ *cup margarine*
- ¼ *cup all-purpose flour*
- 1 *12 ounce can evaporated milk*
- 1½ *cups chicken broth*
- 2½ *cups diced, cooked chicken*
- 1 *3 ounce can sliced mushrooms, drained*
- ⅓ *cup chopped green pepper*
- ¼ *cup chopped pimiento*
- *Salt to taste*
- ¼ *cup slivered almonds*

Prepare rice mix according to package directions, set aside. Melt butter in a heavy saucepan. Stir in flour until well blended. Gradually stir in milk and broth. Cook, stirring constantly over medium heat until mixture is smooth and thickened. Add sauce to cooked rice, mix in chicken, mushrooms, pepper, pimiento and salt. Spoon into a greased 2 quart casserole. Sprinkle top with almonds and bake at 350 degrees for 30-40 minutes. Serves 8

Annette Holeyfield

Crab and Artichoke Casserole

3 tablespoons butter
3 tablespoons flour
1½ cups milk
1 teaspoon salt
⅛ teaspoon pepper
½ teaspoon Worcestershire sauce
½ cup Parmesan cheese
Dry mustard, to taste
Hot sauce, to taste
4 hard-cooked eggs, chopped
1 pound can artichoke hearts, drained
2 cups crabmeat (one pound)
¼ cup or more Parmesan cheese

Make white sauce by melting butter, adding flour, gradually adding milk, and stirring constantly. Season with salt, pepper, Worcestershire, cheese, mustard, and hot sauce. Add eggs, artichokes, and crabmeat. Pour into a greased 1½ quart casserole. Sprinkle top with ¼ cup or more Parmesan cheese. Bake at 350 degrees for 30 minutes. Serves 4 for dinner, 6 for luncheon

Connie Neumeier

Crab Casserole

¼ cup soft bread crumbs
⅓ cup evaporated skim milk
⅓ cup skim milk
2 tablespoons flour
3 tablespoons low fat mayonnaise
1½ teaspoons dry mustard
⅛ teaspoon ground red pepper
1 pound frozen crabmeat
2 hard-cooked eggs, whites chopped
½ teaspoon salt
¼ teaspoon pepper

Spread bread crumbs on baking sheet, bake at 350 degrees for 5-8 minutes. Set aside. In a saucepan, combine skim milk, evaporated milk and flour. Cook and stir over medium heat, until thick and bubbly. Stir in mayonnaise, mustard and red pepper. Combine crab, egg whites, sauce, salt and pepper. Toss to mix well. Spoon into individual shells or baking dishes (or greased 8 x 8 casserole dish). Sprinkle with bread crumbs. Bake 350 degrees for 15-20 minutes for individual servings or 20-25 minutes for casserole. Serves 12

Cathy Andrasik

Shrimp Casserole

- 1 *stick oleo*
- 1 *medium bell pepper, chopped*
- 1 *onion, chopped*
- 1 *pound shrimp, boiled and peeled*
- 1 *can onion soup*
- 1 *can cream of chicken soup*
- 1 *10 ounce can tomatoes with green chilies*
- 2 *cups rice, uncooked*
- *Salt and pepper to taste*

Melt oleo and sauté bell pepper and onion. Add shrimp and remaining ingredients, seasoning to taste. Bake 1½ hours at 350 degrees. After 45 minutes, stir well and continue baking. Can easily substitute chicken.

Kay Roberts

Shrimp and Spinach Casserole

- 1 *8 ounce package spinach noodles, cooked and drained*
- 2 *pounds shrimp, peeled and deveined*
- ½ *cup clarified butter*
- 1 *can cream of mushroom soup*
- 1 *cup sour cream*
- 1 *tablespoon chives, chopped*
- 1 *cup mayonnaise*
- ½ *teaspoon Dijon mustard*
- 4 *tablespoons sherry*
- ½ *cup grated sharp cheddar cheese*

Line the bottom of an oiled 3 quart casserole with noodles. In a large frying pan, sauté the shrimp in clarified butter until pink and tender, about 5 minutes. Cover noodles with shrimp. Combine soup, sour cream, chives, and mayonnaise. Add mustard and sherry. Pour sauce over shrimp and sprinkle cheddar cheese over all. Bake at 350 degrees until heated through and cheese is melted. Serves 6

Toni Weatherford

Chicken Enchilada Casserole

- 8 *chicken breasts, boiled and boned*
- 2 *cups chicken broth (from boiled chicken)*
- 1 *large onion, chopped*
- 1 *teaspoon minced garlic*
- 1 *cup chopped celery*
- 1 *can cream of celery soup*
- 2-4 *chopped jalapeño peppers, remove stems and seeds*
- *Salt and pepper to taste*
- 1 *12 count package corn tortillas*
- 1 *pound grated cheddar cheese*

Skim fat off the broth from boiled chicken and use to sauté onion, celery and garlic. Add broth, soup, chicken and peppers. Add salt and pepper to taste. In a buttered casserole, layer tortillas, chicken mixture, and top with cheese. Repeat. Bake at 350 degrees for 30-40 minutes or until bubbly. Serves 8

Tamara Laws

Creamy Enchiladas

1 onion, chopped
1½ pounds ground chuck
1 can cream of mushroom soup
1 can cream of chicken soup
1 8 ounce carton sour cream
1 4 ounce can diced green chilies
2 cups grated cheddar cheese
1 8 count package flour tortillas

Sauté chopped onion and meat, drain. Mix soups, sour cream, and chilies with meat mixture. On each tortilla place 1-2 tablespoons meat mixture and 1 tablespoon cheese. Roll and place in greased shallow baking dish. Pour extra sauce and cheese on top. Cover and bake about 20 minutes at 350 degrees. Serves 4-6

Carol Hill

Sour Cream Enchiladas

4 chicken breasts, cooked and boned
1½ cans cream of chicken soup
2 4 ounce cans whole green chilies, cut into strips
1 dozen flour tortillas
1 16 ounce carton sour cream
1 pound cheddar cheese, shredded

Cut cooked chicken into bite-sized pieces and mix with ½ can soup. Place some of the chicken mixture and a strip of green chilies on the outer edge of a tortilla. Roll up tortilla and place seam side down in a greased 9 x 13 pan. Repeat for all tortillas. In a large bowl, mix 1 can soup, sour cream and cheese, reserving ¼ cup cheese for top after baking. Pour this mixture over tortilla rolls. Bake in 350 degree oven for 20-30 minutes or until cheese and cream start to bubble. Remove from oven and sprinkle remaining cheese on top immediately. This recipe is excellent for left over turkey and will freeze.

Bonnie Haines

Spanish Lasagna

2 cups cooked and shredded chicken
1 cup sour cream
1 cup whipped cream cheese
1½ cups salsa
1 8-12 count package 6" flour tortillas
1 cup shredded hot pepper cheddar cheese
Chopped green chilies
Chopped black olives
Chopped green onions

Line a greased 9 x 13 casserole dish with tortillas. Top with first four ingredients. Repeat process until all tortillas are used. Sprinkle with hot pepper cheese and bake at 350 degrees for 20-25 minutes. Garnish with chilies, olives, and onions. Serves 4-6

Patti Nickels

Dian's Lasagna

1½ pounds ground beef
1 pound pepperoni, sliced
½ teaspoon garlic powder
1 large can Italian tomatoes
1 envelope onion soup mix
1 teaspoon salt
¼ teaspoon pepper
1 6 ounce can tomato paste
1 package lasagna noodles
1 tablespoon vegetable oil
2 eggs
1 16 ounce carton cottage cheese
2 8 ounce packages Mozzarella cheese slices
½ cup Parmesan cheese (optional)

Brown ground beef, add pepperoni and garlic. Simmer for 10 minutes or until liquid evaporates. Drain grease that is left. Drain liquid from tomatoes and add to meat. Mash with fork. Add soup mix, salt, pepper and tomato paste to meat mixture. Mix well and simmer for one hour or until slightly thick. While sauce simmers, place lasagna noodles in boiling salt water (do not break noodles); add 1 tablespoon vegetable oil to keep noodles from sticking. Cook, stirring often for 15 minutes or until tender. Drain, cover with cold water until ready to layer in baking dish. Next, beat eggs slightly in a medium bowl. Stir in cottage cheese. Line bottom of a slightly oiled 9 x 13 baking dish with a single layer of drained noodles. Cover noodles with a third each of cottage cheese mixture, meat sauce, Mozzarella slices and Parmesan cheese. Repeat to make two more layers. Bake at 350 degrees for 30 minutes or until bubbly hot. Let stand about 15 minutes, then cut into squares and lift out with wide spatula. Serves 12-15

Gaye Croom

Ham and Swiss Spinach

1 10 ounce package frozen spinach
2 tablespoons margarine, melted
2 beaten eggs
⅓ cup milk
2 tablespoons chopped onion
½ teaspoon dry mustard
¼ teaspoon basil
⅛ teaspoon salt
6-8 slices ham, chopped
1 cup shredded Swiss cheese
1 can French fried onions

Cook spinach according to package directions; drain. Stir in margarine. In medium bowl, combine eggs, milk, onion, mustard, basil and salt. Stir in ham, cheese and spinach. Pour into a buttered 10 x 6 baking dish. Top with onions. Bake in 350 degree oven about 30-40 minutes, or until set. Serves 4-6

Linda Bewley

Bob Parker's Vintage Lasagna

1 medium zucchini, thinly sliced
1 medium onion, thinly sliced
2 tablespoons olive oil
1 teaspoon garlic powder
1 pound ground round
1 medium onion, chopped
1 15 ounce jar spaghetti sauce
2 8 ounce cans tomato sauce
1 teaspoon basil
1 tablespoon oregano
Salt and pepper to taste
1 tablespoon hot sauce
4 ounces mushrooms, sliced
1 1 pound package lasagna noodles
3 hard boiled eggs, sliced
½ cup sliced green olives
1 12 ounce carton cream style cottage cheese
1 cup shredded Mozzarella cheese

Sauté zucchini and onion in olive oil until crisp. Remove from skillet and sprinkle with garlic powder. Set aside. Cook beef and chopped onion in skillet, stirring to crumble meat. Drain well. Add spaghetti sauce, tomato sauce, basil, oregano, salt, pepper, hot sauce, and mushrooms. Simmer 30 minutes. Cook noodles according to package directions and drain. Reserve 1 cup of the meat sauce. Put alternate layers of meat sauce, noodles, egg slices, olives, cottage cheese, Mozzarella cheese, and zucchini mixture. Repeat layers 3 times in a 13 x 9 x 2 baking dish. Spread reserved meat sauce on top. Bake at 350 degrees for 35 minutes. Let cool for 15 minutes after baking to set lasagna. Serves 10-12

Judy Thacker

Greek Spinach Pie

15 sheets phyllo pastry (½ box)
1½ sticks butter, melted
2 10 ounce packages frozen spinach, thawed and squeezed
1 cup chopped onion
4 eggs
½ pound feta cheese, crumbled
1 pound ricotta cheese
Salt and pepper to taste
3 tablespoons olive oil

Sauté onion in olive oil until golden. Mix with spinach and set aside. Arrange seven sheets of phyllo, brushing each layer with butter, to fit the bottom of a 9 x 13 pan. Mix eggs, cheeses, salt, pepper and spinach mixture. Pour half onto the pastry. Layer on the remaining sheets of phyllo dough, brushing each with butter. Pour on remaining spinach filling. Bake at 400 degrees for 40 minutes, until golden. Can be served with salad for a luncheon or cut into small squares and served as an appetizer. Serves 8-10

Linda Fenech

Chicken Pot Pie

Filling

2 tablespoons butter
2 tablespoons flour
1 cup milk
2 cups cooked, cubed chicken
1 15 ounce can mixed vegetables, drained
1 teaspoon thyme
1 teaspoon basil
Salt and pepper to taste
Hard-boiled eggs, optional
Pimiento, optional

Pie Crust

1 cup flour
¾ teaspoon salt
¼ cup oil
⅛ cup milk

Melt butter in saucepan and stir in flour. Gradually add milk. Cook over medium heat until thickened. Add drained vegetables and chicken. Add basil and thyme along with salt and pepper to taste. (May also add sliced hard-boiled eggs and pimiento.) Pour into pie pan. To make crust, mix flour and salt together. Add milk and oil. Stir well. Roll out between sheet of plastic wrap and sheet of wax paper. Pull wax paper off and mold onto top of pie. Cut holes in top of crust to vent. Bake at 375 degrees until lightly browned.

Linda Hill

Tomato Tart

1 pie crust, unbaked
1 tablespoon Parmesan cheese
5 large tomatoes, sliced
Salt and pepper to taste
½ teaspoon oregano
1 cup chopped green onions
1 4 ounce can chopped green chilies
1 cup mayonnaise
2 cups grated sharp cheddar cheese
½ cup grated Parmesan cheese

Preheat oven to 400 degrees — when heated, reduce to 325 degrees. Drain slices of tomato on paper towels for 15 minutes. Sprinkle crust with one tablespoon Parmesan cheese. Cover with two layers of tomato, using half of the slices. Sprinkle with salt, pepper, oregano, ½ cup of green onions and half the chilies. Repeat layers. In a bowl, combine mayonnaise and cheddar cheese and spread over top of pie. Top with one half cup grated Parmesan. Bake 50 minutes. Serves 6-8

This is good warm as well as at room temperature.

Toni Weatherford

Joellen's Tomato Pie

1 *9" pie shell*
1 *cup mayonnaise*
2 *cups shredded cheddar cheese*
1 *bunch fresh basil, minced*
6 *Roma tomatoes or 4 regular ripe tomatoes*

Bake pie shell in 400 degree oven about 5-10 minutes, until shell just starts to turn golden. In a large bowl mix mayonnaise, cheddar cheese and basil. Cut tomatoes into pieces and place in pie shell. Cover with cheese mixture and bake until bubbly at 350 degrees for about 30-45 minutes.

Maysel Teeter

A Gardener's Vegetable Pie

2 *cups sliced fresh broccoli or cauliflower*
½ *cup chopped onion*
½ *cup chopped green pepper*
1 *cup shredded cheddar cheese*
1½ *cups milk*
¾ *cup biscuit baking mix*
3 *eggs*
1 *teaspoon salt*
¼ *teaspoon pepper*

Cook or steam broccoli about 5 minutes. Drain. In a pie plate, mix broccoli, onion, green pepper and cheese. In a separate bowl, beat remaining ingredients together. Pour over vegetables. Bake at 400 degrees for 35-40 minutes. Let stand 5 minutes before cutting. Serves 6

Jane Barnes

Hungarian Cabbage Roll

2 *heads of cabbage*
4 *pounds ground beef*
1 *pound ground pork*
2-3 *cups long grain rice, uncooked*
1 *bell pepper, chopped*
1 *medium onion, chopped*
1 *egg*
Salt and pepper to taste
1 *teaspoon garlic powder*
2 *quart jars sauerkraut*
2 *46 ounce cans tomato juice*

In a large pot, boil 2 heads of cabbage until leaves are tender. Remove from water and let cool. In large mixing bowl, add beef, pork, rice, peppers, onions, egg and seasonings. Mix well. Roll mixture into balls and cover with tender cabbage leaves by wrapping tightly around meat. In a large pot, layer the tomato juice, cabbage rolls, sauerkraut. Repeat until pot is full. Cook on medium heat for 4-5 hours, covered.

Cathy Andrasik

Stromboli

- 2 *frozen bread loaves*
- 1 *pound browned ground beef*
- 1 *pound chopped ham*
- 1 *cup chopped onion*
- ¾ *cup chopped bell pepper*
- 1 *8 ounce package Mozzarella cheese*
- 1 *8 ounce package cheddar or American cheese*

Let bread thaw completely. Roll out dough about the length of French bread. Mix all other ingredients together. Put ½ the mixture into the middle of each rolled-out loaf. Fold over one side, then the other. Place on cookie sheets and bake at 400 degrees for 15-20 minutes. Serves 10-12

Linda Bewley

Western Meal-in-One

- 1 *pound ground beef*
- 1 *tablespoon oil*
- 1 *clove garlic, minced*
- 1 *teaspoon salt*
- 1 *large onion, chopped*
- 1 *large green pepper, chopped*
- 1 *teaspoon chili powder*
- 1 *10 ounce can tomatoes with green chilies, chopped*
- 1 *15 ounce can kidney beans*
- ¾ *cup uncooked rice*
- ½ *cup tomato juice*
- ¼ *cup ripe olives, chopped*
- ¾ *cup cheddar cheese, grated*

Brown ground meat in oil until crumbly. Add garlic, salt, onion, green peppers and chili powder. Sauté for 5 minutes or until vegetables are limp. Mix in tomatoes, kidney beans, rice and tomato juice. Pour into a greased 2 quart casserole. Bake covered in 350 degree oven for 45 minutes. Sprinkle with olives and cheese. Bake uncovered an additional 15 minutes until cheese melts. Serves 8

Becky Ellison

Florentine Spaghetti

- 1 *package tangy Italian spaghetti dinner*
- 1 *pound ground beef*
- 1 *6 ounce can tomato paste*
- 1½ *cups water*
- 1½ *cups cottage cheese*
- 1 *10 ounce package frozen spinach, thawed*
- 8 *ounces Mozzarella cheese, shredded*

Cook spaghetti noodles according to package directions. Set aside. Brown ground beef and drain off grease. Add tomato paste, water and small can Parmesan cheese from package dinner. Cook over low heat about 15 minutes. In casserole dish, layer noodles, beef mixture, cottage cheese, spinach and Mozzarella cheese. Repeat layers. Bake at 350 degrees for 20 minutes. Serves 6-8

Patti Nickels

Chicken Spaghetti

1 *8 ounce package ready-cut or elbow spaghetti*
1 *stick oleo*
1 *medium onion*
½ *cup stuffed olives*
6 *small cloves garlic*
1 *medium green pepper*
1 *can tomato soup*
1 *can cream of chicken soup*
½ *teaspoon chili powder*
3 *chicken breasts, cooked, boned and chopped*
½ *cup grated cheddar cheese*

Cook spaghetti according to package directions and set aside. Chop onion, olives, garlic and green pepper and sauté in melted oleo. When vegetables are tender, add cans of soup, chili powder and chicken. Mix well and add spaghetti. Place in casserole dish and bake for 30 minutes at 325 degrees. Remove from oven and sprinkle cheese on top. Bake for an additional 15 minutes. Note: After boiling chicken, cook spaghetti in the broth.

Jackie Gardner

BBQ Seasoning Mix

2 *tablespoons plus 1 teaspoon chili powder*
1 *tablespoon plus 1 teaspoon paprika*
2 *teaspoons dried oregano*
½ *teaspoon sugar*
½ *teaspoon dry mustard*
½ *teaspoon ground cloves*
½ *teaspoon celery seed*
½ *teaspoon garlic powder*
½ *teaspoon black pepper*
¼ *teaspoon cayenne pepper*
¼ *teaspoon thyme*
¼ *teaspoon tarragon*
¼ *teaspoon salt*
¼ *teaspoon MSG*
2 *bay leaves, crushed*

Combine all ingredients and mix well. Use as a dry rub or seasoning on meat to be smoked or grilled. Especially good on ribs.

Toni Weatherford

Mustard Sauce

½ *cup sugar*
1 *teaspoon flour*
1 *pinch salt*
½ *cup oil*
½ *cup mustard*
½ *tomato soup*
3 *egg yolks*

Mix all ingredients in saucepan and cook over medium heat for five minutes. Good to serve with ham.

Connie Neumeier

Raisin Sauce

- ⅓ *cup raisins*
- ½ *cup water*
- ⅓ *cup currant jelly*
- ½ *teaspoon orange rind*
- ½ *cup orange juice*
- 2 *tablespoons packed brown sugar*
- 1 *tablespoon cornstarch*
- ¼ *teaspoon salt*
- ¼ *teaspoon allspice*

Bring first 5 ingredients to a boil and cook until raisins are soft. Add remaining ingredients and bring to a boil. Cook slowly until thickened and serve with ham.

Karen Dunn

GARDEN VARIETY

Curried Fruit

1 *29 ounce can peach halves, drained*
1 *29 ounce can pineapple chunks, drained*
1 *29 ounce can pear halves, drained*
1 *10 ounce jar maraschino cherries, drained*
½ *cup butter*
2 *teaspoons curry powder*
¾ *cup brown sugar*

Mix fruit in greased 8 x 8 casserole dish. Melt butter and blend in curry and sugar. Pour over mixed fruit. Bake at 375 degrees for 1 hour.

Annette Holeyfield

Apple Soufflé

1 *16 ounce can applesauce*
½ *cup sugar*
1 *cup crushed graham crackers*
1 *cup milk*
2 *eggs*
¼ *cup oleo, melted*

Combine all ingredients in a medium mixing bowl. Pour into a greased 2 quart dish. Bake at 350 degrees for 1 hour 15 minutes. Serve instead of sweet potatoes.

Tonia Beavers

Scarlett's Pineapple Soufflé

1 *20 ounce can pineapple chunks, drained*
4 *cups fresh bread crumbs or crushed round buttery crackers*
3 *eggs, beaten*
2 *cups sugar*
1 *cup butter, melted*

Toss bread crumbs or crackers with pineapple and place in greased 2 quart baking dish. Combine remaining ingredients and pour over pineapple mixture. Bake at 350 degrees for 30 minutes. Can be made day before.

Maysel Teeter

Asparagus à la Parmigiana

2 *pounds of asparagus, trimmed and peeled*
4 *tablespoons butter, melted*
Salt and pepper to taste
½ *cup freshly grated Parmesan cheese*

Preheat oven to 400 degrees. Blanch asparagus and drain on paper towels. Arrange asparagus in a shallow oven proof serving dish. Pour melted butter over asparagus. Sprinkle with salt and pepper to taste. Spoon cheese evenly over top. Bake until lightly browned, about 20 minutes. Serves 4

Betsy Harris

Artichoke-Asparagus Casserole

1 *large can asparagus tips*
1 *large can artichoke hearts, sliced*
2 *cups cracker crumbs*
½ *cup butter, melted*
8 *ounces grated cheddar cheese*
1 *cup almonds, sliced*
1 *can cream of mushroom soup*
Salt and pepper to taste

Mix cheese with cracker crumbs. Stir juice from asparagus and artichokes into soup; add salt and pepper. Put ⅓ of crumb-cheese mixture on bottom of buttered 8 x 8 casserole, then half of asparagus and half of artichokes. Sprinkle ⅓ of almonds. Pour ½ of butter on top, then ½ of soup mixture. Layer again in same order ending with ⅓ of crumb-cheese mixture and almonds on top. Bake at 350 degrees for 20 minutes or until bubbly. This can be made a day ahead and refrigerated before baking.

Tamara Laws

Asparagus Casserole

1 *16 ounce can asparagus spears*
4 *tablespoons butter*
4 *tablespoons all purpose flour*
Salt and pepper to taste
½ *cup milk*
½ *teaspoon Worcestershire sauce*
Dash of cayenne pepper
4 *hard boiled eggs, sliced*
¼ *pound sharp cheddar cheese, cut in chunks*
½ *cup blanched almond halves*
Cracker crumbs

Drain asparagus and reserve liquid. In a heavy saucepan, melt butter. Add flour, salt and pepper and blend thoroughly. Gradually add ¾ cup of asparagus liquid and milk, and cook until thickened and smooth, stirring constantly. Sauce should be thick, but a bit more milk or asparagus liquid may be needed. Add Worcestershire sauce and cayenne. Remove from heat. Butter a 9 x 12 casserole dish. Layer asparagus, eggs, cheese and almonds. Repeat layers until all of ingredients are used. Spoon sauce over all and sprinkle with crumbs. Bake in a 350 degree oven for about 25 minutes, until bubbly and lightly browned.

Vickie Hale

Broccoli Casserole

2 *packages frozen broccoli, cooked*
2 *eggs, beaten*
1 *can cream of mushroom soup*
1 *cup round buttery cheese flavored cracker crumbs*

Mix all together and pour into buttered casserole. Sprinkle with cracker crumbs and bake 350 degrees for 45 minutes.

Georganne Peel

Pimiento Broccoli

1½ pounds fresh broccoli
½ cup chopped green onions
¼ cup margarine, melted
⅜ cup or 2 ounce jar pimiento, chopped
¾ tablespoon grated lemon rind
¼ cup lemon juice
¼ teaspoon salt
⅛ teaspoon pepper

Trim off leaves of broccoli; wash thoroughly and cut stalks about 1" from florets. Steam florets in a small amount of boiling water 10-15 minutes or until tender crisp. Sauté green onions in margarine in a saucepan until tender. Stir in remaining ingredients, reduce heat and simmer 5 minutes. Place broccoli in a large serving dish; spoon sauce over broccoli and toss gently. Serves 6

Annette Holeyfield

Broccoli Puff

1 10 ounce box chopped broccoli
1 10 ounce can cream of mushroom soup
2 ounces shredded American cheese
¼ cup milk
¼ cup salad dressing
1 egg, beaten
¼ cup fine dry bread crumbs
1 tablespoon melted oleo or butter

Cook broccoli according to package directions, omitting salt; drain thoroughly. Place in a 1½ quart baking dish. Mix soup with shredded cheese. Stir in milk, salad dressing and beaten egg until well blended. Pour over broccoli. Toss bread crumbs with melted butter. Sprinkle evenly over mixture. Bake at 350 degrees until crumbs are lightly browned.

Marcia Godown

Baked Beans

4 tablespoons white corn syrup
2 onions, finely chopped
2 garlic cloves, chopped
½ green bell pepper, chopped
2 tablespoons Worcestershire sauce
2 tablespoons prepared mustard
2-3 cups ketchup
1 cup brown sugar
2 42 ounce cans pork and beans
3-4 bacon strips

Mix all ingredients except bacon. Pour into a Dutch oven. Place bacon strips on top. Cover and bake at 325 degrees for 2-3 hours. For crispy bacon, uncover for the last 20 minutes. Serves 20

Jane New

Best Ever Baked Beans

- 3 *15 ounce cans pork and beans*
- ½ *cup ketchup*
- 1 *tablespoon Worcestershire sauce*
- 1 *tablespoon white vinegar*
- ½ *cup brown sugar*
- 1½ *pounds ground beef*
- 1 *bell pepper, chopped*
- 1 *onion, chopped*

Brown beef with onion and pepper. Mix all ingredients together and bake at 350 degrees for 1 hour.

Bonita Church

Donna's Green Beans

- ⅓ *cup ground pork or chicken, optional*
- 1 *teaspoon soy sauce*
- 1 *teaspoon water*
- 1 *pound fresh green beans, strings removed*
- 1 *cup cooking oil*
- 1 *teaspoon water*
- 2 *cloves garlic, cut into strips*
- 1 *teaspoon sugar*
- 2 *tablespoons soy sauce*
- 1 *teaspoon vinegar*
- 1 *teaspoon chili paste*
- ½ *teaspoon sesame seed oil*
- 1 *green onion, chopped*

Marinate meat for 30 minutes in 1 teaspoon soy sauce and 1 teaspoon water. Drain. Fry beans in 1 cup oil in wok or electric skillet until tender. Remove beans. Pour off oil, except 2 tablespoons. Stir fry meat, adding 1 teaspoon water. Remove. Stir fry garlic. Return green beans and meat to wok. Add other ingredients, except onion and stir fry. Add green onion, toss briefly and serve.

Tonia Beavers

Pizza Green Beans

- 2 *cans French cut green beans, drained*
- 2 *8 ounce packages sliced Mozzarella cheese*
- 1 *2.5 ounce can Italian croutons*
- 1 *10 ounce can tomato bisque*

Layer first three ingredients in greased 1½ quart dish. Pour bisque over top. Bake 350 degrees for 30-45 minutes. Serves 6-8

Marcia Godown

Plantation Green Beans

80 fresh long pole green beans
8 slices bacon
8 toothpicks

Partially cook green beans in salted water until tender; drain. Arrange 10 beans in a bundle, wrapping with bacon. Secure with a toothpick. Place on foil covered cookie sheet and bake at 400 degrees until bacon is done on all sides, about 10-15 minutes. Pour sauce over beans and serve hot.

Sauce

4 tablespoons bacon grease
3 tablespoons cider
2 tablespoons tarragon vinegar
1 teaspoon salt
½ teaspoon paprika
1 tablespoon chopped parsley
1 tablespoon grated onion

Boil over medium heat for 5 minutes. Pour 1 to 1½ tablespoons over each bundle.

Maysel Teeter

Swiss Green Bean Casserole

1 4 ounce can sliced mushrooms
1 tablespoon minced onion
¼ cup cashew nuts
½ cup butter
⅓ cup flour
½ teaspoon dry mustard
1 teaspoon salt
¼ teaspoon pepper
2 cups milk
1 cup processed Swiss cheese, shredded
⅛ teaspoon hot pepper sauce
1 tablespoon lemon juice
1½ pounds or 2 packages green beans, cooked and drained
¼ cup chopped cashews

Melt butter in large skillet and sauté mushrooms, onion, and ¼ cup nuts. Add flour and seasonings and blend. Add milk, stirring constantly, and cook until sauce is smooth and thickened. Add ¾ cup cheese, hot pepper sauce, and lemon juice; cook over low heat until cheese is melted. Add beans. Pour into a buttered 2 quart casserole dish. Bake in a 350 degree oven for 15-20 minutes. Sprinkle remaining cheese and chopped nuts over the top; bake only until cheese is slightly melted. Serves 8

Lou Adams

Marinated Beans

1 can French cut green beans, drained
1 can yellow wax beans, drained
1 4 ounce can sliced mushrooms, drained
3 tablespoons dried onion flakes
1 cucumber, sliced
1 cup cauliflower florets
¼ cup vinegar
¼ cup water
¼ teaspoon pepper
½ teaspoon salt
¼ teaspoon garlic powder
¼ teaspoon seasoned salt
3-4 drops artificial sweetener

Combine first 6 ingredients in large bowl and set aside. Make marinade in bowl with the remaining ingredients. Pour over vegetables. Marinate overnight. Drain off liquid before serving.

Patti Nickels

Harvard Beets

1 tablespoon cornstarch
⅓ cup sugar
¼ cup beet juice
¼ cup vinegar
1 16 ounce can sliced beets, drained, reserve ¼ cup
2 tablespoons margarine

Dissolve cornstarch and sugar in beet juice and vinegar in a saucepan, boiling until thickened. Add beets and margarine. Simmer until thick.

Mary Noel Mabry

Bonnie's Brussels Sprouts

½ cup sliced almonds
¼ teaspoon crushed thyme
2 tablespoons butter
1 can cream of chicken soup
1 2 ounce jar chopped pimiento
Black pepper, to taste
2 10 ounce packages frozen Brussels sprouts

In saucepan, brown almonds and thyme in butter. Stir in soup. Blend well and add pimiento and pepper. Cook Brussels sprouts as directed on package, drain, and stir into sauce.

Betsy Harris

Carrot Soufflé

3 tablespoons cornstarch
1½ cups milk
2 cups cooked mashed carrots
4 eggs, beaten
¼ cup oleo, melted
1 teaspoon salt
½ teaspoon honey

Heat oven to 400 degrees. Grease a 1½ quart casserole dish. In a large bowl, add cornstarch to milk stirring until dissolved. Stir in carrots; add remaining ingredients. Pour into dish. Bake for 45 minutes.

Tonia Beavers

Baked Bacon Corn

2 tablespoons chopped onion
2 tablespoons melted butter
2 tablespoons all purpose flour
1 8 ounce carton sour cream
2 12 ounce cans shoepeg corn, drained
¼ teaspoon salt
6 slices bacon, cooked and crumbled

Sauté onion in butter in large skillet. Stir in flour. Cook 1 minute over low heat. Stir in sour cream, corn and salt. Cook over medium heat, stirring constantly until thoroughly heated. Do not boil. Stir in ½ of the crumbled bacon. Pour into greased shallow pan. Sprinkle with remaining bacon. Bake at 350 degrees for 25-30 minutes.

Susie Nicholson

Hondo Corn Casserole

1 can cream style corn
1 cup grated sharp cheddar cheese
1 11 ounce can whole kernel corn, drained
1 cup crushed round buttery crackers
1 onion, chopped
1 egg, beaten
3 tablespoons sugar
⅔ cup evaporated milk
½ pound butter or margarine
Salt and pepper to taste
Hot pepper sauce, to taste

Preheat oven to 350 degrees. In a mixing bowl, mix all ingredients together. Bake in a greased 3 quart oven proof casserole for 50-60 minutes. Variations: add green chilies or bell pepper to taste.

Joyce R. Laws

Jalapeño-Corn Casserole

1 *cup uncooked rice*
1 *medium onion, chopped*
1 *medium green pepper, chopped*
½ *cup butter or margarine, melted*
1 *tablespoon sugar*
1-2 *large jalapeño peppers, finely chopped*
2 *cans cream style corn*
1½ *cups shredded mild cheddar cheese*

Cook rice according to package directions; set aside. Sauté onion and green pepper in butter until tender. Combine rice, sautéed vegetables and next 4 ingredients, stirring well. Spoon mixture into a lightly greased 12 x 8 x 2 inch baking dish. Bake at 350 degrees for 40-45 minutes.

Terri Knight

Mexi-Corn Casserole

1 *can whole kernel corn, drained*
1 *can cream style corn*
1 *8 ounce carton sour cream*
½-1 *cup chopped onion*
1 *stick butter, melted*
1 *cup shredded cheese*
1 *6 ounce package Mexican cornbread mix*

Mix all ingredients except cheese. Pour into lightly greased 9 x 13 dish. Bake at 350 degrees for 20-30 minutes. Sprinkle on cheese and bake until melted.

Jane New

White Corn Casserole

4 *cans white corn, drained*
1 *teaspoon black pepper*
1½ *cans cream of celery soup*
1½ *cups sour cream*
1½ *cups shredded cheddar cheese*
1 *white onion, chopped*
2 *tablespoons butter*
1 *roll buttery crackers, crushed*
½ *cup sliced almonds*
½ *cup melted butter*

Pour corn into buttered 9 x 13 casserole dish. Sprinkle with pepper. In a bowl, mix together soup, sour cream and cheddar cheese. Set aside. Sauté onion in butter until it becomes soft and transparent. Pour over corn. Pour soup mixture over onions. Sprinkle crackers and almonds on top, then pour ½ cup melted butter over all. Bake for 45 minutes at 300 degrees.

Tamara Laws

Corn Pudding Supreme

3 large eggs, room temperature
2½ cups corn (2 10 ounce packages frozen, thawed)
½ cup whipping cream
½ cup milk
2 tablespoons flour
1 teaspoon salt
2 tablespoons brown sugar
2 tablespoons melted butter

Beat eggs until light and add remaining ingredients. Pour into a 1 quart buttered casserole. Bake for 1 hour at 350 degrees.

Kay Ewing

Eggplant Casserole

1 medium eggplant
3 tablespoons melted butter
¾ cup cornbread crumbs
2 eggs, beaten
1 small onion, chopped
Salt and pepper to taste
¼ cup milk
1 cup grated cheddar cheese

Peel and cube eggplant. Boil until tender, drain and mash. In a separate bowl, add butter to cornbread crumbs. Mix and reserve half for topping. Mix mashed eggplant with half of cornbread crumbs and all remaining ingredients. Pour into a buttered casserole dish. Sprinkle top with reserved corn bread crumbs. Bake at 350 degrees for 25-30 minutes.

Becky Ellison

Microwave Ratatouille

1½ cups peeled and diced eggplant
½ cup thinly sliced onion
1 clove garlic, minced
3 tablespoons olive oil or vegetable oil
1½ cups sliced zucchini
1 medium green pepper, cut into ½" strips
1 16 ounce can stewed tomatoes
1 teaspoon Italian seasonings
1 teaspoon salt
Dash of pepper

Place first four ingredients in casserole dish and cover. Microwave on high for 5 minutes. Layer zucchini and green pepper on top. Mix last four ingredients and pour over top. Cover and cook on high for 8-10 minutes until tender. Let stand, covered for 5 minutes.

Jane Barnes

Hot Hominy

1 stick margarine
¼ cup chopped onion
1 jalapeño pepper, chopped
¾ cup grated American cheese
1 can cream of mushroom soup
2 cans yellow hominy, drained

Sauté onion in margarine in a large skillet. Add remaining ingredients and stir well. Pour into a 1 quart baking dish. Bake for 30 minutes in a 350 degree oven.

Kay Roberts

Dr. Mark's Baked Onions

5 yellow onions, preferably Vidalia
Butter
Lemon pepper
Milk
Parmesan cheese

Thickly slice onions. Layer in a deep casserole dish. Dot with butter and sprinkle with lemon pepper. Repeat layers until all onions are used. Pour enough milk to cover onions, 1½-2" deep. Cover and bake at 350 degrees for one hour. Remove cover, sprinkle with Parmesan cheese, cover and bake another 7 minutes. Can be served over a grilled steak.

Donna Myers

Baked Onions

6 yellow onions, thinly sliced
½ cup crushed potato chips
½ pound Colby cheese, grated
2 cans cream of mushroom soup
1 cup milk
⅛ teaspoon cayenne pepper

Place in alternate layers: onions, potato chips and grated cheese in greased 3 quart casserole dish. Mix the soups and milk together, pour over the layers. Sprinkle pepper over all. Bake uncovered at 350 degrees for one hour.

Tonia Beavers

Barbecued Black-Eyed Peas

1 pound dried black-eyed peas
1½ quarts water
6 slices bacon, cut in half, or 1 smoked ham hock
2 teaspoons salt
½ cup barbecue sauce
1 small onion, chopped
1 tablespoon light molasses

Sort peas and wash thoroughly. Place in a heavy saucepan or Dutch oven; cover with water. Bring to a boil, and boil for 2 minutes. Cover and let soak overnight. Drain and rinse well. Combine 1½ quarts water, peas, bacon and salt in Dutch oven. Cover and bring to a boil; reduce heat. Simmer 45 minutes or until just tender, stirring often; add water, if needed. Stir barbecue sauce, onion and molasses into peas. Cover and simmer 2 hours or until done; stir occasionally. Add water, if needed. Yield 6-8 servings

Annette Holeyfield

Pickled Black Eye Peas

3 18 ounce cans black eye peas, drained and rinsed
2 bunches scallions, sliced diagonally, including green part
1 red pepper, julienned
2-3 jalapeño peppers, diced finely
¼ cup fresh chopped chervil or parsley

Vinaigrette

½ cup olive oil
¼ cup champagne vinegar
1 large shallot, minced
2 teaspoons grainy mustard
Salt and pepper to taste

Combine black eye peas, scallions, red pepper, jalapeño peppers and fresh chervil in a large bowl. Mix together vinaigrette ingredients and pour over black eye pea mixture. Toss and season to taste. Chill before serving. Toss again and check for seasoning.

Betsy Harris

Peas Continental

2 *10 ounce packages frozen English peas*
¼ *cup chopped onion*
2 *tablespoons butter, melted*
1 *4 ounce can sliced mushrooms, drained*
2 *tablespoons dry sherry*
¼ *teaspoon salt*
¼ *teaspoon ground nutmeg*
⅛ *teaspoon ground marjoram*
Dash of pepper

Cook peas according to package directions, omitting salt. Drain and set aside. Sauté onion in butter in a medium saucepan until tender. Add peas and remaining ingredients; cook, stirring occasionally, just until thoroughly heated. Yields 6 servings

Annette Holeyfield

Fluffy Potato Casserole

2 *cups mashed potatoes*
1 *8 ounce package cream cheese, softened*
1 *tablespoon onion flakes*
2 *eggs, well beaten*
1 *tablespoon all purpose flour*
¼ *teaspoon salt*
⅛ *teaspoon pepper*
1 *3 ounce can French fried onion rings*

Combine first 7 ingredients; beat with electric mixer until well blended. Pour into a greased 1 quart casserole. Bake, uncovered for 25 minutes at 300 degrees. Add French fried onion rings and bake an additional 10 minutes.

Susie Kroencke

Golden Parmesan Potatoes

6 *large potatoes*
¼ *cup flour*
¼ *cup Parmesan cheese*
¾ *teaspoon salt*
⅛ *teaspoon pepper*
⅓ *cup butter*

Peel and quarter potatoes. Combine flour, cheese, salt and pepper in a bag. Moisten potatoes with water and shake. Coat with flour mixture. Melt butter in a 9 x 13 pan. Place potatoes in one layer in pan. Bake at 375 degrees for 45 minutes to 1 hour. Turn one time. Add more Parmesan cheese if you like cheese. More butter may be added while baking.

Bonnie Haines

Scalloped Potatoes

6 large potatoes, baked or boiled
½ cup melted butter
1 green onion, chopped
2 cups grated cheddar cheese
2 8 ounce cartons sour cream
Salt and pepper to taste

Peel and slice potatoes. Place in casserole. Mix remaining ingredients and cover potatoes and bake for 30 minutes at 350 degrees.

Carolyn Srygley

Turmeric Potatoes

3 large potatoes
½ cup chopped onion
1 cup chicken broth
½ bell pepper, chopped
1 clove garlic, minced
1 teaspoon turmeric
Salt to taste

Bring all ingredients to a boil and simmer for 30 minutes.

Kay Roberts

Sweet Potato Casserole

5 medium sized sweet potatoes
3 eggs
¾ cup sugar
2 sticks oleo, melted
1 teaspoon vanilla
½ cup evaporated milk
¼ teaspoon cinnamon
⅛ teaspoon nutmeg

Topping

1½ cups crushed corn flakes
½ cup brown sugar
½ cup chopped pecans
½ stick oleo, melted

Boil, peel and mash the sweet potatoes. Beat potatoes with electric mixer on high until smooth and creamy. Clean off beaters and throw potato strings away. Add the rest of the ingredients and beat. Pour into a 3 quart casserole dish and cover with the topping. Bake at 350 degrees for 40-45 minutes.

Jane Fore

Sweet Potato Balls

4-5 sweet potatoes
Brown sugar to taste
1 teaspoon vanilla
40 marshmallows
2 cups corn flake crumbs

Cook sweet potatoes in small amount of water until done; drain and mash. Sweeten to taste with brown sugar. Add vanilla. Roll mixture into ball using a large marshmallow as the center. Repeat until all potato mixture has been used. Roll balls in corn flake crumbs. Bake at 350 degrees for 20 minutes. Makes 40

Marlene Newton

Squash Casserole

12 medium yellow squash
1 bunch green onions, sliced
2 tablespoons butter
1 can cream of celery soup
2 whole eggs
⅓ cup bread crumbs
¼ teaspoon garlic powder
Pinch of basil
1 tablespoon Worcestershire
1 teaspoon salt
Grated cheese
Bread or cracker crumbs and butter

Cook squash in salted water until tender. Drain and break up, but do not mash. Brown green onions in butter and stir in celery soup. Add eggs, bread crumbs and seasonings. Combine the soup mixture with the squash. Put into a 3 quart buttered casserole and cover with the grated cheese and additional bread crumbs. Dot with butter. Cook at 375 degrees for 45 minutes. Serves 8-10

Laurie Bibler

Italian Squash Casserole

2 small zucchini
1 medium onion, sliced
2 tablespoons butter
1 medium green pepper, diced
1 3 ounce can mushrooms
Pepper to taste
1 teaspoon garlic salt
1 teaspoon oregano
2-3 tablespoons Parmesan
1 16 ounce jar spaghetti sauce
1 cup grated Mozzarella

Slice zucchini and simmer in water until tender. Drain zucchini. Sauté onion and green pepper in butter and add mushrooms. In a buttered 2 quart casserole dish, mix zucchini and sautéed vegetables. Sprinkle with pepper, garlic salt, oregano and Parmesan cheese. Pour spaghetti sauce over this; top with grated Mozzarella. Put in 350 degree oven until cheese melts and casserole is bubbly.

Cathy Andrasik

Plantation Squash

12 medium yellow squash
2 10 ounce packages frozen chopped spinach
1 3 ounce package of cream cheese, softened
3 eggs, well beaten
6 tablespoons of butter, melted
1 heaping tablespoon of sugar
½ teaspoon seasoned salt
½ teaspoon onion salt
1 tablespoon cracked black pepper
1 cup buttery cracker crumbs
1 cup crumbled crisp bacon
Paprika to taste

Scrub squash; cut green stem away. Cook whole in boiling water just until tender, testing with a fork. Cut in half and scoop out pulp with a spoon and place pulp in a large bowl. Boil spinach in lightly salted water until tender; drain well in a colander; add to squash pulp. Add cream cheese to warm squash-spinach mixture. Add all except last three ingredients to mixture and mix well. Lightly salt squash shells and fill with mixture, mounding the top; garnish each with crumbs, paprika and bacon. Place on a lightly greased cookie sheet or in a shallow casserole. Cover with foil and bake at 325 degrees for 30 minutes or until hot. May be prepared a day ahead.

Betsy Harris

Easy Spinach Casserole

2 pounds fresh spinach or two 10 ounce frozen packages
1 8 ounce package cream cheese
¼ pound butter
Salt and pepper to taste
1 cup bread crumbs

Preheat oven to 350 degrees. Cook spinach as directed, 5-8 minutes. Drain. Mix with cream cheese, 4 tablespoons butter, salt and pepper. Pour into casserole. Melt remaining butter, toss with bread crumbs, sprinkle over casserole. Bake for 20-30 minutes. Serves 4

Marilyn Moores

Spinach Soufflé

2 8 ounce packages cream cheese, softened
¾ cup butter, softened
2 14 ounce cans artichoke hearts
2 packages frozen spinach soufflé

Blend cream cheese and butter together. Butter loaf pan. Cut artichoke hearts into two pieces and layer in loaf pan. Spread cream cheese and butter mixture over artichoke hearts. Break frozen soufflé into pieces and lay on top. Bake at 350 degrees for 60 minutes.

Joyce R. Laws

The Perfect Tomato Recipe

1 good sized, fully ripe tomato on vine, preheated by sun
1 salt shaker

Pick tomato. Wipe on shirt sleeve. Bite, then sprinkle with salt. Serves 1

The Committee

Marinated Tomatoes

3 medium tomatoes
1 clove garlic, minced
1 teaspoon salt
1 teaspoon sugar
1/8 teaspoon cayenne pepper
2 tablespoons vinegar
2 tablespoons prepared mustard
1/4 cup salad oil
1/4 cup parsley flakes

Slice tomatoes. Mix all other ingredients together and baste tomatoes. Chill for 4 hours or more.

Jane New

Fresh Vegetable Bake

2-3 yellow squash, sliced
2-3 zucchini, sliced
1 large red or Vidalia onion, sliced
2-3 tomatoes, sliced
10 okra pods, sliced
3 ears of corn
Salt and pepper to taste
Spices to taste
6 slices bacon

Spray 9 x 13 baking dish with non stick spray. Arrange squash and zucchini slices on bottom. Layer onion, tomatoes, then okra. Cut corn from cob and place on okra. Sprinkle with salt and pepper and other spices as desired. Arrange bacon on top and cover tightly with foil. Bake for about one hour in 300 degree oven.

Marie Biggers

Vegetable Casserole

1 can shoe peg corn, drained
2 cans French style green beans, drained
1 can sliced water chestnuts, rinsed and drained
1 8 ounce carton sour cream
1 can cream of celery soup
1/3 cup chopped onion
1/3 cup chopped celery
1 roll buttery crackers, crushed
1/2 cup margarine, melted

Combine first seven ingredients. Pour into a greased 2 quart round dish and bake at 350 degrees for 30 minutes, until bubbly. Mix crumbs and margarine together; sprinkle on top of casserole and bake another 15 minutes.

Debbie Bell

Marinated Vegetables

1 cauliflower head, separated into florets
3-4 carrots, sliced
10 cherry tomatoes, sliced
1 4 ounce can black olives
1 3 ounce jar whole mushrooms
½ cup vegetable oil
⅔ cup vinegar
1 teaspoon pepper
2½ teaspoons sugar
2 cloves garlic, minced
1 teaspoon lemon juice

Place first five ingredients into large bowl with a lid. Mix together oil, vinegar, pepper, sugar, garlic and lemon juice. Pour dressing over vegetables and stir well. Cover and marinate for one hour or more. Stir or shake occasionally.

Marcia Godown

Vegetable in Pastry Shell

1 onion, diced
3 tablespoons oil
1 teaspoon salt
1 tablespoon paprika, optional
1 pound fresh mushrooms, sliced
1 tablespoon cornstarch
¼ cup water
½ cup chicken broth
1 pound fresh or frozen peas, or other desired vegetable
1 package pastry shells, baked according to directions

Sauté onion in oil, sprinkle on salt and paprika. Add mushrooms and cook slightly. In a saucepan combine cornstarch and water. Pour in broth and mushroom/onion mixture. Add peas. Stir until thickened over medium heat. Fill baked pastry shells. This sauce is very good with ¼ teaspoon dill weed added to it.

Linda Fenech

Lemon Dressing for Vegetables

¼ cup lemon juice
¼ teaspoon paprika
¼ cup vegetable oil
1 tablespoon sugar
1 clove garlic, minced
½ teaspoon salt
1 tablespoon chopped onion

Mix all ingredients well. Refrigerate several hours or overnight. Shake well and pour over freshly cooked vegetables. Makes ¾ cup

Teresa Wilkins

SAY CHEESE, EGGS AND RICE

Cheese Grits

- 6 *cups boiling water*
- 1 *teaspoon salt*
- 1½ *cups quick grits*
- ½ *cup butter*
- 1 *pound grated pasteurized process cheese spread*
- 3 *eggs, beaten*
- 1 *teaspoon hot pepper sauce*
- 2 *teaspoons seasoned salt*
- ⅛ *teaspoon pepper*

Add salt and grits to boiling water. Cook two minutes and then add remaining ingredients. Pour into a buttered 9 x 13 casserole dish. Bake at 300 degrees for 45 minutes. Serves 8-10

Linda Richardson

Mushroom Rarebit

- ½ *pound fresh mushrooms*
- 6 *tablespoons butter*
- 1 *small onion, chopped*
- ¼ *cup all-purpose flour*
- 1 *cup milk*
- ⅛ *teaspoon nutmeg*
- ½ *teaspoon Worcestershire sauce*
- *Salt and pepper*
- 1½ *cups shredded Swiss cheese, divided*
- 8 *slices bread*
- *Chopped parsley*

Slice mushrooms. Melt butter over medium heat and cook onions until tender. Stir in mushrooms and cook four minutes. Sprinkle with flour and remove from heat. Gradually blend in milk. Add nutmeg, Worcestershire sauce, salt and pepper. Return to heat and bring to a boil; simmer three minutes. Remove from heat and stir in one-half cup cheese. Toast one side of bread. Top toasted side with mixture. Sprinkle remaining cheese on top, broil until cheese melts. Garnish with parsley. Serves 4

Kay Ewing

Company Tortellini

- 1 *8 ounce package tortellini*
- 2 *zucchini, sliced*
- ¼ *cup butter*
- 10 *to 12 fresh mushrooms, sliced*
- ¼ *teaspoon garlic powder*
- 1 *14 ounce can artichoke hearts, drained and quartered*
- ½ *pint whipping cream*
- 1 *tablespoon cornstarch*
- 4 *ounces Parmesan cheese, fresh*

Cook tortellini, drain, and set aside. Microwave or steam zucchini just until tender crisp. Sauté mushrooms in butter with garlic powder. Add artichoke hearts; then add cream and cornstarch. Heat until thickened (may add more cornstarch for thicker consistency). Add shredded cheese and cook until melted. Pour sauce over tortellini and zucchini, which has been tossed in a large casserole dish.

Camille Thurlby

Exceptional Macaroni and Cheese

1 8 ounce package elbow macaroni
2 tablespoons vegetable oil
1 medium onion, diced
1 tablespoon flour
1¼ cups milk
1 8 ounce package cheddar cheese, shredded
1 24 ounce can whole peeled tomatoes, drained and chopped
1 8 ounce tub small curd, low-fat, cottage cheese
Salt and pepper to taste
¼ cup herb stuffing mix
2 tablespoons Parmesan cheese

Preheat oven to 350 degrees. Lightly grease a 2½ quart casserole. Cook macaroni according to package directions; drain. In same pan, heat oil, add onion and sauté until tender. Add flour and cook one minute, stirring constantly. Gradually add milk and stir over low heat until sauce thickens. Remove from heat. Stir in cheddar cheese, tomatoes, cottage cheese, salt and pepper. Add cooked macaroni. Spoon into dish. Sprinkle with Parmesan cheese and bread crumbs. Bake 35-40 minutes. Serves 4 as a main course

Jackie Gardner

Egg Baskets

2 packages frozen pastry shells (12)
12 eggs
12 slices tomato
12 slices Canadian bacon
Pimiento strips

Bake pastry shells according to directions, undercooking slightly, so shells are light brown. Cool. Cut off tops and scoop out middle dough, being careful not to make holes in shell. Place shells on large cookie sheet. Carefully crack raw egg into each shell. Bake at 325 degrees until egg is set, 20-25 minutes. Remove from oven. To serve, place tomato slice on slice of heated Canadian bacon, top with cooked shell. Spoon Hollandaise sauce over egg baskets and garnish with crossed strips of pimiento.

Hollandaise Sauce

1 cup butter
6 egg yolks
¼ cup fresh lemon juice
¼ teaspoon cayenne pepper

Heat butter until almost boiling. Remove from heat and let rest five minutes. Place egg yolks, lemon juice and pepper in blender. Using high speed, blend until thick, pouring in melted butter a little at a time until smooth. Place in double boiler over warm, not boiling water, until ready to serve. Serves 6

Good for a brunch or spring buffet!

Terri Knight

Cheese-Egg Bake

1 *cup sliced onion*
1 *tablespoon butter*
8 *hard-cooked eggs, sliced*
2 *cups shredded process Swiss cheese (about 8 ounces)*
1 *can condensed cream of mushroom soup*
¾ *cup milk*
1 *teaspoon prepared mustard*
½ *teaspoon seasoned salt*
¼ *teaspoon dill weed*
¼ *teaspoon pepper*
6 *slices caraway rye bread, buttered and cut diagonally into four pieces*

Preheat oven to 350 degrees. Sauté onion in butter until it is tender. Spread in ungreased 11 x 7 baking dish. Top with egg slices; sprinkle with cheese. Beat remaining ingredients except bread. Pour soup mixture over cheese; overlap bread slices buttered side up on top of casserole. Bake uncovered 30-35 minutes or until heated through. Set oven control at broil or 550 degrees and broil 5" from heat one minute or until bread is toasted. Serves 6

Mary Noel Mabry

Fancy Egg Scramble

2 *cups diced ham or Canadian bacon*
½ *cup chopped green onions*
3 *tablespoons butter or oleo*
12 *eggs, beaten*
1 *3 ounce can chopped mushrooms*
4 *teaspoons butter or oleo*
2¼ *cups soft bread crumbs*
⅛ *teaspoon paprika*
1 *recipe Cheese Sauce*

In large skillet, combine first three ingredients and sauté until onion is tender. Add eggs and cook until soft set. Stir in mushrooms and Cheese Sauce. Pour into a greased 9 x 13 pan; top with combined butter and bread crumbs. Sprinkle paprika on top. Cover and refrigerate at least one hour to overnight. Bake at 350 degrees for 30 minutes.

Cheese Sauce

2 *tablespoons butter or oleo*
2 *tablespoons flour*
½ *teaspoon salt*
⅛ *teaspoon pepper*
2 *cups milk*
1 *cup grated cheddar or American cheese*

Stir flour, salt and pepper into melted butter in a saucepan. Slowly stir in milk. Cook until thick and bubbly. Pour in cheese and stir until melted.

Marlene Newton

Breakfast Pizza

1 pound sausage
1 8 ounce package refrigerated crescent dinner rolls
1 cup shredded sharp cheddar cheese
6 eggs, beaten
½ cup milk
¾ teaspoon dried whole oregano
⅛ teaspoon pepper

Cook sausage, drain and set aside. Separate dough into eight triangles; place with elongated points toward center of a greased 12" pizza pan. Press bottom and sides to form a crust, sealing perforations. Bake at 375 degrees for five minutes on lower rack. Crust will be puffy when removed. Reduce oven temperature to 350 degrees. Spoon sausage over dough; sprinkle with cheese. Combine eggs and next three ingredients. Pour over sausage mixture. Bake at 350 degrees on lower rack 30-35 minutes. Serves 6-8

Ann Ray

Eggs à la Benedict

1 tablespoon margarine
4 eggs
2 tablespoons milk
4 slices Canadian-style bacon
½ cup margarine
3 egg yolks
2 tablespoons lemon juice
Dash cayenne pepper
4 English muffins, buttered

In a one quart casserole, micro-melt one tablespoon margarine 30-40 seconds. Beat eggs with milk and add salt and pepper to taste. Pour into casserole with melted butter. Micro-cook covered, until desired doneness, about two minutes; stir through entire mixture every 30 seconds. Cover and set aside. Wrap Canadian bacon in waxed paper; place ½ cup butter in a two cup glass measuring cup. Micro-cook bacon and margarine until margarine is bubbly and bacon is hot, about one minute. Remove from oven; do not unwrap bacon. In blender container, combine egg yolks, lemon juice, and cayenne. Cover; quickly turn blender on and off. Then blend on high speed for about 30 seconds, while slowly adding hot margarine until fluffy. To assemble, place a muffin on each plate; top each with a Canadian bacon slice. Spoon eggs over, spoon sauce over eggs. Serves 4

Annette Holeyfield

Swiss-Zucchini Quiche

1½ cups zucchini, shredded
Vegetable cooking spray
¼ pound fresh mushrooms, sliced
1 small onion, chopped
3 eggs, beaten
½ cup evaporated skim milk
¼ cup water
½ teaspoon salt, optional
¼ teaspoon pepper
¾ cup (3 ounces) shredded Swiss cheese, divided
1 10" pie crust, baked for 10 minutes

Cook zucchini in small amount of unsalted boiling water for three minutes. Drain and press gently to remove excess water. Spray a small skillet with cooking oil. Sauté mushrooms and onion in skillet over low heat until vegetables are tender but not brown; set aside. Combine eggs, milk, water, salt and pepper; mix well. Add zucchini, mushroom mixture and one-half cup cheese; stir well. Pour mixture into pie shell. Top with remaining ¼ cup cheese. Bake at 375 degrees for 40 minutes, or until set.

Patti Nickels

Sausage and Mushroom Quiche

1 9" unbaked pie shell
1 pound pork sausage
1 pound small, whole mushrooms
½ cup minced parsley
2 eggs
1 cup cream
½ cup Parmesan cheese
¼ teaspoon salt
½ cup diced onion

Crumble sausage in large skillet, adding mushrooms and onion. Cook over high heat 15 minutes, stirring frequently until meat and mushrooms are lightly browned and all liquid from mushrooms has evaporated. Drain grease. Add parsley. Beat eggs with cream and cheese. Blend in the mushroom mixture. Stir in salt. Pour mixture into pastry shell arranging mushrooms stem side down. Bake at 400 degrees for 25-30 minutes or until crust is well browned and filling is set. Let pie stand about 10 minutes before cutting. Serves 8

Linda Fenech

Sunshine Omelet Roll

Sauce

1 cup mayonnaise
2 tablespoons mustard
2 tablespoons green onions, chopped

Roll

½ cup mayonnaise
2 tablespoons flour
1 cup milk
12 eggs, separated
⅛ teaspoon pepper

Filling

1½ cups ham
1 cup Swiss cheese
¼ cup green onions, chopped

For the sauce, mix all three ingredients together; refrigerate. To make the roll, separate eggs; mix mayonnaise and flour; gradually add milk, pepper and beaten egg yolks. Cook in a double boiler over low heat; stir constantly until thick. Remove, cool 15 minutes. To make the filling, use food processor or grinder to process the ham, cheese and onions. Add enough sauce to filling to make it spreading consistency. Set aside. Beat egg whites until stiff peaks form. Fold the whites into the cooled egg yolk mixture along with the seasonings. Carefully pour onto jellyroll pan that has been lined with wax paper and oiled. Bake at 425 degrees for 20 minutes. Invert on towel. Spread with filling. Roll up from the short end. Seal with plastic wrap. Can be refrigerated or frozen at this point. To serve, slice roll and top with a dollop of sauce. Serves 6-8

Kay Stephens

Wake-Up Call

1 dozen eggs, beaten
1 pound ground sausage
6 slices white bread
5 ounces cheddar cheese, grated
1 cup green onions, chopped
1 cup mushrooms, chopped
1 cup fresh jalapeños, chopped

Preheat oven to 350 degrees. With butter, lightly grease a 9 x 13 pan. Arrange bread slices to cover bottom of dish. In a skillet, brown sausage and spread evenly over bread. Sprinkle on mushrooms and jalapeños. Pour eggs into dish evenly. Sprinkle on onion and top with cheese. Bake 30 minutes. (For best results, prepare casserole in advance and allow to set overnight.) Serve with chilled fruits and sliced tomatoes.

Vickie Hale

Scrambled Eggs in Pastry Shells

1 package pastry shells
2 tablespoons butter or margarine
¾ cup chopped onion
1 16 ounce can whole peeled tomatoes, drained and chopped
1 tablespoon butter
¼ cup chopped onion
1 teaspoon dried basil leaves
6 large eggs
2 tablespoons milk or cream
Salt and pepper to taste

Prepare frozen pastry shells according to directions. In large frying pan, melt two tablespoons butter and sauté ¾ cup chopped onion until tender; set aside. In small saucepan, simmer tomatoes, 1 tablespoon butter, ¼ cup chopped onion, and basil for 15-20 minutes — do not overcook. Beat eggs with milk, salt and pepper, add to frying pan and cook, stirring occasionally until scrambled, but still moist. To serve: Spoon eggs into warm shells and serve with tomato sauce spooned over. Serves 6

Great for brunch.

Jackie Gardner

Rice Chili Verde

1 pint sour cream
1 4 ounce can chopped green chilies
¼ teaspoon salt
3 cups cooked rice, salted
½ pound Monterey Jack cheese, cut into strips
Grated Parmesan cheese

Mix sour cream, chilies and salt together. Layer ingredients in a greased 1½ quart casserole; rice, sour cream mixture, then cheese. Bake 350 degrees for 25 minutes. Remove from oven and top with Parmesan cheese. Bake five minutes more. Serves 6

Judy Thacker

Chinese Fried Rice

5 cups cooked rice (medium grain)
1 cup small raw shrimp, optional
1 teaspoon salt
2 tablespoons oil
⅔ cup cooked ham, cubed
3 eggs, beaten
½ cup cooked, fresh or frozen, green peas
1 tablespoon chopped green onion

Using a wok or large deep skillet, heat two tablespoons oil. Stir fry ham, shrimp and peas for about two minutes, or until heated. Add salt and onion and stir fry another 1-2 minutes. Add the cooked rice and beaten eggs to the wok. Constantly stir until done, approximately 4-6 minutes.

Laura Harrison

Fiesta Rice

3-4 tablespoons oil
1 cup uncooked rice
1 celery rib, chopped
1 fresh or canned green chili, chopped
1 tablespoon chopped green onion
1 fresh tomato, peeled, seeded, and chopped
1 teaspoon salt
2 cups chicken broth

Heat oil in large, heavy skillet. Add rice, cooking and stirring until rice begins to turn golden in color. Stir in celery, green chili, onion, tomato, salt and broth. Cover and simmer 15 minutes or until rice is tender and liquid absorbed. Serves 4-6

Connie Neumeier

Rice à la Grecque

2 tablespoons butter
1 onion, finely chopped
½ clove garlic crushed
4 leaves green lettuce, shredded
4 mushrooms, sliced
4 tomatoes, peeled, seeded, and chopped
3 fresh sausage links
1½ cups rice
3 cups chicken stock
1½ teaspoons salt
Dash pepper
1 tablespoon butter
¾ cup cooked peas
1 pimiento, diced
3 tablespoons raisins

Melt two tablespoons butter in a casserole, add onion and cook until it is soft, but not brown. Add garlic, lettuce, mushrooms and tomatoes. Peel and mash sausage and add to mixture. Add rice and mix together. Bring chicken stock to a boil. Then add stock, salt and pepper to other ingredients. Cover tightly and cook in a 400 degree oven for one hour or until liquid is absorbed and rice is tender. Toss together with remaining ingredients. Serves 8-10

Good and pretty.

Lou Adams

Spinach Rice

- *4 10 ounce packages chopped spinach*
- *¼ cup oleo*
- *3 tablespoons flour*
- *2 cups milk*
- *1 cup spinach liquid*
- *1 onion, chopped*
- *1 teaspoon each celery salt, salt and garlic salt*
- *1 4 ounce roll jalapeño cheese*
- *1 cup cooked brown rice*
- *2 14 ounce cans artichoke hearts*
- *1 cup herb seasoned stuffing*
- *1 16 ounce can sliced mushrooms*

Cook spinach, drain; save one cup liquid. Melt oleo in a medium size saucepan. Stir in flour; slowly pour in milk and spinach liquid. Continue stirring until thick and bubbly. Remove from heat and add seasonings. Cut cheese into small slices and stir into sauce. Stir in drained spinach. Sauté onion in one tablespoon oleo; stir in artichokes, rice, mushrooms and stuffing. Add spinach sauce. Pour into a greased three quart casserole and bake at 350 degrees until bubbly. Serves 20

This was served at the provisional dinner on November 13, 1984

Kay Stephens

Wild Rice Casserole

- *1 pound wild rice*
- *¾ pound butter*
- *1 pound processed cheese spread, cut into 1" cubes*
- *2 medium cans sliced mushrooms*
- *2 large green peppers, chopped*
- *1 large onion, chopped*
- *1 pint cream*

Place rice in pan of warm water. Stir thoroughly and drain. Wash in strainer under flowing water. To cook, put rice in pan of hot water. Boil about five minutes. Drain. Put fresh hot water in the pan with rice (3 parts water to 1 part rice). Add salt and boil until flaky. Drain. Sauté pepper and onion in ¼ pound butter. Mix with cooked rice. Add cubes of cheese, mushrooms, cream and remaining butter to rice. Pour into a greased 3 quart casserole. Bake uncovered for one hour in a 350 degree oven. Serves 12-15

Connie Neumeier

Spanish Rice

1 large onion, chopped
3 tablespoons bacon grease (or oil)
1 cup uncooked rice
1 10 ounce can tomatoes with chilies
1¼ cups V-8 juice
Salt and garlic powder to taste

Sauté onion in grease until clear. Add rice and stir until golden. Add remaining ingredients and simmer, covered, 25-30 minutes. Add water if necessary. Turn off heat and let stand 5-10 minutes.

Susan Barefield

Wonderful Rice

1½ cups raw rice, cooked
½ cup chopped green onions
2 cups grated cheddar cheese
½ teaspoon each salt and pepper
1 can cream of celery soup
1 8 ounce carton sour cream
⅓ cup oleo, melted
2 cups crispy rice cereal, crushed

Combine first six ingredients in a large bowl. Spoon into a greased two quart baking dish. Top with crushed rice cereal and drizzle with oleo. Bake at 350 degrees for 40 minutes. Serves 8-10

Tonia Beavers

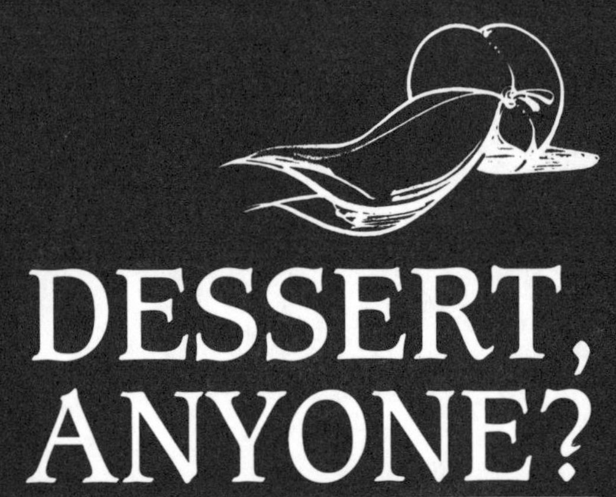

DESSERT, ANYONE?

Fall Apple Dapple Streusel Cake

1 cup margarine, softened
¾ cup sugar
¾ cup brown sugar
2 eggs
2½ cups flour
1¼ teaspoons baking powder
1 teaspoon baking soda
½ teaspoon salt
1 teaspoon cinnamon
1 cup buttermilk
2 cups shredded apples (with peel)
⅓ cup raisins

Streusel Topping

⅓ cup sugar
⅓ cup brown sugar
3 tablespoons butter
½ cup flour
⅓ cup oatmeal
2-3 tablespoons sesame seeds
⅓ cup chopped nuts

Cream together first four ingredients. Combine and add next six ingredients. Stir in shredded raw apples and raisins. Set aside. Mix together all streusel ingredients. Spread half of the batter in a greased 9 x 13 pan. Sprinkle with half of the streusel topping. Spread remainder of batter on top and sprinkle on remaining topping. Bake 30-40 minutes at 350 degrees. Drizzle on a glaze of ½ cup powdered sugar, ⅓ cup orange juice, and ¼ teaspoon orange extract (optional) over warm cake.

Jane Barnes

Apple Cake

4 apples, peeled and cubed
1 cup vegetable oil
2 eggs
2 cups sugar
1 teaspoon salt
1 teaspoon baking soda
1 teaspoon cinnamon
2½ cups flour
1 cup chopped nuts

Combine oil, eggs, and sugar and beat well. Add salt, soda, cinnamon and flour. Mix well. Combine and stir in apples and nuts. The batter will be stiff. Pour into a greased and floured bundt pan and bake at 350 degrees for one hour. Serves 10-12

Brown Sugar Glaze

1 cup light brown sugar, packed
½ cup evaporated milk
1 teaspoon vanilla

Bring sugar and milk to a boil, stirring occasionally. Remove from heat and add vanilla. Beat with a spoon until cool. Pour over cake.

Cathy Andrasik

Applesauce Cake

½ cup butter, softened
1½ cups sugar
2 eggs, beaten
1 cup applesauce
2 cups flour
¼ teaspoon salt
1 teaspoon baking powder
½ teaspoon baking soda
1½ teaspoons cinnamon
¾ teaspoon ground cloves
1 cup chopped pecans
1 cup raisins

Grease and flour tube pan, set aside. In a large mixing bowl, cream butter and sugar. Add eggs, beat well. Add applesauce. Sift together dry ingredients and add to mixture slowly. Beat until smooth. Stir in pecans and raisins. Pour into pan and bake for 45-60 minutes at 350 degrees. Serves 10-12

Teresa Wilkins

Banana Pudding Cake

1-2 small bananas, mashed
1 box yellow cake mix
1 3 ounce package banana cream pudding
4 eggs
1 cup water
¼ cup oil
½ cup finely chopped pecans, optional

In large mixing bowl, mash bananas. Add remaining ingredients. Beat with mixer two minutes. Pour into a greased and floured tube pan. Bake 60-70 minutes. Cool in pan 15 minutes before removing. Serves 10-12

Tonia Beavers

Blueberry Cake

2 boxes blueberry muffin mix
1 large can blueberries, drained and rinsed

Prepare muffin mix as directed on box and add extra can of blueberries. Pour into a greased and floured bundt pan and bake 45 minutes at 350 degrees.

Sauce

1 cup oleo
2 cups sugar
2 half pint cartons whipping cream
1 teaspoon vanilla

In saucepan, melt oleo. Add whipping cream and sugar. Bring to a boil and simmer for 10 minutes, stirring constantly. Remove from heat and add vanilla (this can be frozen and reused). Serve cake hot or cold with the sauce hot.

Jane New

Carrot Cake

2 cups sugar
1 teaspoon salt
2 teaspoons baking soda
1½ cups vegetable oil
2 cups flour
2 teaspoons cinnamon
4 large eggs
2 cups grated carrots

Mix dry ingredients and sift. Beat eggs and oil together. Add to dry ingredients and mix well. Add carrots last and mix well. Pour into a greased and floured 9 x 13 pan and bake for 30 minutes at 350 degrees. Let cool before frosting.

Cream Cheese Frosting

1 8 ounce package cream cheese, softened
2 tablespoons butter
1 box powdered sugar
1 teaspoon vanilla
1 cup chopped walnuts

Cream together cream cheese and butter. Add remaining ingredients and mix well until smooth and creamy. Frost cooled carrot cake.

Becky Ellison

Velvet Almond Fudge Cake

1 box chocolate fudge cake mix
1½ cups slivered almonds (can use pecans)
1 12 ounce package chocolate chips
1 3 ounce package chocolate or fudge instant pudding mix
4 eggs
1 cup sour cream
½ cup water
¼ cup oil
½ teaspoon vanilla
½ teaspoon almond extract

Grease bottom of 10" tube cake pan. Toast almonds at 350 degrees for 3-5 minutes. Spread ½ cup nuts in bottom of pan. Put cake mix, pudding mix, eggs, sour cream, water and oil in large mixing bowl. Blend, then beat at medium speed four minutes. Stir in extracts, chocolate chips and rest of nuts. Pour batter into greased pan and bake 70 minutes at 350 degrees or until cake begins to pull away from sides of pan. Do not underbake! Cool in pan 15 minutes. Serves 10-12

Judy Thacker

Perfect Chocolate Cake

- *1 cup cocoa*
- *2 cups boiling water*
- *1 cup butter (or margarine), softened*
- *2½ cups sugar*
- *4 eggs*
- *1½ teaspoons vanilla*
- *2¾ cups flour*
- *2 teaspoons soda*
- *½ teaspoon baking powder*
- *¼ teaspoon salt*

Combine cocoa and water; stir until smooth. Set aside to cool. Cream butter, sugar, eggs and vanilla; beat until light and fluffy (5 minutes). Combine dry ingredients and add alternately to the creamed mixture with the cocoa water. Beat at low speed, just until mixed. Pour into three greased and floured 9" cake pans. Bake at 350 degrees for 25-30 minutes. Cool in pan 10 minutes; remove. Cool completely. May be frozen at this point. Ice with your favorite frosting. Serves 10-12

Tonia Beavers

Death by Chocolate

- *1 devil's food cake mix*
- *1 12 ounce tub frozen whipped topping*
- *3 Skoar candy bars*
- *2 boxes chocolate mousse mix*
- *½ cup Kahlúa*

Prepare and bake cake according to directions in two pans. While cake is cooling, prepare chocolate mousse mix according to directions. *Only use one layer of the cake in this recipe.* Poke holes in the layer with a fork. Pour Kahlúa over cake, letting it soak into cake. In a large glass bowl, crumble one half of the one layer of cake into the bottom of the bowl. Next, use one half of the chocolate mousse and layer it over the cake. Take one half of the whipped topping and spread it over the layer of mousse. Break up one candy bar and sprinkle it over the whipped topping. Repeat the layering, ending up with two candy bars. Refrigerate. Remember, use only one layer of cake.

Jalia Lingle

Fruit Cocktail Cake

1½ cups sugar
2 cups flour
2 teaspoons baking soda (scant)
2 eggs
½ teaspoon salt
1 No. 2 can fruit cocktail
¼ cup brown sugar
1½ cups chopped pecans

Mix first six ingredients well (for two minutes) — pour into greased 9 x 13 pan. Sprinkle brown sugar and pecans over top. Bake 40 minutes at 350 degrees.

Icing

¾ cup sugar
½ cup whipping cream
⅓ cup butter
1 3½ ounce can coconut

Boil first three ingredients two minutes; add coconut. Spread on cake while both are hot. This was served at the very first Russellville Junior Auxiliary fund raiser — a bridge benefit.

Joyce Wilkins

Granny's Date Cake

2 cups sugar
½ cup oleo, softened
2 cups boiling water
2 teaspoons baking soda
4 eggs, beaten
3 cups flour
1 cup chopped pecans
2 teaspoons vanilla
1 teaspoon salt
1½ pounds dates, chopped

Pour water over dates; set aside. Cream oleo, sugar and eggs. Mix together flour, dates, soda, pecans and vanilla; then mix all together. Oil and flour three 8" pans. Pour into pans and "drop" to level and release air. Bake 325 degrees 30-40 minutes. Cool.

Filling

¼ cup lemon juice
½ cup oleo
Zest of one lemon
1 box powdered sugar

Melt oleo, add lemon juice and zest. Beat in powdered sugar. Spread on cake and stack.

Kay Stephens

Orange Cake

1 box orange cake mix or orange chiffon cake mix

Mix and bake cake in 9 x 13 pan, according to package directions. When cooled, cut cake in half, then cut each half in half horizontally.

Icing

1 can sweetened condensed milk
2 lemons, juice only
1 8 ounce tub frozen whipped topping
1 15 ounce can crushed pineapple, drained well

Mix icing ingredients together and spread between layers and on top of cake; refrigerate. Very good!!

Marlene Newton

Orange Slice Cake

1 pound orange slice candy
1 8 ounce package pitted dates
2 cups chopped walnuts or pecans
1 3¼ ounce can flaked coconut
3½ cups flour
1 cup butter, softened
2 cups sugar
4 eggs
1 teaspoon baking soda
½ cup buttermilk

Cut orange slice candy into small pieces. Add ½ cup flour to fruit, nuts and candy and mix well. Cream butter and sugar; add eggs one at a time. Dissolve soda in the buttermilk — add alternately with the flour to the creamed mixture. Stir in the coated candy, fruit and nuts. Bake in a 10" greased and floured tube pan at 300 degrees for one hour and 45 minutes. Remove cake from oven and pour icing over while hot. Cool and let set in refrigerator overnight before removing from pan.

Icing

1 cup orange juice
2 cups powdered sugar

Mix well. Let set 15-20 minutes before pouring over cake so that sugar will be dissolved.

Bobbie Moore

"Rush" Party Cakes

- ¾ *cup milk*
- 2 *teaspoons vanilla*
- 2 *eggs*
- 1 *cup sugar*
- ½ *cup biscuit baking mix*
- 2 *8 ounce packages cream cheese, softened*

Pour all ingredients into a blender. Blend on high speed two minutes. Pour into greased mini-muffin pans, about ¼" from the top. Bake at 325 degrees 35-45 minutes, or until toothpick comes out clean. Cool.

Topping

- 1 *cup sour cream*
- 2 *tablespoons sugar*
- 2 *teaspoons almond extract*

Invert cakes and ice the bottom with topping in a cake decorator syringe. These can be frozen at this point on cookie sheets until hard then placed in sealable bags until ready to serve. Place frozen cakes on cookie sheet, garnish with a slice of fruit (strawberry, grape, banana, etc.).

Kay Stephens

Mom's Plum Cake

- 2 *cups flour*
- 2 *cups sugar*
- 1 *large jar baby food plums*
- 1 *teaspoon allspice*
- 1 *cup corn oil*
- 3 *eggs (room temperature)*
- 1 *cup chopped pecans*

Combine all ingredients, except pecans, and beat for four minutes. Fold in nuts. Grease and flour tube pan. Bake for 70 minutes in 325 degree oven. Sprinkle with powdered sugar when cool.

Jeannine Sawyer

Vanilla Wafer Cake

- 1 *cup margarine, softened*
- 2 *cups sugar*
- 6 *eggs*
- 1 *12 ounce box vanilla wafers, crushed*
- 1 *3½ ounce can coconut*
- 1 *cup chopped pecans*
- 1 *teaspoon vanilla*

Cream margarine and sugar. Add eggs, beating well. Add rest of ingredients. Put in well-greased tube pan and bake at 275 degrees for 1½ hours. Cake comes out of pan easier if you grease pan, line bottom with waxed paper and grease again.

Marlene Newton

Fuzzy Navel Cake

1 box white cake mix
1 8 ounce tub orange yogurt
1 8 ounce tub peach yogurt
⅓ cup vegetable oil
¾ cup peach schnapps or peach nectar
2 eggs

Combine all ingredients in a large bowl, beat on high three minutes. Pour into two greased and floured 9" cake pans. Bake at 350 degrees for 35 minutes, testing for doneness. Cool on wire rack.

Filling

1 8 ounce jar orange marmalade
½ cup peach schnapps or nectar
2 tablespoons sugar

Heat all ingredients in saucepan until bubbly. Cool completely. Spread between layers.

Frosting

1 8 ounce tub frozen whipped topping
4 ounces cream cheese, softened

Beat together on high for about three minutes. Spread on top and sides of cake. The cake bakes flat and looks beautiful frosted and garnished with violets.

Kay Stephens

Strawberry Cake

1 box white cake mix
1 3 ounce box wild strawberry gelatin
1¼ cups vegetable oil
1¼ cups flour
⅓ cup water
4 eggs
1½ cups fresh or frozen strawberries
1 cup flaked coconut
1 cup chopped pecans

Mix cake mix, gelatin, oil, flour, water and eggs together. Stir in strawberries, coconut and nuts. Place batter in two greased and floured 9" cake pans. Bake at 325 degrees for 30 minutes. Remove from pans and cool slightly.

Frosting

1 box powdered sugar
¾ cup fresh or frozen strawberries
¾ cup flaked coconut
½ cup chopped pecans
⅓ cup butter, melted

Combine all ingredients together. Mix well and spread over and between layers of cake while they are still warm.

Jane Fore

German Chocolate Cake Icing

⅔ cup sugar
¼ cup oleo
⅔ cup evaporated milk
1 egg, beaten
1 3.5 ounce can coconut
½ cup finely chopped pecans
1 teaspoon vanilla

Mix first four ingredients in a 2 quart saucepan. Stir over medium heat until mixture thickens and bubbles. Remove from heat and stir in coconut, pecans and vanilla. Let cool slightly. Frost tops of two 8-9" cake layers.

Teresa Wilkins

Spumoni Frosting

1 cup milk
2 tablespoons flour
Pinch salt
½ cup butter or margarine, softened
½ cup shortening, softened
1 cup granulated sugar
1 4 vial box food colors
¼-½ teaspoon each almond extract, coconut extract, strawberry extract
3 tablespoons cocoa
¼ teaspoon vanilla

In small saucepan, combine milk, flour and salt. Cook over medium heat about 5-7 minutes, until thick. Cool. Combine butter, shortening and sugar in a medium bowl. Beat well. Add to milk mixture, beating constantly, for about 7 minutes. Divide mixture among four bowls. In first bowl, add green food coloring and almond extract. In second bowl, add yellow food coloring and coconut extract. In third bowl, add red food coloring and strawberry extract. Add cocoa and vanilla to the fourth bowl. Cut chocolate or white cake layers horizontally to make four layers. Frost each layer with a different color. Stack. Do not frost sides.

Tonia Beavers

Vanilla Frosting

¼ cup shortening
¼ teaspoon salt
2 teaspoons vanilla
3 cups powdered sugar
¼ cup milk

Mix shortening, salt, vanilla and about a third of the sugar. Add milk and remaining sugar alternately. Mix until smooth and creamy. Add sugar to thicken, milk to thin to desired consistency. Frosts two 8-9" round cakes or one 9 x 13 cake.

Teresa Wilkins

Fluffy White Icing

1 cup white corn syrup
½ cup sugar
3 stiffly beaten egg whites

Mix corn syrup and sugar in a heavy saucepan. Heat slowly until sugar is dissolved, then bring to a boil. Pour immediately over egg whites. Beat with mixer until cool. Spread on two 8-9" layers or one 9 x 13 pan. Keeps well and does not get weepy.

Tonia Beavers

Chocolate Cheese Cake

Graham Crust

1¼ cups graham cracker crumbs
½ cup butter, soft
¼ cup sugar

Preheat oven to 350 degrees. Mix ingredients; press evenly over bottom and sides (½" from top) of a 9" springform pan. Refrigerate crust until needed.

Cream Filling

3 eggs
3 8 ounce packages cream cheese
1 cup sugar
1 12 ounce package chocolate chips, melted
1 teaspoon vanilla
⅛ teaspoon salt
1 cup sour cream

In a large bowl, at high speed, beat eggs with sugar until light. Beat in cream cheese until mixture is smooth. Add melted chocolate, vanilla, salt and sour cream. Beat until smooth. Turn into crumb crust and bake one hour, or until cake is just firm, when the pan is shaken gently. Cool cheesecake in pan on a wire rack. Then refrigerate, covered, overnight.

Cream Topping

1 cup heavy cream
2-4 tablespoons powdered sugar

Beat cream with sugar just until stiff. Remove the side of the pan and decorate cake with whipped cream. Sprinkle with grated chocolate if desired.

Bonnie Haines

Cream Cheese Pound Cake

- *1 8 ounce package cream cheese*
- *1½ cups oleo, softened*
- *3 cups sugar*
- *6 large eggs*
- *3 cups cake flour*
- *1 teaspoon vanilla*
- *¼ teaspoon salt*

In mixing bowl, cream sugar, oleo and cream cheese well. Add one egg at a time, beating after each. Add vanilla. At slower speed, add flour, a little at a time. Pour into a large greased and floured tube pan. Place in cold oven and bake at 300 degrees for 1½ hours.

Marlene Newton

Arkansas Apple Pie

- *8-10 cups red or green apples*
- *1½ cups sugar*
- *½ cup water*
- *1 9" pie crust and top*
- *1 tablespoon lemon juice*
- *½ teaspoon cinnamon*
- *¼ cup butter*

Peel and slice apples very thinly. Cook apples until tender in sugar and water. Drain apples, reserving juice. Pile cooked apples in pie shell. Sprinkle with lemon juice, cinnamon and dot with butter. Cover with top crust. Bake 45 minutes at 350 degrees or until crust is brown. While pie is cooking, return juice to a low burner and let juice cook down (it will still be thin when pie is done). Pour hot juice over hot cooked pie (use as much juice as possible). I pour what I can over pie, wait 10-15 minutes and pour on remaining juice. Sometimes it will not take all of the juice depending on how much the apples cooked down. Do not refrigerate — it is not as good cold.

Jalia Lingle

Sugar-Free Apple Pie

- *1 8" crust, baked*
- *5 green Granny Smith apples, peeled and sliced thinly*
- *½ package butter flakes*
- *¼ teaspoon nutmeg*
- *½ teaspoon cinnamon*
- *Squirt of lemon juice*
- *2 tablespoons flour*
- *½ cup fructose granules*
- *½ cup Sugar Twin brown sugar*
- *Whipped topping*

Mix apples, artificial butter, spices, flour and lemon; tossing to coat. Put in a covered dish and bake in 350 degree oven for 30 minutes (to test for doneness, prick with knife in center). Cool completely. Stir in fructose and brown sugar. Pour into baked crust. Top with cream substitute just before serving.

Kay Stephens

Nanny's Apple Sack Pie

- ½ *cup sugar*
- 2 *tablespoons flour*
- ½ *teaspoon cinnamon*
- 1 *can pie-sliced apples (not apple pie filling)*
- ½ *cup sugar*
- ½ *cup flour*
- ½ *cup margarine, softened*
- 1 *9" unbaked pie crust*

Mix first four ingredients together and place in pie crust. Mix sugar, flour and margarine (should be crumbly) and place over top of pie to form topping. Slide pie into a grocery sack that has been placed on its side and fold under open end, securing with paper clips. Place sack on cookie sheet and place in 425 degree oven for one hour. Don't worry if you smell the paper during baking. Just make sure the sack is not touching the oven interior anywhere. Top each slice with a scoop of vanilla ice cream for a mouth-watering dessert.

Ann Ray

Old Time Buttermilk Pie

- 1 *9" unbaked pie shell*
- ½ *cup butter, softened*
- 1¼ *cups sugar*
- 3 *rounded tablespoons flour*
- 3 *eggs, beaten*
- 1 *cup buttermilk*
- 1 *teaspoon vanilla*
- *Dash nutmeg*

Cream butter and sugar; add flour and eggs and beat well. Stir in vanilla, buttermilk and nutmeg. Pour into unbaked pie shell and cook at 350 degrees for 45-50 minutes. Cool before serving.

Jalia Lingle

Chess Pie

- 3 *egg yolks*
- 1½ *cups sugar*
- 1 *tablespoon cornstarch*
- 1 *12 ounce can evaporated milk*
- ¼ *cup butter, partially melted*
- 1 *teaspoon vanilla*

Beat the egg yolks by hand; beat in the sugar. Add cornstarch, milk, butter and vanilla. Mix well and pour into a 9" unbaked pie shell. Bake 10 minutes at 425 degrees and then lower temperature to 325 degrees and bake 45 minutes.

Gaye Croom

Caramel Pie

- 2 *baked pie shells*
- 1 *8 ounce package cream cheese*
- 1 *16 ounce tub frozen whipped topping*
- 1 *can sweetened condensed milk*
- ¼ *cup butter*
- 1 *7 ounce can coconut*
- 1 *cup sliced almonds*
- 1 *jar caramel ice cream topping*

Melt butter in skillet. Add coconut and almonds; brown, then cool. Mix cream cheese, whipped topping and milk on medium speed with mixer until smooth. Pour ¼ filling in each shell, then layer with ¼ of the butter mixture and top with ¼ caramel. Repeat all three layers to fill pie shell. Freeze until ready to serve. Let pie set at room temperature for 10 minutes before slicing, then return to freezer.

Debbie Bell

Chocolate Ice-Box Pie

- 2 *cups milk*
- ½ *cup chocolate chips*
- 1½ *cups sugar*
- 2 *cups milk*
- ¾ *teaspoon salt*
- ½ *cup flour*
- ¼ *cup cornstarch*
- ½ *cup egg whites*
- 2 *tablespoons vanilla*
- ½ *cup oleo*
- 2 *baked pie crusts*

Bring milk, chocolate chips and sugar to a boil. Combine and add to boiling mixture: milk, salt, flour, cornstarch and egg whites. Cook until thick, stirring to keep from lumping or sticking. When thick, remove from heat, add vanilla and oleo. Cool and put in crusts. Chill and top with whipped cream. Makes two pies.

Marilyn Moores

Fudge Swirl Pie

- ½ *cup chocolate chips*
- 2 *tablespoons milk*
- 1 *8 ounce package cream cheese, softened*
- 1 *7 ounce jar marshmallow creme*
- 1 *8 ounce tub frozen whipped topping*
- ½ *cup sugar*
- 1 *chocolate wafer crumb crust*

Melt chocolate chips with milk over low heat. Cool. Combine cream cheese, marshmallow creme and sugar until well blended. Fold in 2½ cups of whipped topping. Combine chocolate mixture with rest of the whipped topping. Spread ½ marshmallow mixture into crust, spread on chocolate topping mixture, then rest of marshmallow mixture and freeze.

Bonnie Haines

Chocolate Eggnog Pie

1⅓ cups (22) chocolate wafers, crumbled
2 tablespoons sugar
¼ cup butter, melted
1 envelope unflavored gelatin
¼ cup cold water
⅓ cup sugar
2 tablespoons cornstarch
⅛ teaspoon salt
2 cups eggnog
1 teaspoon vanilla
½ teaspoon rum extract (optional)
1 cup whipping cream, whipped
1 cup whipping cream
2 tablespoons powdered sugar

Combine crumbs, sugar and butter. Press into a 9" pie pan. Bake five minutes at 350 degrees and let cool. Sprinkle gelatin over water to soften. Combine sugar, cornstarch and salt in a heavy saucepan. Slowly add eggnog. Stir over medium heat until thickened; cook two minutes more. Remove from heat. Stir in gelatin until dissolved. Add extract and chill until slightly thickened. Fold in whipped cream. Pour into crust and chill several hours or overnight. Before serving, beat one cup whipping cream and powdered sugar until soft peaks form. Spread over pie. Garnish with chocolate curls.

Virginia Berner

French Silk Pie

3 egg whites
¼ teaspoon cream of tartar
⅛ teaspoon salt
¾ cup sugar
½ cup chopped pecans
½ teaspoon vanilla
1 4 ounce package sweet baking chocolate
3 tablespoons water
2 cups whipped cream, divided
Grated sweet chocolate

Beat egg whites (at room temperature), cream of tartar and salt until foamy. Gradually add sugar, beating well until stiff peaks form. Fold in chopped pecans and vanilla. Spoon meringue into a well-greased 9" pie pan. Use a spoon to shape meringue into a pie shell, swirling sides high. Bake at 300 degrees for one hour. Cool. Combine chocolate and water in a medium saucepan; over low heat, cook, stirring often, until chocolate melts. Let cool. Beat one cup whipping cream until stiff peaks form; fold into chocolate mixture. Pour chocolate mixture into meringue shell; chill at least three hours. Beat remaining whipping cream until stiff peaks form; spread evenly over top of pie. Garnish with grated chocolate.

Annette Holeyfield

Japanese Fruit Pie

2 eggs, unbeaten
1 cup sugar
½ cup margarine, softened
⅓ cup white corn syrup
1 teaspoon vanilla
1 tablespoon vinegar
½ cup coconut
½ cup raisins
½ cup chopped pecans
1 9" unbaked pie crust

Cream margarine and sugar; add eggs, corn syrup, vanilla and vinegar. Beat until well mixed. Stir in coconut, raisins and nuts. Pour into pie crust. Bake at 375 degrees for 15 minutes, then reduce temperature to 325 degrees and bake for 45 minutes more. Cool completely before serving.

Linda Bewley

Fresh Peach/Blueberry Pie

7-8 peaches, peeled and sliced
⅔ cup water
1 cup sugar
3 tablespoons cornstarch
1 tablespoon lemon juice
1 tablespoon butter
Dash salt
½ cup blueberries (or more)
1 9" pie crust, baked

Purée one cup of peaches with water in a blender. Pour into a saucepan and cook four minutes. Mix sugar and cornstarch; add to fruit mixture and cook until thick and clear. Remove from heat and add lemon juice, butter and salt. Let cool. Arrange remaining peaches in cooked pie shell and sprinkle with blueberries. Pour cooled glaze over fruit and refrigerate.

Susie Kroencke

Peanut Butter Pie

Crust

1 cup flour
½ cup oleo, softened
2 tablespoons sugar

Mix well and press into a 9" pie plate. Bake at 400 degrees for 10 minutes. Cool.

Filling

1 8 ounce package cream cheese, softened
2 cups powdered sugar
1 cup peanut butter
1 12 ounce tub frozen whipped topping

Mix cream cheese, sugar and peanut butter until smooth with a mixer. Add 8 ounces of topping and mix well. Pour into crust. Refrigerate one hour. Garnish with remaining topping and crushed peanuts.

Marcia Godown

Southern Pecan Pie

3 eggs
⅔ cup sugar
Dash salt
1 cup dark corn syrup
⅓ cup butter, melted
1 cup pecan halves
1 9" unbaked pie crust

Beat eggs thoroughly with sugar, salt and corn syrup. Add melted butter and pecans. Pour into pie crust. Bake at 350 degrees for 50 minutes or until knife inserted halfway comes out clean. Cool.

Vickie Hale

Pecan-Cheese Pie

1 9" unbaked pie crust

Cheese Layer

1 8 ounce package cream cheese, softened
⅓ cup sugar
¼ teaspoon salt
1 teaspoon vanilla
1 egg
1½ cups chopped pecans

Custard

¼ cup sugar
1 cup light corn syrup
1 teaspoon vanilla
3 eggs

Combine all cheese layer ingredients, except pecans, beat until smooth. Pour into pie crust. Sprinkle with pecans. Combine custard ingredients and pour on top of pecans. Bake at 375 degrees for 35-40 minutes or until top is firm. Cool and refrigerate before serving.

Tonia Beavers

Pecan Delight Pie

3 egg whites
1 cup sugar
1 teaspoon baking powder
1 cup graham cracker crumbs
1 teaspoon vanilla
2 cups chopped pecans
1 tub frozen whipped topping, optional

Beat egg whites until stiff, then fold in sugar. Add baking powder. Fold in graham cracker crumbs. Add vanilla and chopped pecans. Pour in an ungreased pie pan and bake at 325 degrees for 30 minutes. Let cool. Top with whipped topping and refrigerate.

Jane Fore

Pumpkin Chiffon Pie

3 egg yolks
½ cup sugar
1¼ cups canned pumpkin
½ cup milk
½ teaspoon salt
½ teaspoon ginger
½ teaspoon cinnamon
½ teaspoon nutmeg
1 envelope unflavored gelatin
¼ cup cold water
3 stiffly beaten egg whites
½ cup sugar
1 9" pastry shell, baked

Beat egg yolks and ½ cup sugar until thick; add pumpkin, milk, salt and spices. Cook in double boiler until thick. Soften gelatin in cold water, stir until dissolved. Add to pumpkin mixture. Cool. Beat egg whites with remaining ½ cup sugar and add to pumpkin mixture. Blend and pour into cooled baked shell. Chill and top with sweetened whipped cream before serving.

Kathy Smith

Sammye's Sweet Potato Pie

1¾ cups cooked and mashed sweet potatoes
½ teaspoon salt
1½ cups milk
2 large eggs, beaten
1 cup sugar
1 teaspoon cinnamon
½ teaspoon nutmeg
¼ cup butter
1 9" unbaked pie shell

Blend all ingredients together. Pour into a 9" unbaked pie shell. Bake at 425 degrees for 45-55 minutes, or until browned and set. Serve with whipped cream.

Kathleen Fullerton

Soda Cracker Pie

6 egg whites
1 teaspoon cream of tartar
2 cups sugar
32 saltine crackers, crushed finely
2 teaspoons vanilla
2 cups chopped pecans
1 pint whipping cream

Beat egg whites until foamy, add cream of tartar, beat until stiff. Add sugar gradually, continue beating as sugar is added. Fold in crackers, pecans and vanilla. Grease a 9 x 13 pan with a generous amount of butter. Pour ingredients into pan and bake at 325 degrees for 35 minutes. Cool. Top with sweetened whipped cream and chill for several hours in refrigerator. This is extra special topped with your favorite fruit.

Joyce Wilkins

Strawberry Pie

3 egg whites
½ teaspoon baking powder
1 cup sugar
10 soda crackers
½ cup chopped pecans
1 quart fresh strawberries, washed, stemmed, and drained
1 pint whipped topping

Beat egg whites and baking powder until stiff. Gradually add sugar. Fold in cracker crumbs and pecans. Spread in a well buttered 9" pie plate. Bake at 300 degrees for 30 minutes. Cool thoroughly. Place berries in cooled shell and cover with whipped cream. Chill up to an hour before serving.

Bobbie Moore

Never Fail Pie Crust

3 cups flour
1¼ cups shortening
1 teaspoon salt
5 tablespoons water
1 tablespoon lemon juice or vinegar
1 egg

Mix flour, shortening and salt until crumbly (the size of peas). Add water, lemon juice or vinegar and egg. Stir with spoon until all is moist and rolls away from the bowl. This crust is never tough when re-rolling. Can be kept in refrigerator for up to two weeks — also freezes well.

For Spicy Pie Crust, add

¼ cup sugar
½ teaspoon cinnamon
½ teaspoon nutmeg
¼ teaspoon allspice

Bobbie Moore

Country Vanilla Ice Cream

4 eggs
2¼ cups sugar
5 cups milk
4 cups heavy cream
4½ teaspoons vanilla
½ teaspoon salt

Add sugar gradually to beaten eggs. Continue to beat until mixture is very stiff. Add remaining ingredients and mix well. Pour into a gallon freezer and freeze as directed. If you use less cream, it doesn't get as thick. It may not cause the electric ice cream freezer to stop. Substitutions: 2 cups heavy cream and 7 cups 2% milk or 4 cups half and half and 5 cups 2% milk.

Marlene Newton

Granny's Vanilla Ice Cream

3-4 eggs, beaten
2½ cups sugar
1 quart of instant milk, as directed on powdered milk box
2 12 ounce cans evaporated milk
Whole milk to fill
Dash salt

Mix all ingredients in ice cream freezer and freeze. Better than store bought!

Sue McCoy

Ice Cream

1 can sweetened condensed milk
1 gallon ± whole milk
2 eggs
2 tablespoons vanilla extract
1-2 cups sugar
1 12 ounce can evaporated milk (very cold)
2 cups fruit, if desired

Refrigerate large mixing bowl and beaters along with evaporated milk in can. Blend together condensed milk, sugar, eggs, vanilla and fruit (if desired). Whip cold evaporated milk on high until peaks stand. Fold in condensed milk mixture. Pour in ice cream freezer, fill to full line with whole milk. Freeze as usual adding ice cream salt and ice as needed.

Kay Stephens

Tutti-Frutti Ice Cream

2½ cups sugar
1 pint whipping cream
1 12 ounce can evaporated milk
1 tablespoon vanilla
6 eggs
1 cup crushed pineapple, drained
3-4 sliced bananas
1 6 ounce jar maraschino cherries, sliced
1 cup chopped pecans
Milk to fill

Mix together sugar, whipping cream, evaporated milk, eggs, and vanilla. Add other ingredients. Add enough milk to come to fill line on ice cream freezer. Freeze. Let mellow in freezer at least one hour.

Linda Bewley

Fruit Slush

3 bananas, mashed
3 cups sugar
Juice of three oranges (1½ cups)
Juice of three lemons (½ cup)
3 cups water
1 16 ounce can crushed pineapple with juice
1 6 ounce jar maraschino cherries with juice

Mix together and freeze until almost solid. Serve in sherbet cups. Yields 24 servings

Patricia Peters

Apple Dessert

1 yellow cake mix
½ cup margarine, softened
1 egg
1 cup sour cream
½ cup coconut
1 teaspoon cinnamon
½ cup sugar
2 cans apple pie filling

Cut margarine into cake mix, then add coconut. Press into bottom of a 9 x 13 pan and up sides. Bake 10 minutes at 350 degrees. Spread apple filling over crust. Mix cinnamon and sugar together and sprinkle over apples. Blend sour cream and egg and drizzle over top. Bake 25 minutes at 350 degrees.

Marie Biggers

Bavarian Apple Torte

Pastry

½ cup butter, softened
⅓ cup sugar
¼ teaspoon vanilla
1 cup flour

Cream butter, sugar and vanilla. Blend in the flour. Spread dough on the bottom and 1" up the sides of a 9" springform pan.

Filling

12 ounces cream cheese, softened
¼ cup sugar
1 egg
1 teaspoon vanilla

To make filling, beat together cream cheese and sugar. Blend in egg and vanilla. Pour into pastry-lined pan.

Topping

⅓ cup sugar
½ teaspoon cinnamon
4 cups peeled and sliced tart apples
¼ cup slivered almonds
1 cup heavy whipping cream, whipped
Pinch of cinnamon

Combine sugar and cinnamon; toss with apples. Arrange apples in concentric circles on pastry. Sprinkle with almonds. Bake at 450 degrees for 10 minutes, then reduce heat to 400 degrees and continue baking about 25 minutes. Cool before removing rim. Serve with a bountiful amount of whipped cream laced with cinnamon.

Terri Knight

Cherry Jubilee

½ cup sugar
¼ cup margarine, softened
12 graham crackers (1¾ cups crumbs)
1 8 ounce package cream cheese
1 cup powdered sugar
1 cup whipped topping
1 can cherry pie filling (or fruit of choice)

Crush graham crackers and mix with sugar and margarine. Line a 9-10" pie plate with mixture and chill while preparing filling. Cream together the cream cheese, powdered sugar and whipped topping. Pour over crust and chill one hour. Cover with cherry pie filling and serve. Yields 6-8 slices

Bobbie Moore

Apple Blueberry Cobbler

½ cup butter
1 cup self-rising flour
⅔ cup milk
1 cup sugar
1 teaspoon vanilla
6 apples, peeled and chopped
1½ cups blueberries
1 tablespoon cinnamon
½ cup sugar
½ cup butter
2 tablespoons cornstarch
½ cup milk
½ teaspoon almond extract
1 teaspoon vanilla

For the pastry, melt butter in the oven while preheating to 300 degrees in a 3 quart dish. Mix flour, sugar and milk together. Add vanilla and pour over melted butter. For the filling, place apples, blueberries, sugar, butter and cinnamon in a saucepan and cook over medium heat until apples are tender. Combine cornstarch with milk and stir into the fruit mixture, cooking until thick. Remove from heat and stir in vanilla and almond extract. Pour over pastry. Bake at 300 degrees for 30 minutes or until brown. Serves 10

Lynda Hill

Date Torte

4 eggs, separated
1 cup sugar
1 cup chopped dates
1 cup chopped nuts
3 tablespoons flour
½ teaspoon baking powder

Whip egg whites, gradually adding ½ cup sugar. Whip until stiff but not dry. Beat yolks and add remaining sugar. Add dates, nuts, flour and baking powder to yolk mixture. Fold in egg whites. Bake in a 2 quart dish at 300 degrees for 50-60 minutes. Top with whipped cream.

Jane Fore

Linden Date Loaf

1 pound package of pitted dates
2 cups sugar
1 cup milk
2 cups pecans, chopped
Lump of butter the size of a small egg

Place sugar, milk and butter in a small pan and cook until it reaches soft ball stage (238 degrees). Add dates and cook until thoroughly done. Add pecans and pour into a wet napkin (use a tea towel) and roll into a loaf. Refrigerate until firm. Remove from towel, wrap in plastic wrap, and keep refrigerated. Slice to serve. *This recipe dates back to 1840 and is named for the home called Linden in Natchez, Mississippi, that was purchased by Mrs. Boyce's great-great-great grandmother.

Arden Boyce

Frozen Lemon Cream

1 cup whole milk
1 cup whipping cream
1 cup sugar
3 lemons - juice and rind
6 large lemons
Mint leaves
Chocolate curls

Stir milk, whipping cream and sugar until sugar is thoroughly dissolved. Pour mixture into a refrigerator tray and freeze it until it is mushy. Add grated rind and juice of three lemons; beat mixture well with mixer and freeze it again for two hours. Beat cream mixture again thoroughly and return it to the freezer, and freeze until it is solid. Slice off tops of six large lemons and with a grapefruit knife and spoon, remove all pulp. Cut a thin slice from the bottom of each lemon so that it will stand upright. Fill the shells with frozen cream piling it high. Serve on individual plates, garnished with mint leaf and chocolate curls.

Sue H. Streett

Lime Melon Balls

1 cup water
2 tablespoons sugar
2 tablespoons lime juice
2 cups assorted melon balls
Pomegranate seeds, mint springs, and/or thin lime slices

Boil together water and sugar. Cool to room temperature and add lime juice. Pour over melon balls in sherbet glasses. Garnish with pomegranate seeds and sprig of mint, or lime slices. Serves 4, with approximately 55 calories per serving.

Bonnie Haines

Lemon Roll

10-12 egg yolks
1 cup cake flour
6 tablespoons cold water
1 cup sugar
3 teaspoons baking powder
1 teaspoon vanilla
1 can lemon pie filling (or your favorite pie filling)

Beat yolks until thick and lemon-colored. Add sugar gradually. Add water. Sift dry ingredients together and fold into first mixture, a little at a time. Add vanilla. Bake on waxed paper-lined jellyroll pan for 15 minutes. Turn out on towel sprinkled with powdered sugar. Roll up in towel until cake is cool. When cool, unroll and spread with pie filling and roll up. Refrigerate. Serve with a dollop of whipped cream. This is a light and delicious dessert that was kept secret by a caterer in my hometown for many years. Use the remaining egg whites for an angel food cake.

Ann Ray

Peach Cobbler

Filling

1 29 ounce can peaches (Elberta best), drained, reserve juice
½ cup sugar
4 tablespoons flour
1 teaspoon vanilla
¼ of a lemon
Margarine
1 recipe of pie crust

Cut peaches into small pieces. Place them in an 11 x 8 baking dish. Mix together sugar and flour and stir in the drained juice. Pour evenly over the peaches. Sprinkle vanilla and juice of lemon quarter over the mixture. Dot with margarine. Add strips of pie dough for top. Bake at 400 degrees for 20 minutes and then lower temperature to 350 degrees and finish baking about 30 minutes. It should be brown on top. Serves 6

Pie Crust

1 cup flour
⅓ cup shortening
½ teaspoon salt
Up to ¼ cup ice cold water

Mix flour, shortening and salt together with pastry cutter or two forks. Gradually add water until dough leaves the side of the bowl. Roll out on lightly floured surface. Cut into strips and place on peach mixture.

Mary Dean Lyford

Peach Delight

1 *cup flour*
2 *tablespoons sugar*
½ *cup oleo, softened*
¼ *cup chopped pecans*
1 *cup sugar*
1 *8 ounce package cream cheese, softened*
1 *8 ounce tub frozen whipped topping*
3 *cups peaches*
1 *cup sugar*
1½ *cups water*
4 *tablespoons cornstarch*
1 *3 ounce package peach gelatin*

Mix first four ingredients well and press into a 9 x 13 baking dish. Bake at 350 degrees for 20 minutes. Cool. Beat cream cheese and sugar. Fold in whipped topping. Spread over cooled crust. Top with peaches. Combine sugar and cornstarch in saucepan. Add water slowly and cook until thickened, beating well so it does not get lumpy. Stir in peach gelatin. Cool. Spoon glaze over peaches. Refrigerate. Cut into squares to serve. Yields 12-15 servings

Connie Neumeier

Yarbrough's Stove-Top Peach Dumplings

4 *cups fresh sliced very ripe peaches*
¾ *cup sugar*
2 *tablespoons flour*
½ *teaspoon cinnamon*
Squirt of lemon juice
1 *can biscuits*

In a large saucepan, bring sliced peaches and their juices to a boil. If peaches aren't really ripe you may need to add ¼ cup water. Mix together flour, sugar, and cinnamon and add to boiling peaches. Add a squirt of lemon juice. Cut biscuits into quarters and add to peaches, a few at a time. Cover and let simmer 12-15 minutes. Serve warm, plain or with ice cream.

The Committee

Fruit Dessert

1 *cup sour cream*
1 *8 ounce can crushed pineapple, drained*
1 *tablespoon lemon juice*
Pinch salt
½ *cup sugar*
2 *bananas, sliced*
2 *10 ounce boxes sliced frozen strawberries, slightly thawed*
1 *cup pecans*

Mix all ingredients together — spoon into molds or casserole dish. Freeze. Set out 10-15 minutes before serving. Serves 6-8

Laurie Bibler

Heavenly Clouds

1 16 ounce bag marshmallows
1 cup milk
1 15 ounce can crushed pineapple, drained well
1 cup pecans, chopped
1 large tub frozen whipped topping
Maraschino cherries
Mint leaves, optional

In a saucepan, melt marshmallows with milk. Do this slowly, over low heat and do not burn. Cool slightly and add pineapple, pecans and whipped topping.

Crust

2 packages graham crackers, crushed
½ cup oleo, softened
¼ cup sugar

Mix well. Pour into a greased 9 x 13 pan and press. Pour pineapple mixture over crust and cool several hours. Cut into squares and garnish with a cherry and mint leaf. Serves 12-15

Kay Ewing

Pumpkin Nut Cream Roll

3 eggs
1 cup sugar
⅔ cup pumpkin
1 teaspoon lemon juice
¾ cup flour
½ teaspoon salt
1 teaspoon baking powder
½ teaspoon nutmeg
½ teaspoon ginger
2 teaspoons cinnamon
1 cup chopped pecans
2 cups powdered sugar, divided
6 ounces cream cheese
4 tablespoons margarine
1 teaspoon vanilla

Beat eggs on high speed for five minutes. Gradually add sugar. Add pumpkin and lemon juice. Sift flour, salt, baking powder, nutmeg, ginger and cinnamon. Add to pumpkin mixture and blend well. Pour into a well greased 10 x 15 x 1 jellyroll pan. Top with chopped pecans and press lightly into batter. Bake at 375 degrees for 15 minutes. Spread one cup of powdered sugar over a tea towel. Turn baked cake onto towel. Roll cake and towel together and let cool completely. Mix cream cheese, margarine, one cup powdered sugar and vanilla. Cream well. Unroll cooled cake and spread with filling. Roll cake again (without towel). Chill and slice.

Becky Ellison

Strawberry Meringue Nut Torte

- 1½ *cups finely rolled soda crackers*
- 2 *cups chopped pecans*
- 2 *teaspoons baking powder*
- 6 *egg whites*
- 2 *cups sugar*
- 2 *tablespoons almond extract*
- 2 *cups whipped cream*
- 2 *tablespoons sugar*
- 1-2 *pints fresh strawberries*

Beat egg whites until stiff while adding sugar, one tablespoon at a time. Add almond extract. Fold in cracker crumbs, nuts and baking powder. Prepare two 9" or three 8" round cake pans by greasing, lining with wax paper, and greasing and flouring. Spread mixture in pans and round slightly in the center. Bake 35 minutes at 325 degrees. Remove from oven and cool in pans on cake rack. When cool, put layers together with sliced strawberries and sweetened whipped cream. Reserve about one cup of whipped cream for the top. Allow some of the strawberries to show by not completely covering the layer with whipped cream. Cover well and put in the refrigerator to mellow. Before serving, cover top meringue with whipped cream and garnish with whole uncapped strawberries. Place more berries around the bottom of the torte. You may make this torte with other fruits such as peaches or blueberries. However, other fruits are just not as spectacular as the strawberry version. Make this torte when you want to show off. It is a beautiful thing, especially on a cake stand. This recipe was on the agenda of a French cooking class I took in Memphis about 20 years ago.

Suzanne Singleton

Strawberry Cheese Cake Trifle

- 2 *8 ounce packages lite cream cheese, softened*
- 2 *cups powdered sugar*
- 1 *cup sour cream*
- ¼ *teaspoon almond extract*
- ¼ *teaspoon vanilla extract*
- 1 *8 ounce carton whipped cream*
- ¼ *teaspoon vanilla*
- 1 *tablespoon sugar*
- 1 *angel food cake, torn into bite-sized pieces*
- 2 *quarts fresh strawberries*
- 3 *tablespoons sugar*
- 1½ *tablespoons almond extract*

In a large bowl, cream together cream cheese and sugar; then add sour cream, vanilla and almond extract. Set aside. In a small deep bowl, whip cream, vanilla and sugar. Fold whipped cream into cream cheese mixture. Add cake pieces, and set aside. Slice strawberries thinly, then combine with the sugar and almond extract. Layer in trifle bowl, starting with the strawberries, then cake mixture. Continue layering, ending with strawberries on top. Cover with plastic wrap and refrigerate for a couple of hours to overnight.

Tamara Laws

Strawberry Pizza

- 1 *cup self-rising flour*
- ¼ *cup powdered sugar*
- ¼ *cup butter or oleo*
- 1 *8 ounce package cream cheese, softened*
- 1 *can sweetened condensed milk*
- ⅓ *cup lemon juice*
- 1 *teaspoon vanilla*
- ½ *cup sugar*
- 2 *tablespoons cornstarch*
- ½ *cup water*
- 2 *pints strawberries, hulled and sliced*

Combine flour, powdered sugar and butter. Mix well and press dough in a 14" pizza pan. Bake 350 degrees for 10 minutes or until lightly browned. Combine cream cheese, condensed milk, lemon juice and vanilla. Mix well and spread on cooled crust. Chill. Combine sugar and cornstarch in a saucepan; add water, cook over medium heat until thickened, about five minutes, stirring constantly. Cool and add strawberries. Spread strawberry mixture over cream cheese layer and chill. Serves 8-12

Jalia Lingle

Family Secret Chocolate Cookies

- 1 *cup brown sugar*
- ½ *cup shortening*
- 2 *squares semi-sweet chocolate, melted*
- 1 *egg*
- ½ *cup milk*
- 2 *cups flour*
- ¼ *teaspoon salt*
- ¼ *teaspoon baking soda*
- 1 *teaspoon baking powder*
- 1 *cup nuts, chopped*
- 1 *teaspoon vanilla*

Cream sugar and shortening. Add melted chocolate squares, egg and milk. Combine in a separate bowl: flour, salt, soda and baking powder. Add this to creamed mixture. Add nuts and vanilla. Drop by teaspoonsful on lightly greased cookie sheets. Bake at 350 degrees until lightly brown, about 15 minutes. Cool and ice. Yields 4-5 dozen

Icing

- ½ *cup butter, softened*
- 1 *box powdered sugar*

Zest of one orange

- 1 *6 ounce can orange juice, thawed*

Mix butter with sugar, add rind. Add orange juice, one teaspoon at a time, until spreading consistency.

Kay Ewing

Colossal Cookies

½ cup butter or margarine
1½ cups sugar
1½ cups brown sugar, firmly packed
4 eggs
1 teaspoon vanilla
1½ teaspoons baking soda
1 18 ounce jar chunky-style peanut butter
6 cups old fashioned oats
1 6 ounce package semi-sweet chocolate chips

In large bowl beat together butter and sugar, blending well. Beat in eggs and vanilla. Stir in soda, peanut butter and oats. Add chocolate chips last. Drop by scant one-half cup on ungreased cookie sheets. Flatten with a fork to 2½" in diameter. Bake 10-12 minutes at 350 degrees. Remove to wire cooling rack. This also works well to make regular sized cookies. Makes 4½ colossal or 9 dozen regular sized cookies

Pat Gordon

Chocolate Sugar Cookies

2 eggs
⅔ cup oil
1 teaspoon vanilla
¾ cup sugar
1¾ cups flour
½ teaspoon salt
½ teaspoon soda
6 tablespoons cocoa

Beat eggs with fork until well blended. Stir in oil and vanilla. Blend in sugar until mixture thickens. Sift together flour, soda, salt and cocoa; add to egg mixture. Drop by teaspoonsful about 2" apart on *ungreased* cookie sheets. Stamp each cookie flat with a bottom of a glass dipped in sugar. Lightly oil glass, then dip in sugar and continue pressing cookies. Bake at 375 degrees for 8-10 minutes. Yields three dozen

Judy Taylor

Lemon Cookies

1 lemon cake mix
1 8 ounce tub frozen whipped topping
2 eggs, beaten
½ teaspoon lemon extract
Powdered sugar

Combine first four ingredients. Stir until blended. Drop from teaspoon onto greased cookie sheets. Bake at 350 degrees for 15 minutes. While still warm, sprinkle with powdered sugar. Makes about 48 cookies

Great with tea — hot or cold!

Patti Nickels

Betsy's Special Fruitcake Cookies

3½ cups flour
1 teaspoon baking soda
1 teaspoon salt
1 pound dates, chopped
2 cups red and green cherries, quartered
4 slices pineapple, chopped
1 cup white raisins
2 cups chopped pecans
1 cup butter-flavored oil
1 pound light brown sugar
2 eggs
½ cup buttermilk

Mix first eight ingredients. Set aside. Mix last four ingredients, then combine all. Drop batter 2" apart on greased cookie sheet. Bake 10 minutes at 375 degrees. Makes six dozen.

These are delicious even to those who do not like fruitcake. They improve with age, so make them early.

Toni Weatherford

Molasses Crinkles

1 cup packed dark brown sugar
¾ cup butter or margarine
¼ cup molasses
1 egg
2¼ cups all purpose flour
2 teaspoons baking soda
1½ teaspoons cinnamon
1½ teaspoons ginger
½ teaspoon cloves
¼ teaspoon salt
Granulated sugar

Mix brown sugar, butter, molasses and egg. Mix dry ingredients together and combine with sugar mixture. Chill for at least 1 hour. Shape into balls (about 1 teaspoonful). Roll balls until completely covered in sugar. Bake on greased cookie sheet, just until set, about 8-10 minutes. Remove immediately from cookie sheets to cool. Makes about 4 dozen

Jeannine Sawyer

Pecan Cookies

½ cup shortening
½ cup butter
2½ cups brown sugar
2 beaten eggs
2½ cups flour
¼ teaspoon salt
½ teaspoon baking soda
1 cup or more chopped pecans

Cream shortening, butter and sugar. Add beaten eggs. Sift together all dry ingredients. Add to butter mixture and mix well. Add pecans. Drop by teaspoonsful on greased cookie sheets. Bake in 350 degree oven for 12-15 minutes. (Don't make the cookies too large or they won't be crispy!)

Connie Neumeier

Peanut Butter Cup Cookies

1¼ cups flour
½ teaspoon baking soda
¼ teaspoon salt
½ cup butter, softened
¾ cup sugar
½ teaspoon vanilla
1 egg
18 miniature peanut-butter cup candies

Preheat oven to 325 degrees. Combine flour, soda and salt. Beat butter and sugar until light and fluffy. Beat in vanilla and egg. Stir in flour mixture. Drop dough by level tablespoon measures onto ungreased baking sheets, eight cookies per sheet. Cut each candy into four pieces and push three pieces of candy into each cookie, flattening dough slightly. Bake until cookies are a light golden color, about 12 minutes; center will still be pale and a little soft. Let cookies stand one minute on baking sheets before removing. Yields 24 cookies

Patti Nickels

Butter Meltaways

Cookie

⅓ cup powdered sugar
1¼ cups flour
¾ cup cornstarch
1 cup butter, softened

Blend the cookie ingredients together in a mixer. Separate the dough into two halves and roll each half into two logs on wax paper. (If dough is sticky, use a little powdered sugar or flour on wax paper and hands.) Refrigerate six hours to overnight, wrapped in wax paper. Slice dough and place on greased cookie sheets; bake at 350 degrees for 12-15 minutes. Cool on a wire rack.

Frosting

1 3 ounce package cream cheese, softened
1 cup powdered sugar
½ teaspoon vanilla
Food coloring

Mix first three ingredients. Color as desired. Drop a dollop of frosting on top of each cookie. These cookies melt in your mouth!

Mary Smith

Spritz Cookies

- 1 *cup shortening*
- ¾ *cup sugar*
- 2 *eggs, beaten*
- 1 *teaspoon almond extract*
- 2¼ *cups flour*
- ½ *teaspoon baking powder*
- ¼ *teaspoon salt*

Cream shortening and sugar thoroughly. Add eggs and almond extract, beat well. Add sifted dry ingredients two tablespoons at a time, mixing well after each addition. Bake approximately three minutes at 375 degrees. Cookies should not brown.

Icing

- ½ *cup oleo*
- 2½ *cups powdered sugar, sifted*
- 1 *teaspoon vanilla*
- *Milk*

Beat together oleo and sugar. Add vanilla. Add small amounts of milk slowly until icing is of a firm texture for decorating. Cookie press is required for this recipe, also decorating equipment for icing in order to decorate with small dots of icing. These cookies are very pretty and delicious.

Kathy Soto

Grandmother Davis' Old Fashioned Sugar Cookies

- 1 *cup shortening*
- 4 *cups flour*
- ½ *cup milk*
- 2 *eggs*
- 1½ *cups sugar*
- 2 *teaspoons baking soda*
- ½ *teaspoon salt*
- ½ *teaspoon almond extract*

In a large bowl, mix flour and shortening to the consistency of cornmeal or small peas. Combine remaining ingredients in a small bowl and add to first mixture. Roll dough on floured board to ⅛" thickness. Cut with cookie cutter of choice. Bake at 350 degrees for 8-10 minutes on ungreased cookie sheets. Yields six dozen

Icing

- 1 *pound powdered sugar*
- ⅓ *cup shortening*
- 1 *teaspoon cream of tartar*
- ½ *teaspoon salt*
- 1 *teaspoon flavoring of choice*
- ¼ *cup water*

Cream all ingredients with half of the water. Gradually add remaining water. Beat 5-7 minutes until fluffy. Keep covered when not in use.

Maysel Teeter

Yummy Whole Grain Cookies

- 1 *cup butter*
- 1 *cup white sugar*
- 1 *cup brown sugar*
- 2 *eggs*
- 1 *teaspoon vanilla*
- 2 *cups whole wheat pastry flour**
- 1½ *teaspoons cinnamon*
- 1 *teaspoon baking soda*
- ½ *teaspoon salt*
- 3 *cups quick oats*
- 1 *cup nuts*
- 1 *cup raisins*

Cream butter and sugars. Add eggs and vanilla. Sift flour, cinnamon, soda and salt. Blend into creamed mixture. Stir in nuts, oats and raisins. Drop by rounded teaspoonsful onto greased cookie sheets. Bake 12-14 minutes in a preheated 375 degree oven. Makes six dozen

**Flour available at health food stores. Ideal for baking cookies and pie crusts.*

Suzanne Singleton

Neiman-Marcus Brownies

- 1 *box Swiss chocolate cake mix*
- 1 *egg*
- 1 *stick butter or margarine*
- 2 *cups chopped pecans*
- *Coconut, to taste*
- 3 *eggs, beaten*
- 1 *8 ounce package cream cheese, softened*
- 1 *box powdered sugar*

Mix together first four ingredients. Press mixture in bottom of greased 9 x 13 pan. Sprinkle coconut on top. Mix together eggs, cream cheese and powdered sugar; pour on top. Bake at 350 degrees for 45 minutes. Makes 12-15 bars

Laurie Bibler

Peanut Brownies

- ⅔ *cup crunchy peanut butter*
- ¼ *cup oleo*
- 1 *cup packed brown sugar*
- ⅔ *cup sugar*
- 1 *teaspoon vanilla*
- 3 *eggs*
- 1 *cup self-rising flour*
- 2 *cups chocolate chips*

Cream peanut butter, oleo, brown sugar, sugar and vanilla in a large bowl. Beat in eggs. Combine dry ingredients; add to creamed mixture. Stir in chips. Spread stiff dough in a greased 9 x 13 pan. Bake at 350 degrees for 30-35 minutes. Cool. Cut into small pieces. Yield 36 pieces

Kay Stephens

Lisa's Sinful Brownies

Brownie

4 eggs
2 cups sugar
1 cup margarine
3 tablespoons cocoa
1½ cups flour
1 cup chopped nuts
1 tablespoon vanilla
1 7 ounce jar marshmallow creme

In a large bowl, beat eggs; combine with sugar. In a saucepan, melt margarine and cocoa over low heat. Combine flour with the cocoa mixture. Pour into bowl with sugar and eggs. Add nuts and vanilla and mix. Bake at 350 degrees for 30 minutes. Cool for 10 minutes and then spread marshmallow creme over brownie.

Icing

½ cup margarine, melted
2 tablespoons cocoa
2½ cups powdered sugar
1 tablespoon milk

Mix icing together and spread over the marshmallow creme.

Susan Dishner

Three Layer Brownies

1 package brownie mix
¾ cup butter
3 cups powdered sugar
3 tablespoons milk
¾ teaspoon vanilla
3 1 ounce squares semi-sweet chocolate
3 tablespoons butter

Prepare brownie mix according to directions and bake in 9 x 13 pan. Let cool.

Browned Butter Icing Layer

Microwave ¾ cup butter on high until melted. Add sugar, milk, and vanilla. Stir and spread on top of cooled brownies.

Chocolate Glaze Layer

Microwave chocolate squares and 3 tablespoons butter on high for three minutes. Stir. Cool slightly and drizzle over icing on brownies. Refrigerate until cool and icing and glaze are set.

Patti Nickels

Grandma's Brownies

- 2 *cups sugar*
- ½ *cup cocoa*
- 4 *eggs*
- 1 *cup margarine, melted*
- 1 *cup flour*
- ½ *teaspoon salt*
- 2 *teaspoons vanilla*
- 1 *cup nuts, chopped (pecans best)*

Mix all ingredients and pour into an ungreased 9 x 13 pan. Bake 50 minutes at 325 degrees. Cut while still hot.

Toni Laws

Magic Coconut Squares

- ½ *cup margarine*
- 1½ *cups graham cracker crumbs*
- 2 *cups coconut*
- 1 *cup chopped nuts*
- 1½ *cups miniature marshmallows*
- 1 *can sweetened condensed milk*
- 3 *squares semi-sweet chocolate, melted*

Preheat oven to 350 degrees. Place margarine in a 9 x 13 pan and place in oven to melt. Remove pan from oven and sprinkle crumbs over margarine, pressing down with a fork. Sprinkle coconut over crumbs. Add a layer of nuts and a layer of marshmallows. Drizzle sweetened condensed milk evenly over the top. Bake for 25-30 minutes or until golden brown. Remove from oven and drizzle with melted chocolate. Cool before cutting. Yields 48 bars

Renae Bailey

Conga Bars

- 1 *pound box brown sugar*
- 1 *cup oil*
- 3 *eggs*
- *Pinch salt*
- 3 *teaspoons baking powder*
- 1 *teaspoon vanilla*
- 2½ *cups flour*
- 1 *6 ounce package chocolate chips*
- 1 *cup walnuts or pecans*

Mix oil, vanilla, eggs and sugar. Add dry ingredients. When mixed, add chips and nuts. Spoon mixture into greased 9 x 13 pan and bake at 350 degrees for 30-40 minutes. Bars may be soft in the middle, but will harden when cooled. Cut into squares after cooling for at least 30 minutes. Yields 24 bars

Georganne Peel

Pecan Bars

Filling

2/3 cup yellow or white cake mix
1/2 cup brown sugar, packed
3 eggs
1 1/2 cups dark corn syrup
1 teaspoon vanilla
1 cup pecans, chopped

Crust

Remaining cake mix
1/2 cup melted oleo
1 egg

Mix crust ingredients until crumbly. Spread in a greased 9 x 13 pan. Bake at 350 degrees for 15-20 minutes or until brown. Combine all filling ingredients, except pecans. Beat at medium speed for 1-2 minutes. Pour over baked crust and sprinkle with pecans. Return to oven and bake 30-35 minutes or until filling is set. Cool. Cut into 36 bars. Serve plain or with ice cream.

Bonnie Haines

Pumpkin Bars

1 cup flour
1/2 cup oats
1/2 cup brown sugar
1/2 cup butter
2 cups canned pumpkin
1 12 ounce can evaporated milk
2 eggs
3/4 cup sugar
1/2 teaspoon sugar
1 teaspoon cinnamon
1/2 teaspoon ginger
1/4 teaspoon cloves

Combine flour, oats, brown sugar and butter. Mix until crumbly. Press into an ungreased 9 x 13 pan. Bake at 350 degrees for 15 minutes. Combine remaining ingredients. Beat well. Pour over crust and bake 20 minutes.

Topping

1/2 cup pecans, chopped
1/2 cup brown sugar
2 tablespoons butter

Mix topping ingredients, sprinkle over pumpkin and bake 15-20 minutes more. Serve with a dollop of whipped cream or ice cream. Serves 12-15

Kay Ewing

Pineapple Sour Cream Bars

1 box yellow cake mix
½ cup margarine
1 egg
1 cup nuts, chopped coarsely
1 box powdered sugar
1 8 ounce carton sour cream
2 eggs, beaten
1 15 ounce can crushed pineapple, drained

Mix first four ingredients and pat into an 11 x 15 pan (will be stiff). Mix the remaining ingredients and pour this over the crust. Bake at 325 degrees for one hour. Yields 30 bars

Bobbie Moore

Date Balls

3 tablespoons butter
1 cup sugar
1½ cups chopped dates
Pinch salt
2 eggs
1 cup chopped nuts
3 cups crispy rice cereal
Coconut

Melt butter over low heat. Add sugar, dates, eggs and salt. Stir briskly for about 15 minutes until mixture pulls away from pan. Remove from stove and add nuts and rice cereal. Shape into balls (use two spoons if the mixture is too hot to handle) and roll in coconut. Makes 20 balls

Kay Roberts

Peppermint Creams

1 pound almond bark, cut into pieces
¼ cup shortening
¾ cup finely crushed peppermint candy
Several drops red food coloring, optional

Line a 9 x 9 pan with waxed paper. In a medium microwave safe bowl, combine bark and shortening. Microwave on medium (50%) 4-6 minutes or until candy is melted. Stir often during cooking. Stir until smooth. Stir in crushed peppermint and food coloring. Spread into prepared pan. Allow candy to stand at room temperature until firm; cut into 1" squares. Allow candy to harden completely. Yields 81 1" squares

Patti Nickels

Chocolate Drops

1 box powdered sugar
2½ cups graham cracker crumbs
1 cup flaked coconut
1 cup nuts, chopped
⅓ cup crunchy peanut butter
2 teaspoons vanilla

In a large bowl, mix sugar, graham crackers, coconut and nuts until well blended. Add peanut butter and vanilla. Mix with hands to form walnut-sized balls. Set aside.

Glaze

1 12 ounce package chocolate chips
½ block paraffin

Melt chips and paraffin. Dip balls and coat in chocolate. Dry on wax paper. Store in an air-tight container or freeze for future enjoyment.

Kay Stephens

Buttermilk Fudge

2 cups sugar
1 cup buttermilk
½ cup oleo
2 tablespoons white corn syrup
1 teaspoon baking soda
1 teaspoon vanilla
½ cup pecans

Cook sugar, buttermilk, oleo, syrup and baking soda in a saucepan until a drop forms a soft ball in water. Add vanilla and pecans and beat until creamy. Pour into a greased 9 x 5 loaf pan. Let cool, then cut into squares. Yields 9-12 pieces

Mary Noel Mabry

Cheesy Chocolate Fudge

1 pound oleo
1 pound pasteurized process cheese spread, cubed
1 cup cocoa
4 pounds powdered sugar
2 cups chopped nuts
1 teaspoon vanilla

Melt oleo and cheese together. Sift together cocoa and powdered sugar. Add melted cheese mixture to cocoa mixture and mix well. Add vanilla and nuts and pat into a 9 x 13 pan. This recipe can be halved easily. Yields six pounds

Jane Fore

Peanut Butter Fudge

3 cups sugar
½ cup corn syrup
¼ teaspoon salt
½ cup milk (evaporated milk is best!)
1 cup peanut butter

Mix all ingredients except peanut butter. Cook to soft ball stage. Add peanut butter and stir well. Pour into a 7 x 11 pan and cool. Yields 36 pieces

Connie Neumeier

Pistachio Lemon Fudge

1 pound white chocolate, chopped
1 cup sifted powdered sugar
½ cup corn syrup
¼ cup oleo
1 cup chopped unsalted pistachios
1 tablespoon whipping cream
1 tablespoon lemon juice
1 teaspoon vanilla

Pour the first four ingredients into a glass bowl. Microwave on high three minutes. Stir after 1½ minutes, then beat until chocolate melts and is smooth. Add nuts, cream, lemon and vanilla. Stir until smooth. Pour into a buttered 9 x 13 pan, spread, chill, and cut into squares. Yields 50 + pieces

Kay Stephens

Chocolate Ritz

1 28 ounce package chocolate candy coating
1 box round buttery crackers
Peanut butter

Spread peanut butter on one cracker. Top with another. Melt the candy. Dip each cracker, removing the excess. Lay on wax paper. Store in an airtight container. Yields about 75 pieces

Tonia Beavers

Sopaipillas

6 cups all-purpose flour
2 teaspoons salt
4½ teaspoons baking powder
4½ tablespoons sugar
3 tablespoons shortening
1¾ cups milk

Sift flour, measure and sift again with salt, baking powder and sugar. Cut in shortening. Add milk. Cover bowl and let dough stand 30 minutes. Roll ¼" thick on lightly floured board. Cut into diamond-shaped pieces. Fry a few pieces at a time in frying pan with 1-1½" of hot oil. Turn at once so they will puff evenly, then turn back to brown both sides. Drain on paper towels. Serve with butter and honey. An excellent addition to your next fish fry!

Ann Ray

Bread Pudding

4-6 pieces buttered toast
¼ teaspoon cinnamon
¼ cup sugar
2 eggs
½ cup sugar
⅛ teaspoon salt
2½ cups milk
1 teaspoon vanilla
Raisins, optional

Butter 12-14" baking pan that is at least 3" deep. Tear toast into small pieces and cover bottom of pan. Combine cinnamon with ¼ cup sugar. Sprinkle over toast. Cook remaining ingredients in a medium saucepan over medium heat, until smooth and well heated. Pour over toast. Bake at 350 degrees for approximately 45 minutes, or until set.

Sauce

2 tablespoons butter
2 tablespoons flour
½ cup sugar
1 cup milk
1 teaspoon vanilla

Melt butter in a saucepan. Stir in flour until smooth. Add sugar, then gradually add milk and vanilla. Pour over bread pudding while hot.

Kathy Soto

Oreo Ice Cream Dessert

24 Oreos
½ cup butter, melted
½ gallon vanilla ice cream
1 German chocolate bar
½ cup butter
⅔ cup sugar
⅔ cup evaporated milk
⅛ teaspoon salt
1 teaspoon vanilla
Nuts, chopped, optional
Frozen whipped topping, optional

Crush Oreos and place in a 9 x 13 pan, pour butter over cookie crumbs and mix together to form crust. Soften ice cream and place on the crust. (I usually buy ice cream that comes in a box and slice it — this makes it easier to spread on the crust.) Melt chocolate bar and add next five ingredients; cook four minutes. Cool this mixture, then pour onto frozen ice cream and refreeze. Top with whipped topping and nuts.

Gaye Croom

Heath Bar Dessert

2 *cups round buttery crackers, ground*
2 *teaspoons sugar*
½ *cup oleo melted*
2 *cups milk*
2 *3.4 ounce packages instant vanilla pudding*
1 *quart vanilla ice cream*
3-4 *Heath bars*
2 *packages powdered whipped topping mix*

Mix crackers, sugar and melted butter together. Pat in bottom of 9 x 13 dish. Crunch candy bars and sprinkle half over crust. Chill. Mix milk with pudding mixes. Let stand until thickened. Add ice cream and stir together. Pour mix over crust. Mix whipped topping mix as directed on box. Pour over mixture. Top with remaining candy bars. Keep refrigerated.

Marcia Godown

Hot Fudge Sauce

2 *squares semi-sweet chocolate*
1 *5.33 ounce can evaporated milk*
½ *cup butter*
2-3 *cups powdered sugar*

In double boiler, heat all ingredients until melted. Serve over ice cream or cake. This is ***the best*** ever!

Susie Nicholson

Rum Sauce

1 *pound powdered sugar*
½ *pint whipping cream*
4 *ounces melted butter*
Rum to taste (up to ½ cup)

Heat sugar and whipping cream until bubbly. Don't caramelize. Add butter and rum. Serve over apple dumplings.

Susie Nicholson

OH, BY THE WAY

Sugared Violets, Rose Petals and Mint Leaves

Violets, rose petals or mint leaves
1 egg white, slightly beaten
Granulated sugar

With a small brush, coat each petal or leaf on all sides with egg white. Dip in sugar and place on a plate that has been liberally sprinkled with sugar. Set in warm place to dry overnight. Use within a few days or freeze on layers of paper towels in a tightly covered container. Will keep for about 6 months. Can use ¼ cup corn syrup instead of egg white.

Teresa Wilkins

Frosted Grapes

Egg whites
Small bunches of grapes
Granulated sugar

Beat egg whites until stiff. Dip small bunches of grapes into egg whites. Let grapes stand until nearly dry on wax paper. Sprinkle with granulated sugar (can use food coloring to color sugar). Refrigerate until dry in a closed container. These are nice to use as garnish on meat, cheese or vegetable trays.

Teresa Wilkins

Bob's Hot Salsa

6 onions
6 bell peppers
4 large stalks celery
4 46 ounce cans tomato juice
14 8 ounce cans tomato sauce
Garlic cloves, to taste
Jalapeño pepper to taste (2-4 cups)
Salt and pepper to taste
Oregano to taste
½ cup vinegar
½ cup sugar

Chop onions, peppers, celery, garlic and jalapeño peppers. Mix all ingredients together and cook slowly until celery is done. Stir occasionally. Place in clean, hot pint jars and seal. Wonderful as a dip for chips. Makes 20 pints

Becky Ellison

Sue Berkemeyer's Jalapeño Jelly

1 pound green peppers
¼ pound jalapeño peppers
5½ cups sugar
1¼ cups white vinegar
⅓ cup fresh lemon juice
2 3 ounce packages liquid fruit pectin

Wash peppers and pat dry. Trim, seed and remove veins in peppers. Cut into quarters and set aside. Position steel blade in food processor bowl or blender. Add peppers and process about 1½ minutes or until smooth. Pulp will be visible. Combine peppers, sugar and vinegar in a Dutch oven. Bring to a boil. Boil 5 minutes stirring constantly. Stir in lemon juice and return to a boil. Add fruit pectin and return to a boil. Boil 1 minute, stirring constantly. Remove from heat; skim off foam with a metal spoon. Quickly pour jelly into hot sterilized jars, filling to ¼ inch from top. Wipe jar rims. Cover at once with metal lids and screw bands. Process in boiling water bath for 5 minutes or let cool 12 hours and store in refrigerator. Serve with cream cheese and crackers.

Renae Bailey

Pickled Jalapeño Peppers

1½ cups jalapeño peppers
¼ cup sliced carrots
¼ cup Bermuda onions, quartered
1 cup vinegar
¼ cup water
¼ cup olive oil
1 teaspoon canning salt
1 teaspoon pickling spices

The above ingredients are for one pint jar. Adjust for the amount you wish to make. Pack cleaned peppers, carrots and onions into hot canning jars and cover with remaining ingredients. Seal with canning lids and process 5 minutes in a boiling water bath.

Bobbie Moore

Sweet Ice Box Pickles

7 cups sliced cucumbers
1 cup chopped bell pepper
1 cup chopped onion
1 tablespoon salt
2 cups sugar
1 tablespoon mustard seed
1 tablespoon celery seed
1 cup cider vinegar

Slice cucumbers thin and do not peel. Mix first four ingredients and let stand four hours. Drain. Mix sugar, mustard seed, celery seed, and vinegar. Bring to a boil, cool and strain if desired. Pour over cucumbers, peppers and onions. Pack in jars and store in refrigerator.

Jalia Lingle

Chocolate Gravy

4 tablespoons flour
2 tablespoons cocoa
1 cup sugar
2 cups milk

Mix flour, cocoa and sugar. Add milk. Cook until thick, stirring constantly. Serve over biscuits, pancakes or waffles. Makes 4 servings

Renae Bailey

Nut Caramels

2 sticks butter
2 cups sugar
1¾ cups light corn syrup
1 12 ounce can evaporated milk
1½ teaspoons vanilla
1 cup nuts, chopped

Melt butter in large saucepan. Add sugar and corn syrup. Cook hard on high heat, then add milk in a stream. (This keeps it from curdling.) Cook for 5 minutes on high heat, stirring constantly. Reduce heat to medium and continue cooking to hard ball stage, about 15-20 minutes. Add vanilla and nuts. Pour in a 9 x 13 buttered pan and cool. Cut and wrap in wax paper.

Marcia Godown

Linda's No Fuss Caramel Corn

3 quarts popped corn
1½ cups peanuts
1 cup brown sugar, packed
½ cup butter
¼ cup light corn syrup
½ teaspoon salt
½ teaspoon baking soda

Place popped corn and peanuts in a paper grocery bag. Set aside. Combine brown sugar, butter, corn syrup and salt in a 2 quart glass bowl. Microwave on high for 3-4 minutes, stirring after each minute until mixture comes to a boil. Microwave 2 minutes more. Stir in baking soda. Pour syrup mixture over popped corn and peanuts in paper bag. Close bag and shake well. Microwave bag on high for 1½ minutes. Shake bag. Repeat 2 times. After third time, remove bag and pour corn into a large roasting pan. Stir to separate. Cool completely.

Teresa Wilkins

Rocky Road Popcorn

¼ *cup butter*
1 *10 ounce package marshmallows*
½ *cup peanut butter*
10 *cups popped corn*
½ *cup peanuts*
½ *cup semi-sweet chocolate chips*

Melt butter in medium saucepan. Add marshmallows and cook over low heat until melted. Remove from heat and add peanut butter. In large bowl, combine popcorn, nuts, chocolate chips and marshmallow mixture. Stir to mix. Spread in buttered 9 x 13 pan. When cool, cut into squares. If preferred, use buttered hands to make mixture into balls. Can be placed in cupcake papers until cool. Another idea is to place a popsicle stick in the center of each one. When cool, peel paper away.

Linda Fenech

Puppy Chow

1 *stick oleo*
1 *12 ounce package chocolate chips*
1 *12 ounce jar creamy peanut butter*
1 *12 ounce box bite size crispy rice cereal squares*
4 *cups powdered sugar*

Melt oleo, chocolate chips and peanut butter in microwave oven for 1 minute. Stir and cook 1 more minute. In a large bowl, pour melted mixture over cereal and stir gently to coat all sides. Pour powdered sugar and cereal into a paper sack and shake. Store in an air tight container.

Sue McCoy *Mary Smith*

No Drip Popsicles

1 *3 ounce package gelatin, any flavor*
1 *0.13 ounce package pre-sweetened drink mix*
4 *cups cold water*
1 *cup sugar*

Mix gelatin as directed on box. Add remaining ingredients and pour into popsicle molds. Freeze.

Susan Dishner

Katie's Wand Bubbles

½ *cup dishwashing liquid*
5 *cups water*
5 *drops glycerine*

Mix together. Dip your wand in and blow lots of bubbles.

Patti Nickels

Play Dough

2 *cups flour*
½ *cup salt*
2 *tablespoons cream of tartar*
2 *cups water*
2 *tablespoons oil*
Food coloring

Mix all ingredients except food coloring. Cook over medium heat until mixture pulls away from sides of pan and becomes doughy in consistency. Knead until glossy and cool. Divide and add food coloring. Keep in covered containers. Keeps well.

Renae Bailey

Finger Paint

5 *cups hot water*
2 *cups flour*
½ *cup soap flakes*
½ *cup salt*
Tempera, for coloring

Combine water and flour. Cook over medium heat about 15 minutes, stirring constantly. Remove from heat and stir in soap and salt. Add four tablespoons tempera to each pint while hot. Makes 4 pints. Liquid starch can be added to consistency of brush paint.

Tonia Beavers

SOUTHERN CELEBRATIONS

Cranberry Brie

1/3 cup cranberry sauce
2 tablespoons brown sugar
1/4 cup pecans
1 tablespoon brandy
2 pounds brie

Mix together first four ingredients. Cut rind off top of brie to within 1" of edge. Put sauce on top of cheese and bake 5 to 8 minutes at 500 degrees. Garnish with holly for a holiday party.

Betsy Harris *Maysel Teeter*

Orange Brandy

1 bottle brandy
4 naval oranges
1⅓ cups honey

Strip peel from oranges and remove as much white pulp from peel as possible. Marinate orange peel in brandy at room temperature for 4 weeks. Remove orange peel and pour in honey. Stir until honey is dissolved. Let stand 4-6 days. Decant and bottle. Brandy will reach its peak flavor in about 4 weeks. Serve after a holiday dinner. Give guest a gift bottle that has a pretty orange ribbon attached.

Joyce R. Laws

Kahlúa

2 cups water
3 cups sugar
1 teaspoon vanilla
1 fifth 100 proof vodka
7 tablespoons instant coffee
2 teaspoons glycerine

Dissolve sugar in water on low heat until clear. Dissolve coffee in ½ cup hot water and add to sugar mixture. Add vanilla, vodka and glycerine. Store in closed container and let age for 5 days.

Marcia Godown

Bonnie's Hot Eggnog

4 eggs
1½ cups sugar
½ gallon of milk
Bourbon to taste (about 1 pint)
Nutmeg, fresh or canned

Beat eggs until foamy. Add sugar and beat until well mixed. Add milk to egg mixture and cook in a heavy saucepan over medium heat. Stir slowly, but constantly, until milk becomes warm. Add bourbon and continue heating until hot. Do not let boil or it will curdle. Serve with grated nutmeg sprinkled on top.

Betsy Harris

Eggnog

- ⅓ *cup sugar*
- 2 *egg yolks*
- ¼ *teaspoon salt*
- 4 *cups milk*
- 2 *egg whites*
- 3 *tablespoons sugar*
- 1 *teaspoon vanilla*
- *Brandy or rum to taste*
- ½ *cup whipping cream, whipped*
- *Ground nutmeg*

Beat ⅓ cup sugar into egg yolks. Add salt and stir in milk. Cook over medium heat, stirring constantly, until mixture coats spoon; cool. Beat egg whites until foamy. Gradually add 3 tablespoons sugar beating until soft peaks form. Add to custard and mix thoroughly. Add vanilla and flavoring. Chill 3-4 hours. Pour in punch bowl. Dot with whipped cream, dash of nutmeg.

Marcia Godown

Orange Slush

- 1 *12 ounce can frozen orange juice*
- 1 *12 ounce can frozen lemon juice*
- 9 *cups water*
- 2 *cups sugar*
- 2 *cups vodka*

Mix together in large container. Freeze until slushy.

Marcia Godown

Lemon and Lime Bread with Cashews

- 1 *cup sugar*
- ½ *cup butter, room temperature*
- 2 *eggs, lightly beaten*
- 1¼ *cups sifted flour*
- 1 *teaspoon baking powder*
- ½ *teaspoon salt*
- ½ *cup milk*
- 1 *cup salted, toasted, chopped cashews*
- *Peel of one lemon, grated*
- *Peel of one lime, grated*

Glaze

- 1½ *tablespoons fresh lemon juice*
- 1½ *tablespoons fresh lime juice*
- 3½ *tablespoons granulated sugar*

Preheat oven to 350 degrees. Cream sugar and butter until fluffy. Blend in eggs. Combine flour, baking powder and salt; sift together. Alternately, add dry ingredients and milk to creamed mixture, stirring well after each addition. Stir in nuts, lemon and lime zests. Pour into a greased and lightly floured 9 x 5 loaf pan and bake at 350 degrees for 1 hour or until a toothpick comes out clean. Remove bread from pan. Make small holes in top of loaf with a toothpick. Mix lemon and lime juices with sugar and pour over the bread while the loaf is still warm.

Betsy Harris

No Knead Holiday Bread

2 cups flour
½ cup sugar
1 tablespoon salt
2 packages yeast
1 cup orange juice
1 cup milk
¼ cup oil
1 egg
1 cup raisins
1 cup chopped dates and candied fruits
2½ cups flour
Powdered sugar

Combine first four ingredients together in large mixing bowl. Set aside. Heat in a saucepan on low heat the next three ingredients, until very warm. Add warm liquid to flour mixture. Add egg and blend on low speed until moistened. Beat 3 minutes on low speed. Fold in remaining ingredients. Mix well. Cover and let rise in warm place until doubled. Stir down and spoon into greased bundt pan. Bake at 350 degrees for 45 minutes or until done. Remove from pan immediately and drizzle with powdered sugar.

Karen Dunn

Mom's Thanksgiving Day Bread

2 packages dry rapid rise yeast
2 cups warm water
½ cup sugar
¼ cup shortening
2 teaspoons salt
6½ cups all-purpose flour
1 egg

Dissolve yeast in water. Add sugar, salt and half of flour. Beat for 2 minutes. Add egg and shortening. Gradually beat in remaining flour. Let rise in large bowl to double in size, covered with a damp cloth. Shape into 2 loaves using small amount of flour to keep from sticking. Butter two loaf pans. Put in dough and let rise again. Bake at 400 degrees until brown, about 30 minutes.

Tamara Laws

Cranberry-Orange Relish

1 cup sugar
1 medium orange (cut into eighths), peeled
2 cups whole cranberries
½ cup slivered almonds

Combine 1 cup cranberries and four orange slices in blender or food processor and blend. Remove and repeat with remaining orange and cranberries. Stir together with sugar and almonds and refrigerate at least 24 hours before serving.

Jeannine Sawyer

Cranberry Delight

4 cups raw cranberries
1 apple, peeled and cored
2 cups sugar
1 3 ounce package strawberry gelatin
1 cup hot water
1 cup miniature marshmallows
1 ¼ ounce envelope unflavored gelatin
3 tablespoons cold water
Juice of one orange
Juice of one lemon
1 cup chopped pecans

Grind cranberries and apple, cover with sugar and refrigerate overnight. Dissolve strawberry gelatin in hot water. Stir into cranberry mixture. Stir in marshmallows. Add unflavored gelatin to cold water, juices of orange and lemon and pecans. Mix thoroughly and refrigerate. Will keep 2 weeks in the refrigerator.

Maysel Teeter

Nancy's Holiday Stuffed Ham

1 5 pound fresh ham, boned
1 cup onion, finely chopped
4 green onions, finely chopped
½ cup fresh parsley, chopped
1½ teaspoons salt
1 teaspoon dried basil leaves
½ dried marjoram
2 cloves garlic, crushed
1 can of beef broth, undiluted

In a bowl combine all of ingredients above, except ham and broth. Spread ham out flat, fat side down, and spread stuffing over ham jellyroll fashion, roll as tight as possible and secure with string. Put in a roaster. Combine beef broth with 1½ cups water and pour over ham. Bake uncovered at 350 degrees until a meat thermometer registers done. You might need to add more water as pan juices evaporate.

Note: You can ask your butcher to bone ham for you.

The Committee

Corn Bread Dressing

1 recipe corn bread, crumbled
4 cups soft bread crumbs
1½ cups finely chopped onion
1½ cups finely chopped celery
7 cups chicken broth
1 teaspoon poultry seasoning
Salt and pepper to taste
10 beaten eggs

Mix all ingredients together, except eggs, in a large bowl. Cover and set in refrigerator overnight. Add beaten eggs to mixture. Mix well. Divide dressing into two 9 x 13 casserole dishes and bake, uncovered, at 350 degrees for 30 minutes. Cut temperature to 300 degrees and bake 30-45 additional minutes until browned.

Kathleen Fullerton

Oyster Dressing

8 cups bread crumbs
4 eggs
1 cup chopped celery
1 cup chopped onion
1 teaspoon salt
1 teaspoon sugar
1½ cups chicken or turkey broth
½ cup milk
1 tablespoon baking powder
½ cup flour
1 pint oysters and liquor

Mix all ingredients together. If mixture seems too dry, add more broth or milk. Bake in a 9 x 13 pan at 425 degrees until browned. Cut into squares and serve with giblet gravy.

Note: Bread crumbs can be corn bread, crackers, biscuits or white bread. I use about half corn bread. I do not recommend stuffing the bird with this dressing.

Joyce Wilkins

Christmas Green Beans

2 10 ounce packages frozen green beans
2 medium onions, chopped
6 tablespoons oil
2 teaspoons salt
2 cups chili sauce

Cook green beans to desired tenderness. Drain and set aside. Sauté onion in oil. Add remaining ingredients and mix together. Heat through or bake with turkey until ready. This is bright red and green in color. Tastes great with any meat. Serves 16

Kay Stephens

Stuffed Sweet Potatoes

6 medium sweet potatoes
¼ cup margarine, softened
1 tablespoon brown sugar
1 teaspoon salt
Dash pepper
Warm milk
¼ cup pecans, chopped

Wash potatoes and bake at 425 degrees for about 1 hour or until done. Cut tops from potatoes and scoop out pulp. Mash pulp and add butter, sugar, salt, pepper and enough warm milk to moisten. Beat with mixer until fluffy. Fold in pecans. Return mixture to potato shells. Bake at 350 degrees for 15 to 20 minutes. These can be prepared the day before and put in the refrigerator. However, increase baking time to 20-30 minutes.

Teresa Wilkins

Coconut Cream Cheesecake

2½ cups grated fresh coconut
1 cup whipping cream, scalded

Crust

⅔ cup all-purpose flour
5 tablespoons plus 1 teaspoon well-chilled butter, cut into ½" pieces
4 teaspoons sugar

Coconut Filling

20 ounces cream cheese, room temperature
1½ cups sugar
4 eggs, room temperature
2 egg yolks, room temperature
2½ tablespoons coconut liqueur
1 teaspoon fresh lemon juice
½ teaspoon vanilla
½ teaspoon almond extract
1 cup sour cream

Topping

¼ cup cream of coconut
½ teaspoon coconut liqueur
Coconut flakes, lightly toasted

Purée coconut with hot cream in blender until finely shredded, about 4 minutes. Cool while preparing crust. Preheat oven to 325 degrees. To make crust, butter bottom of 10" springform pan. Blend flour, butter and sugar until mixture begins to stick together. Press evenly into bottom of prepared pan. Bake until golden brown, about 25 minutes. Set on rack while preparing filling. Keep oven on at 325 degrees. For filling use mixer on low speed to cream cheese and sugar. Mix in cooled coconut mixture. Blend in eggs and yolks one at a time. Mix in sour cream, 2½ tablespoons liqueur, lemon juice, vanilla and almond extract. Pour into prepared crust. Return to oven and bake until sides of cake are dry and center no longer moves when shaken, about 1 hour. Let cake cool on rack until depression forms in center, about 35 minutes. Preheat oven to 325 degrees. To make topping, Mix remaining ingredients. Spread on top of cake. Bake 10 minutes to set topping. Cool completely on rack. Refrigerate until cake is well chilled, about 4 hours. Cover tightly and refrigerate 1 day to mellow flavors. Spread coconut flakes in 1" band around rim.

Betsy Harris

Miniature Coconut Cheesecakes

Double the above crust recipe only. Mold into foil cups and pour in complete recipe as directed above. To make into Easter egg nests, sprinkle toasted coconut on top and garnish with 2 or 3 gourmet jelly beans.

Maysel Teeter

Can't Fail Fruit Cake

2½ cups flour
1 teaspoon soda
2 eggs, lightly beaten
1 28 ounce jar mincemeat
1 can sweetened condensed milk
1 cup walnuts, coarsely chopped
2 cups mixed candied fruits

Butter a 9" tube or springform pan. Line with wax paper. Butter again. Sift flour and baking soda. Combine eggs, mincemeat, milk, walnuts and fruits. Fold in dry ingredients. Pour in pan. Bake in 300 degree oven for 2 hours until cake is golden brown and center springs back when touched. Turn out and remove paper. Decorate with walnuts.

Shirley Mallett

Gingerbread House

⅔ cup butter
2 cups dark brown sugar
3 cups dark molasses
¼ cup strong coffee
3 tablespoons brandy or rum
12 cups sifted flour
4 teaspoons soda
2 teaspoons salt
1 teaspoon allspice
1 teaspoon ground cloves
3 teaspoons ginger
2 teaspoons cinnamon
Egg white glue
Assorted candy

Mix butter with half of sugar. Add molasses, remaining sugar and liquids. Next, mix flour with other dry ingredients. Add slowly to mixer. Dough will get too stiff for mixer and should be finished by hand. Chill. Roll out on floured surface and cut into shapes or divide dough into 4 parts and put into 4 greased jellyroll pans. Bake at 350 degrees for 15 minutes. Cut house shapes as soon as cool enough to touch. You will need to cut 1 front, 1 back, 2 sides and 2 roof pieces. Cool completely before assembling house.

Egg White Glue

2 egg whites
2½ cups confectioners sugar
¼ teaspoon almond extract
¼ teaspoon cream of tartar

Beat egg whites until stiff. Add sugar, ½ cup at a time. Add almond extract and cream of tartar. Put in pastry bag with tip attached to attach pieces of house together. Use prepared frosting and candies to decorate.

Kay Ewing *Marie Biggers*

Pumpkin Pie Cake

1 16 ounce can pumpkin
1 cup sugar
3 eggs
1 12 ounce can evaporated milk
3 teaspoons cinnamon
1 teaspoon salt
1 box yellow cake mix
1½ cups chopped pecans
2 sticks butter, melted
Whipped cream or non dairy topping

Mix pumpkin, sugar, eggs, milk, cinnamon and salt with electric mixer. Pour into 9 x 13 pan. Sprinkle dry cake mix over pumpkin mixture. Sprinkle pecans on top of cake mix. Drizzle melted butter on top of nuts. Bake for 1 hour at 350 degrees or until center is firm. Top with whipped cream or non dairy topping before serving. Serves 16-24

Maysel Teeter

Christmas Confection

1 box powdered sugar
¼ cup milk
1 stick oleo
2 teaspoons almond extract
½ cup mixed, chopped fruitcake fruit

In large bowl place sugar, oleo and milk. Mix on high speed for 2 minutes. Stir in flavoring and fruit. Pour into buttered 8" square dish. Refrigerate to harden. Cut into squares. Makes 36

Kay Stephens

Cranberry-Chocolate Drops

1 28 ounce package chocolate almond bark
1 cup chopped pecans
1 package fresh cranberries

Wash and pick over cranberries. Melt chocolate in microwave. Stir nuts and cranberries into melted chocolate. Drop by rounded teaspoonsful on waxed paper. Refrigerate until firm. Keep refrigerated.

Hazelene King

Sugared Pecans

1 cup sugar
1 tablespoon cinnamon
1 teaspoon vanilla
2 cups pecan halves
Powdered sugar
½ cup milk

In a saucepan, combine sugar and cinnamon. Add milk and bring to a boil. Cook to soft ball stage. Add vanilla. Stir in pecan halves and coat well. Cool on wax paper, then roll in powdered sugar. Makes nice holiday gifts.

Susie Kroencke

Crystal Candy

- 4 *cups sugar*
- 1 *cup water*
- 1 *cup light corn syrup*
- 5-8 *drops food coloring*
- 1 *teaspoon oil of cinnamon*

Combine sugar, water and syrup in a large Dutch oven. Bring to a boil, stirring constantly. Stir in food coloring. Continue to cook, without stirring, until mixture reaches hard crack stage (300 degrees). Remove from heat and stir in oil of cinnamon. Working rapidly, spread mixture onto an oiled 15 x 10 jellyroll pan. Let cool completely. Break into pieces. Can be dusted with sifted confectioners sugar. Choose food coloring for holiday or leave clear.

Tonia Beavers

Mrs. Spaulding's Divinity

In a large pot, combine:

- 3 *cups sugar*
- 1 *cup white corn syrup*
- 1 *cup water*

In a small pot, combine:

- 1 *cup sugar*
- 4 *tablespoons water*

Additional ingredients:

- 4 *egg whites, room temperature*
- 1 *cup chopped nuts (pecans or black walnuts)*
- 1 *teaspoon vanilla*

Start pans cooking at the same time. Cook mixture in large saucepan over high heat until it reaches soft ball stage. Cook mixture in small pan over high heat until it reaches hard ball stage. Pour contents of small pan in a fine, steady stream into egg whites, which have been beaten stiff but not dry, beating all the while you are pouring. Keep beating mixture on high and pour in half of the large saucepan mixture slowly in a fine steady stream. Place the mixture back on heat for a couple of minutes, then pour the rest into the egg whites. Keep beating until thick, and it loses its gloss. Fold in nuts and vanilla. Drop by teaspoonsful onto waxed paper. Decorate with pecan or walnut halves.

Betsy Harris

Microwave Peanut Brittle

1 cup raw peanuts
1 cup sugar
½ cup white corn syrup
⅛ teaspoon salt
1 teaspoon butter
1 teaspoon vanilla
1 teaspoon baking soda

Stir together peanuts, sugar, corn syrup and salt in a 1½ quart casserole. Place in microwave and cook 7-8 minutes on high, stirring after 4 minutes. Add butter and vanilla, blending well. Return to oven and cook 1-2 minutes more. Peanuts will be lightly browned and syrup very hot. Add baking soda and gently stir until light and foamy. Pour mixture onto a lightly greased cookie sheet. Let cool ½-1 hour. When cool, break into small pieces and store in an airtight container. Makes about 1 pound

Note: if using roasted salted peanuts, omit salt and add peanuts after first 4 minutes of cooking.

Annette Holeyfield

English Toffee

1 cup chopped pecans
1½ cups packed brown sugar
1 cup butter
1 cup semi-sweet chocolate bits

Butter jellyroll pan and set aside. Heat sugar and butter until boiling in 2 quart saucepan, stirring constantly. Boil over medium heat until candy thermometer reaches 310 degrees (takes 7-10 minutes). Immediately pour onto buttered pan and spread evenly. Sprinkle chocolate chips on top and cover until chocolate pieces melt (about 2 minutes). Spread chocolate over sugar mixture until completely covered. Sprinkle chopped nuts on top and quickly cut into squares before it sets. Refrigerate until completely set and cool. Store in airtight container.

Jeannine Sawyer

Hot Mustard

¼ pound box dry mustard
1 cup cider vinegar
2 eggs
1 cup sugar

Soak dry mustard overnight in cider vinegar. Beat eggs with sugar. Add mustard mixture and cook in double boiler, stirring until thick. Pour into jars and refrigerate.

Connie Austin

Index

Q

R

S

W

Y

Z

Junior Auxiliary of Russellville, AR, Inc.
P. O. Box 1011
Russellville, Arkansas 72811

Please send ____ copy(ies) @ $ 14.95 each ____________
Postage and handling @ $ 2.50 each ____________
TOTAL ____________

Name ____

Address ____

City ______________________ State _____ Zip ____________

Make checks payable to Junior Auxiliary of Russellville, AR, Inc.

Junior Auxiliary of Russellville, AR, Inc.
P. O. Box 1011
Russellville, Arkansas 72811

Please send ____ copy(ies) @ $ 14.95 each ____________
Postage and handling @ $ 2.50 each ____________
TOTAL ____________

Name ____

Address ____

City ______________________ State _____ Zip ____________

Make checks payable to Junior Auxiliary of Russellville, AR, Inc.

Junior Auxiliary of Russellville, AR, Inc.
P. O. Box 1011
Russellville, Arkansas 72811

Please send ____ copy(ies) @ $ 14.95 each ____________
Postage and handling @ $ 2.50 each ____________
TOTAL ____________

Name ____

Address ____

City ______________________ State _____ Zip ____________

Make checks payable to Junior Auxiliary of Russellville, AR, Inc.

Reorder Additional Copies